# CITIZENSHIP STUDIES

## STEVE JOHNSON
## GRAEME ROFFE

OCR
GCSE
(9–1)

An OCR endorsed textbook

Oxford Cambridge and RSA

AN HACHETTE UK COMPANY

The Publishers would like to thank the following for permission to reproduce copyright material.

**Photo credits**

**p.1** © goodluz/Fotolia; **p.3** *l* © Aardvark/Alamy Stock Photo, *r* Public domain (https://commons.wikimedia.org/wiki/File:Qur%27anic_Manuscript_-_4_-_Hijazi_script.jpg); **p.4** © Purestock – Thinkstock; **p.5** © Jupiterimages/liquidlibrary/Thinkstock; **p.8** © Mark Runnacles/Getty Images; **p.11** © Olivier Asselin/Alamy Stock Photo; **p.12** © Roberto Fumagalli/Alamy Stock Photo; **p.13** © Evgeny Sergeev/iStock/Thinkstock; **p.18** © Xaume Olleros/Alamy Stock Photo; **p.19** © Nikita Sobolkov/Hemera/Thinkstock; **p.20** © Alex Ekins/Alamy Stock Photo; **p.21** © Rohan Van Twest/Alamy Stock Photo; **p.23** © Federation of Small Businesses; **p.24** © BrianAJackson/ iStock/Thinkstock; **p.25** © rrodrickbeiler/iStock Editorial/Thinkstock; **pp.29, 36, 44** *b*, **48, 51** *b*, **53, 62, 76** *l*, **81, 82** *b*, **85,** *l,r*, **88** *r*, **97** *r*, **100, 101** *t*, **108** *b*, **118, 119, 123, 130** *r*, **142** *r*, **154** *r*, **162** *b*, **163, 169** *b*, **175, 177, 178** *tr* © Steve Johnson; **p.32** *l* © Cultura Creative (RF)/Alamy Stock Photo, *r* © Fuse/Thinkstock; **p.33** *l* © Paco Ayala/Fotolia; **p.33** *r* © Kamil Cwiklewski/Fotolia, *c* © Kamil Cwiklewski/Fotolia, *r* © allanswart/iStock/Thinkstock; **p.35** *l* © Image Source/Alamy Stock Photo, *r* © Supreme Court of the United Kingdom; **p.37** © keith morris/Alamy Stock Photo; **p.38** © 67photo/Alamy Stock Photo; **p.40** © Jeffrey Hamilton/DigitalVision/Thinkstock; **p.42** *t* © Photofusion Picture Library/Alamy Stock Photo, *b* © cynoclub/Fotolia; **p.43** © WENN Ltd/Alamy Stock Photo; **p.44** *lt* © Tinastar/iStock/Thinkstock, *rt* © james andrew/Alamy Stock Photo *c* © Graham Underwood/iStock/Thinkstock; **p.46** © Fredex8/iStock/Thinkstock; **p.51** *t* © RTimages/Alamy Stock Photo; **p.52** © Katy Bourne, Police and Crime Commissioner for Sussex. http://www.katybourne.com/; **p.56** © Britpix/Alamy Stock Photo; **p.58** © Kevin Foy/Alamy Stock Photo; **p.59** *t* © Jupiterimages/Stockbyte via Thinkstock/Getty Images, *c* © michael spring/Fotolia, *b* © Ingram Publishing via Thinkstock/Getty Images; **p.60** © Jupiterimages/Stockbyte/Thinkstock; **p.61** © Image Source Plus/Alamy Stock Photo; **p.64** © West Yorkshire Police; **p.68** © Anna Berkut/Alamy Stock Photo; **p.71** © fStop Images GmbH/Alamy Stock Photo; **p.74** © Roger Bamber/Alamy Stock Photo; **p.76** *c* © National Crime Agency, *b* © Crime Stoppers, Open Governement Licence; **p.77** © CEOP; **p.79** © ullstein bild via Getty Images; **p.82** *t* The Polling/painting by William Hogarth is in the public domain; **p.83** © Photos.com/Thinkstock; **p.86** *l* © Conservatives, *r* © Green Party; **p.87** *l* © Labour, *r* © Liberal Democrats; **p.88** *l* © UK Independence Party; **p.97** *l* © Eye Ubiquitous/Alamy Stock Photo; **p.101** *c* © edella/123RF; **p.104** © lloyd fudge/Fotolia; **p.105** © Joe Gough/Fotolia; **p.108** *t* © Keith Larby/Alamy Stock Photo; **p.112** © www.parliament.uk (https://www.flickr.com/photos/uk_parliament/5198455088/in/album-72157625444917696) **p.114** *t* © www.parliament.uk (https://www.flickr.com/photos/uk_parliament/464291565), *c* © newsphoto/Alamy Stock Photo; **p.122** *l* © Adrian Sherratt/Alamy Stock Photo, *r* © Chris Bull/Alamy Stock Photo; **p130** *l* © keith morris/Alamy Stock Photo, **p.131** © Iain Masterton/Alamy Stock Photo; **p.135** © imageBROKER/Alamy Stock Photo; **p.137** © Google; **p.141** *t* © Mark Bassett/Alamy Stock Photo, *l* © Animal Aid, *b* © Migration Watch; **p.142** *l* © Animal Aid; **p.143** © Bexhill Town Forum; **p.144** © Matthew Horwood/Alamy Stock Photo; **p.146** © Yuen Man Cheung/Alamy Stock Photo; **p.147** © 38degrees.org.uk; **p.149** © Team Keyn (https://www.facebook.com/ncsteamkeyn, www.justgiving.com/NcsKeyn-SAD); **p.154** *l* © Marc Mongenet via Wikipedia (Public Domain); **p.156** *l* © sculpies/Fotolia, *r* © Mandoga Media/Alamy Stock Photo; **p.157** © Andyso via Wikipedia Commons; **p.158** *t* © VitalyEdush/iStock/Thinkstock, *c* © Xinhua News Agency/REX/Shutterstock; **p.162** *t* © mandymin/iStock/Thinkstock; **p.164** © Dan Kitwood/Getty Images; **p.168** © epa european pressphoto agency b.v./Alamy Stock Photo; **p.169** *t* © Daily Herald Archive/SSPL/Getty Images; **p.171** Public Domain; **p.174** © ZUMA Press, Inc./Alamy Stock Photo; **p.178** *tl* © Manchester City Football Club (http://www.mcfc.co.uk/Community/Manchester-programmes/Community-Cohesion ),

*b* © Big Society Flip Book (https://dms.cld.bz/BIG-SOCIETY-flipbook#3); **p.180** Reproduced with permission of the Prince's Trust; **p.184** *t* © The Commonwealth, *t* © epa european pressphoto agency b.v./Alamy Stock Photo, *b* Reproduced with permission of the European Union; **p.185** *t* © Council of Europe, *c* © NATO, *b* © World Trade Organization; **p.186** © United Nations; **p.189** *l* © Britain Stronger in Europe, *b* © jorisvo/Fotolia, *r* © Vote Leave; **p.191** © Trinity Mirror/Mirrorpix/Alamy Stock Photo; **p.192** © Images of Africa Photobank/Alamy Stock Photo; **p.194** *l* © ton koene/Alamy Stock Photo, *r* © epa european pressphoto agency b.v./Alamy Stock Photo; **p.195** *t* © Paris 2015 Climate Change Conference; **p.197** © PBWPIX/Alamy Stock Photo; **p.198** Photofusion/Universal Images Group/Getty Images; **p.200** © epa european pressphoto agency b.v./Alamy Stock Photo.

*t* = top, *b* = bottom, *c* = centre, *l* = left, *r* = right

**Acknowledgements can be found on page 204**

Every effort has been made to trace all copyright holders, but if any have been inadvertently overlooked, the Publishers will be pleased to make the necessary arrangements at the first opportunity.

Although every effort has been made to ensure that website addresses are correct at time of going to press, Hodder Education cannot be held responsible for the content of any website mentioned in this book. It is sometimes possible to find a relocated web page by typing in the address of the home page for a website in the URL window of your browser.

Hachette UK's policy is to use papers that are natural, renewable and recyclable products and made from wood grown in well-managed forests and other controlled sources. The logging and manufacturing processes are expected to conform to the environmental regulations of the country of origin.

Orders: please contact Hachette UK Distribution, Hely Hutchinson Centre, Milton Road, Didcot, Oxfordshire, OX11 7HH.
Telephone: +44 (0)1235 827827. Email education@hachette.co.uk
Lines are open from 9 a.m. to 5 p.m., Monday to Friday.
You can also order through our website: www.hoddereducation.co.uk

ISBN: 978 1 4718 6527 5

© Steve Johnson, Graeme Roffe 2016

First published in 2016 by
Hodder Education,
An Hachette UK Company
Carmelite House
50 Victoria Embankment
London EC4Y 0DZ

www.hoddereducation.co.uk

Impression number    10 9 8 7

Year         2025  2024  2023  2022  2021

Cover © Richard Wendt

Illustrations by Aptara Inc.

Typeset in India by Aptara Inc.

Printed in Italy

A catalogue record for this title is available from the British Library.

# Contents

# Introduction

This textbook has been designed specifically to help teachers and learners make a success of OCR's GCSE course in Citizenship Studies but it can be used to support any other citizenship specification.

Our book is fully consistent with the Department for Education's national guidance for citizenship. Its thematic structure helps make learning relevant, enjoyable and relatively straightforward. We've followed OCR's approach to specification content and so start with 'rights, the law and the legal system in England and Wales', a theme familiar to many learners through their own life experience and prior learning. It's here that we establish those key concepts and terms that learners will use throughout the course. We also introduce central citizenship issues linked to rights, responsibilities, equalities, law, decision-making and government. These issues are revisited and developed throughout the book. Special sections on 'citizen action' are a prominent feature of our introductory theme. These sections show how UK law and the legal system depend on people who volunteer as special constables, magistrates, tribunal members, or who give evidence at a trial or serve on a jury. We hope to inspire learners to make such important contributions themselves.

From the familiar context of rights, responsibilities and the law, we move on to study the broad theme of government and politics. Here we consider differences in philosophy and policy between the rival political parties in the UK, the process of decision-making and the mechanisms of government. By comparing the UK political system with those in Switzerland and China, learners have an opportunity to consolidate their knowledge and understanding of the values underpinning Britain's system.

'Citizen participation in the UK and taking citizenship action' is a central component of this second part of our book. It's here that we describe the many opportunities for citizenship action in the UK. We feature case studies of young people's successful action and point the way for learners to engage in a range of citizenship activities from voting and contributing to an online petition, to organising their own campaign or project using our step-by-step guide.

The third and final part of our book supports learners' understanding of British society and the UK's international role. It's here that learners can explore their own identity and place in British society, and debate ways in which patterns of migration have shaped and continue to shape our economy and culture. In our final chapter, we explore the UK's global significance and role. How should the UK, with its economic strength and permanent membership of the United Nations' Security Council, seek to promote human rights internationally and help resolve global conflict?

Informed and active citizens draw on an extensive skill-set incorporating analysis, interpretation, advocacy and evaluation. Such skills are reflected by the national assessment objectives for citizenship and form the basis of OCR's examinations. That's why they feature very prominently in the learner activities throughout our book. Tasks are accessible and relevant. Many involve learners in research, presentations, advocacy and discussion. We hope they're fun too. At the end of each chapter we've included questions similar in style to those used in OCR's examinations. Learners can use these questions to consolidate and evaluate the range and quality of their knowledge, understanding and skills in preparation for their end-of-course exams.

In a rapidly changing world and a forever undulating UK political landscape, it's never been more important to keep up to date. Our book was published just before the EU referendum in June 2016 and was fully up to date at that point. We've included reliable web references throughout so that teachers and learners can check current developments as well as extending their knowledge and understanding of the book's key themes and issues.

Citizenship is controversial and challenging – that's what helps to make it interesting. We introduce learners to some of the most controversial issues of our time including such matters as: assisted dying; forced marriage; UK intervention in the Middle East; media freedom and immigration. By being able to share their ideas in a safe, supportive environment, we hope that learners will understand and appreciate the different perspectives on these and other debates.

We hope that all learners enjoy our book, and that it helps lead them towards bright futures as informed and active citizens.

Steve Johnson and Graeme Roffe

# Chapter 1:
# Rights and responsibilities

This chapter begins with an investigation of rights and responsibilities in a school or college context. From this familiar starting point, we go on to consider the origins of our rights, the ways in which human rights have been extended and safeguarded, and the difficulties that occur when different rights conflict. This chapter links with Chapter 2, *The law* and Chapter 12, *The UK and its relations with the wider world*.

Learning the following key concepts and terms will make it easier to organise your thinking and communicate your ideas:

- moral and legal rights
- moral and legal duties or responsibilities
- human rights, freedoms and equalities
- criminal responsibility
- the rule of law
- political rights
- rights of representation including the terms 'trade union' and 'employers' association'
- balancing rights.

## Citizens' rights, duties and freedoms

### Key learning
Study, understand and analyse the human, moral, legal and political rights, and the duties, equalities and freedoms of citizens.

## What moral rights do people have?

Within a family, people do not usually have to follow written rules. Instead, the way family members behave is governed by the expectations they have of each other. For example, children expect parents to help and support them. Children feel that they have a right to such support. Parents expect children to help around the house. Here too, parents feel they have a right to be helped with the housework. When a parent or a child's expectations are not met, people feel let down and there are likely to be arguments. Some family members may feel that their rights have been ignored.

While families rarely have written rules, schools usually do. However, informal expectations are just as important in school as they are in a family. We expect certain types of action and behaviour from others at school. Learners expect teachers to teach lessons that are interesting and well organised. Learners therefore feel they have a right to interesting and well-organised lessons. Teachers expect learners to listen to instructions. Teachers therefore feel that they have a right to be listened to in class. These are examples of **moral rights** not **legal rights**. There is no law against ignoring a teacher. However, if learners do not listen, then classroom relationships can quickly break down and little progress will be made.

We also have moral rights in our relationships with other people. Just as within our family and at school, we expect other people to behave in ways that show us respect. We expect to walk down the street without other people bumping into us, we expect to be served politely in a shop and we expect help if we need support.

**Figure 1.1** Relationships in school depend largely on moral rights and duties

**Moral rights**   What we expect from others in particular situations. For example, parents expect to be contacted by teachers if their son or daughter misbehaves. This is not a legal right but parents still expect it to happen. Therefore it is a moral right – based on what can be reasonably expected in a school context.

**Legal rights**   Expectations supported by the law. For example, a child would reasonably expect to be educated. Education is so important for a child's development that there are laws requiring parents or carers to arrange a suitable education for their children – making education a legal right.

## Activity

1. Check your understanding of moral rights and responsibilities in school by filling the gaps in a grid like the one below.

| Moral right | Moral responsibility |
|---|---|
| To have work assessed promptly | complete your work |
| To not discriminate | To speak out against bullying |
| To have personal property respected | to respect others private space |
| Respect other people | To support anyone who is upset |
| To work in clean, tidy rooms | keep your areas tidy |

## What moral duties do people have?

We expect to have certain rights in our family, in our school and in the wider community. However, rights come with duties or responsibilities. For example, it is not fair for us to expect to have the right to be listened to unless we exercise the responsibility or duty to listen to others. Just as parents have a duty to support their children, children have a duty to support their parents if they become elderly and frail. Such duties often stem from a 'Golden Rule' that we should treat other people as we would like to be treated ourselves. Many people see this simple principle of **reciprocity** as a foundation stone for positive human behaviour. All five major world religions include a version of the 'Golden Rule' in their teachings.

Most schools have a Home/School Agreement setting out the rights and duties of learners, teachers and parents. A typical agreement might include responsibilities or duties similar to those in Figure 1.2.

**Reciprocity** Giving something in return. We expect other people to behave towards us with generosity and consideration. In return, we should try to be generous and considerate towards others. Reciprocity is often a feature of relationships between people, but it can also underpin relationships between businesses, organisations or nations. For example, trade agreements or military alliances between countries are based on reciprocity.

**Figure 1.2** A Home/School Agreement

### Teachers' responsibilities

➡ Teach good lessons and set suitable class work and homework that will be marked regularly and returned promptly.

### Parents' or carers' responsibilities

➡ Check their son or daughter's homework. Take an interest in the work their children do at home and make sure it is completed.

### Learners' responsibilities

➡ Listen to teachers, and work hard. Keep a careful record of all homework tasks and hand homework in on time.

## Activities

2. Compare your school's Home/School Agreement with the teachers', learners' and parents' responsibilities in Figure 1.2. Select and record three important responsibilities from your Home/School Agreement to add to the responsibilities in Figure 1.2. Discuss your additions, and reasons for choosing them, with other learners and your teacher.

3. The Education Act of 1996 states the following:
   *If it appears to a local education authority that a child of compulsory school age in their area is not receiving suitable education, either by regular attendance at school or otherwise, they shall serve a notice in writing on the parent requiring him to satisfy them within the period specified in the notice that the child is receiving such education.*

   Study the extract above carefully and answer the questions that follow. You will need to carry out further research on the internet to help you with your answers.
   a) State the legal responsibilities (if any) of:
      • children of compulsory school age
      • parents.
   b) Describe what is meant by the phrase 'either by regular attendance at school or otherwise' (lines 3 and 4).
   c) Describe the steps taken by the local education authority in your area to make sure children receive 'suitable education' (line 3).
   d) Explain why local educational authorities may have difficulty enforcing the 1996 Education Act.

# Understanding human and political rights, freedoms and equalities

**Human rights** are the rights people are entitled to simply because they are human. Such rights are universal – they apply to all people, wherever they live, and are the same for everyone. Descriptions of human rights refer to moral behaviour and are based on people's reasonable expectations of how they should be treated. People are only able to enjoy their human rights if all citizens and their governments respect and uphold those rights. National laws usually require all citizens to respect the human rights of others.

People should not expect to have their rights removed unless they ignore other people's rights. When a government removes someone's rights, it must do so legally. For example, a person should have the chance to defend themselves in court before their right to freedom is removed.

> **Human rights** The fundamental rights that apply to all human beings whatever their nationality, place of residence, sex, national or ethnic origin, colour, religion, language, or any other status. Everyone is entitled to their human rights without discrimination. These rights are all interrelated and so if one right is denied, it will have a negative impact on other rights. International human rights set out governments' duties to promote and protect the human rights and freedoms of their citizens.

**Figure 1.3** Even prisoners have rights

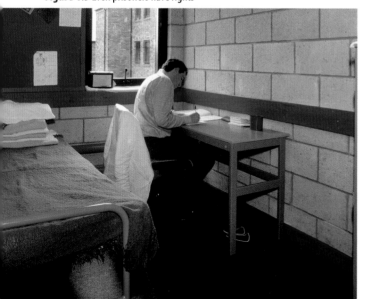

## Constitution of Medina 622 CE

One of the first recorded declarations of human rights was made by the Islamic prophet Muhammad in the Constitution of Medina nearly 1,400 years ago (Figure 1.4). The Constitution was based on the idea that freedom, justice and equality are important principles that everyone should adopt. Sixty-three different articles set out the political rights and privileges the new Muslim state would provide for all its citizens, including non-Muslims, in return for duties. One of the Constitution's most important articles protected all citizens' religious freedom and practices.

**Figure 1.4** The Constitution of Medina was the world's first declaration of human rights

> **Website**
> For a clear and detailed commentary on the Constitution of Medina, which includes interesting details of the historical background and an evaluation of the Constitution's significance, visit: **http://www. constitutionofmadina.com**

## The United Nations Declaration of Human Rights 1948

Today the most widely used human rights declaration is the Universal Declaration of Human Rights agreed by the **United Nations**. This sets out the individual rights and freedoms that all governments have a duty to protect and promote. Among the most important rights and freedoms are the rights to life, liberty and security, and the freedom from slavery, torture and unlawful imprisonment. (See page 10 for more details of the United Nations Declaration of Human Rights.)

The Universal Declaration also safeguards important political rights to enable all citizens to: elect a government, express their opinions freely and to set up their own groups to protect or promote their interests.

**Figure 1.5** The United Nations enables all nations to work together promoting human rights

United Nations (UN)   The UN is an international organisation founded in 1945. It is currently made up of 193 member states. The UN provides a forum for member states to express their views, find areas of agreement and solve problems together. The UN takes action on any issues confronting humanity. (See Chapter 12 for more details.)

### Website

For a the complete text of The Universal Declaration of Human Rights go to: **http://www.un.org/en/documents/udhr/**

## Human rights laws in the United Kingdom

Since 1948, most governments have passed their own national laws to safeguard the rights and freedoms of citizens. Such laws are based on the Universal Declaration of Human Rights. For example, the UK Government referred to the Universal Declaration and to the European Convention on Human Rights when drafting the Human Rights Bill which became law in 1998. In common with similar laws in other countries, the Human Rights Act secures rights for all people. In the UK, this was reinforced by the Equalities Act of 2010. This safeguarded equalities and outlawed discrimination based on a list of '**protected characteristics**' (see Chapter 2 for more details).

Protected characteristics   Particular groups of people are covered against discrimination by the provisions of the Equality Act 2010. The nine characteristics or attributes protected by the Act are: age; disability; gender reassignment; marriage and civil partnership; pregnancy and maternity; race; religion and belief; sex and sexual orientation.

## Understanding legal rights and duties

As we have seen already, governments make laws to safeguard people's rights and to regulate people's duties. As well as having laws to protect key rights linked to citizens' lives and property, governments of **More Economically Developed Countries (MEDCs)** also usually have complex laws to regulate such matters as relationships between businesses and consumers. In the United Kingdom, for example, the Consumer Rights Act (2015) regulates the relationship between traders and consumers. Traders have a legal duty to make sure that items for sale match their description and are of reasonable quality.

Consumers have a legal right to compensation if an item they have bought is faulty.

More Economically Developed Countries (MEDCs)   Countries with a high standard of living, usually in the northern hemisphere. Most citizens of MEDCs work in advanced manufacturing, technology or services.

## Activities

4. As preparation for the next section, imagine that you have discovered a new land where no one has lived before and where there are no laws or rules.
   - List four rights that should be guaranteed for *everyone* in this new country.
   - Discuss your choices and reasoning with other learners.
   - Add further rights to your list following these discussions. (Sort the rights into groups, if possible, and prioritise your list so the most important rights are at the top.)
   - Describe the steps your new government should take to protect and promote these rights for all citizens.
   - Save your list and assess how close you got to reality as you study the chapter sections that follow.
5. Test your understanding of the ideas in this section by matching each term with the correct definition.

| Term | Definition |
|------|------------|
| Human rights | Attributes that must not be the cause of discrimination in British law |
| Constitution of Medina | An international statement of rights and freedoms |
| Universal Declaration of Human Rights | Sixty-three different articles setting out political rights and privileges |
| Protected characteristics | Important entitlements that apply to everyone |

6. Study the information on pages 3 and 4. State at least three different reasons why it is important for governments to protect and promote human rights, freedoms and equalities.

# Age-related rights and responsibilities

## Key learning

Study the age of criminal responsibility and other legal ages when young people become legally entitled to do such things as drive, marry, vote or join the armed forces. Understand and evaluate the justifications for such age laws.

## When can you ...? (Age laws in England and Wales)

### What is the age of criminal responsibility and when should it start?

The UN Convention on the Rights of the Child defines a child as everyone under 18 unless, 'under the law applicable to the child, majority is attained earlier'. Although the Government supports this convention, UK laws set different age limits for matters such as child protection, consent to sexual intercourse and criminal responsibility.

The UN Convention allows countries to decide different ages at which young people should qualify for particular rights and duties. Governments disagree about the age at which people should become responsible for their actions. For England, Wales and Northern Ireland, governments have decided that young people are likely to know the difference between right and wrong by the time they are ten. Ten-year-olds are thought to be capable of committing a crime, and old enough to stand trial and be convicted. Children under ten who break the law regularly can sometimes be taken into care, and their parents can be held responsible for their children's criminal offences. The Scottish Government has decided that children should be twelve years old before they are held responsible for any crimes they commit.

Table 1.1 shows the wide variation in the age of criminal responsibility across the world. This reflects a lack of international agreement. Countries with low ages of criminal responsibility may be giving greater priority to crime victims' rights than to the best interests of offending children.

There is considerable pressure for the age of criminal responsibility in England, Wales and Northern Ireland to be twelve, as it is in Scotland, or even fourteen. The UN supports such a change as do pressure groups such as the Howard League for Penal Reform and the Children's Society but, in 2013, a Private Members' Bill to raise the age of criminal responsibility ran out of debating time in the House of Lords. The Conservative Government, elected in 2015, had no plans to make any changes.

**Figure 1.6** Do ten-year-olds always know the difference between right and wrong?

**Table 1.1** Age of criminal responsibility by country

| Age | Country |
|---|---|
| 7 | India |
| 7 | Nigeria |
| 8 | Indonesia |
| 8 | Kenya |
| 9 | Philippines |
| 10 | England, Wales and Northern Ireland |
| 10 | Ukraine |
| 11 | Turkey |
| 12 | Morocco |
| 12 | Scotland |
| 13 | France |
| 13 | Poland |
| 14 | China |
| 14 | Germany |
| 15 | Egypt |
| 16 | Argentina |
| 18 | Brazil |
| 18 | Peru |

## Website

This official parliamentary research briefing provides politicians and members of the public with a summary of the case for increasing the age of criminal responsibility and a statement of the Government's position: **http://researchbriefings.files.parliament.uk/documents/SN03001/SN03001.pdf**

## Activities

1. Use the information from Figure 1.7 on the next page to help you, design an age laws quiz for younger learners to find out:
   a) What they **know** about what young people **can** do at certain ages
   b) What they **think** about the age at which young people **should** be able to do these things.

   An age laws quiz might have a similar format to the example below.

| Legal rights | At what age do you have this legal right? | At what age should you have this legal right? |
|---|---|---|
| Work up to five hours on a Saturday between 7.00 a.m. and 7.00 p.m. | | |
| Buy a pet | | |
| Leave education and training | | |
| Give consent to medical, dental and surgical treatment | | |

(You can change the examples above and should add some more. Using more than ten examples will make analysis difficult unless you are working in a team.)

2. Analyse the results of your research.
   a) Which age laws were well known by younger learners?
   b) Which age laws were less well known?
   c) Which age laws would the young learners be most and least likely to want to change?

**Some arguments used in the debate on the age of criminal responsibility**

## Leave it at 10

- Ten-year-olds know the difference between bad behaviour and serious wrongdoing and so should be held responsible for what they do.
- Raising the age of criminal responsibility would send the wrong message to young people who would be more likely to break the law if they thought they would get away with it.
- The law can deal with young people in a way that is sensitive to their age and the seriousness of their crime. Until the age of eighteen, young people are usually dealt with by the youth courts and they are not normally placed in adult prisons.

## Increase it to 12 or 14

- Ten-year-olds are often unclear about the difference between right and wrong, and have little knowledge about what is legal or illegal. In other areas of English law, children are not thought able to make sensible decisions until much later in life – whether it involves buying a pet, smoking, drinking, getting a job or marrying.
- In May 2013, the UN Committee Against Torture recommended that the UK should raise its minimum age of criminal responsibility.
- The age of criminal responsibility in England, Wales and Northern Ireland is the lowest in the European Union.

## When should people be able to vote, buy a pet, get married, join the army ...?

At what age should citizens be able to enjoy their rights and freedoms? That's a question that has caused many disagreements in the past and continues to do so today. Figure 1.7 shows some of the age laws for England and Wales in 2016.

Age laws are altered by Parliament according to politicians' changing views about young people's levels of responsibility and the amount of protection they might need. Where changes have been made, age limits have usually increased. For example: the legal age at which a person can buy an animal was raised from twelve to sixteen by the Animal Welfare Act (2006).

### Website

YouthNet UK's guide to life for young people contains a clear summary of age-related rights: **http://www.thesite.org/crime-and-safety/your-rights/what-age-can-i-9102.html**

**Figure 1.7** Age laws for England and Wales in 2016

14+

- Have a part time job, for a maximum of two hours on school days and Sundays, and up to five hours on a Saturday. (No work allowed before 7am and after 7pm. Work in school holidays is allowed for five hours a day from Monday to Saturday.)
- Go into a bar and order soft drinks.
- Be personally responsible for wearing a car seatbelt.
- Use internet services, social media and apps without parental consent ( from age 13).

15+

- Work up to eight hours on a Saturday. (All other working rights are the same as a fourteen-year-old.)
- View, rent or buy a 15 rated film.

16+

- Give personal consent to medical, dental and surgical treatment. (This includes contraceptive advice and treatment.) Choose a doctor.
- Access free full-time further education (at school, sixth form college and city technology college) or job-related training until the age of 18.
- Have sex, gay or straight, if a partner is also 16+, but someone in a position of trust, such as a teacher, is committing an offence if they have sex with someone under 18.
- Apply for legal aid.
- Drink a beer, wine, or cider with a meal in a pub or restaurant if accompanied by an adult.
- Ride a moped, fly a glider, drive an invalid vehicle and use a mowing machine.
- Move out of the family home with parental permission.
- Apply for a passport, and buy lottery tickets and premium bonds.
- Buy a pet.
- Get married or join the armed forces (with parental consent).

17+

- Drive most types of vehicle.
- Apply for a private pilot's licence.
- Become a blood donor.

18+

- Vote in local and general elections.
- Stand for election as a Member of Parliament, local councillor or Mayor.
- Serve on a jury.
- See their original birth certificate if they were adopted.
- Make a will.
- Get married without parental permission.
- View, rent or buy an 18 rated film.
- Buy fireworks and cigarettes, place a bet in a betting shop/casino and have a tattoo.
- Open a personal bank account.
- Buy an alcoholic drink in a pub or a bar.

21+

- Apply to adopt a child.
- Supervise a learner driver if they have had a driving licence for the same type of vehicle for three years.
- Apply for a commercial pilot's licence.
- Drive heavy lorries and buses.

### Activity

3. Explain which five age laws you would change. Give your reasons. Compare your views with other learners in your group or class. Produce an oral or written report on the agreements and disagreements from your discussion.

The minimum age for buying fireworks went up from sixteen to eighteen in 1997 as did the legal age for buying cigarettes (2007).

In contrast, the voting age has decreased. Eighteen-year-olds in the UK were given the right to vote in 1969 (down from twenty-one) and a further reduction to sixteen has now been made in Scotland but not in England, Wales and Northern Ireland.

### Website

Votes at 16 is a well-established pressure group seeking a reduction in the voting age. Their site contains arguments in favour of votes at sixteen, and latest news and views: **http://www.votesat16.org/**

**Figure 1.8** Scottish school students ready to vote in the 2015 referendum to decide whether Scotland should become an independent country

**Some of the arguments for and against allowing sixteen-year-olds to vote in England**

Sixteen-year-olds pay taxes, can work and marry, and are able to join the army. If they can do these things at sixteen, they should also be able to vote.

Sixteen-year-olds took their voting seriously in the 2015 Scottish Referendum.

Sixteen-year-olds are better educated about citizenship than ever before.

Eighteen-year-olds have much more complex adult rights and duties. Sixteen-year-olds do not. They need parental permission to do such things as to marry and join the army.

Most sixteen-years-olds live at home and attend school. They lack the life experience to make voting decisions and will be too easily influenced by parents and friends.

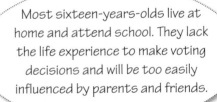

Many sixteen-year-olds lack the maturity to take citizenship seriously because real responsibility is still too far away for them.

## Activities

4. Age laws usually refer to the <u>youngest</u> age at which people gain particular rights. However, there are <u>maximum</u> age limits for joining the armed forces and serving on a jury.

   Find out how these maximum age limits are justified. Explain whether or not you agree with such limits.

   Explain whether or not you think there should also be maximum ages for some other activities.
   a) Which other activities (if any) should have a maximum age limit?
   b) What would be the likely advantages and disadvantages of such maximum age limits?

   c) Would it be necessary to change the Human Rights Act or Equalities Act to allow for maximum age laws? (Consider human rights, freedoms and equalities including the protected characteristics in the 2010 Equalities Act.)
   d) How likely is it that there would be protests and would more maximum age laws be likely to make a government unpopular?

5. Use pages 5 to 8 and your own research to describe the arguments for and against changes to **either** the right to vote **or** the age of criminal responsibility. Advocate your own position using key points and supporting evidence to add weight to your case.

# The Magna Carta of 1215 – why is it so important?

## Key learning

Study the background to Magna Carta and its main provisions. Understand the significance of the Magna Carta in the development of rights.

## What is the Magna Carta and why was it needed?

'Magna Carta' is Latin and means 'Great Charter'. It was an agreement between King John and the English barons signed in June 1215. Barons were wealthy men who had been granted land by the King in return for their support and loyalty.

In 1214, King John's army had been beaten by the French. The barons had already made a large contribution to the army's costs and some had fought in France – but now they would get nothing in return for supporting the King. When John demanded more taxes, the barons rebelled against the King's power and captured London. By the spring of 1215 the two sides were ready to make peace and the Magna Carta was the result. A new and clearer set of principles was agreed for the relationship between the King and his people. The King promised to deal with the English people according to the laws recognised at the time rather than to act as he wanted.

## What did the Magna Carta say and why is it still important today?

The Magna Carta has sixty-three clauses, most of which address particular complaints about King John's rule. However, two clauses in particular have remained important over the last eight hundred years. The Magna Carta stated that everybody, including kings and queens, should be subject to the law. This principle, now known as the **Rule of Law**, remains a key feature of modern English law. It helps to safeguard citizens against the abuse of power by powerful people.

The Magna Carta's core principles are at the heart of the United States Bill of Rights (1791) and influenced both the Universal Declaration of Human Rights (1948) and the European Convention on Human Rights (1950).

> **Magna Carta clauses 39 and 40 gave all 'free men' the right to justice and a fair trial.**
>
> 'No free man shall be seized or imprisoned, or stripped of his rights or possessions, or outlawed or exiled, or deprived of his standing in any other way, nor will we (the King) proceed with force against him, or send others to do so, except by the lawful judgment of his equals or by the law of the land.'
>
> *Clause 39*
>
> 'We will not sell, or deny, or delay right or justice to anyone.'
>
> *Clause 40*

**Rule of Law** Everyone has to obey the law. This applies to politicians, the police and judges as well as to ordinary citizens. If anyone breaks the law, they must expect to be made accountable for their actions and be punished in the same way as everyone else.

9

## Websites

The British Library has a clear, detailed and reliable account of the background to the Magna Carta, and its short-term and long-term significance: **http://www.bl.uk/magna-carta**

See also: *The importance of the Magna Carta* – a short video summary by the BBC of the Magna Carta's significance for rights and freedoms across the world: **http://www.bbc.co.uk/news/uk-11745856**

## Activities

1. The most famous clauses in the Magna Carta are clauses 39 and 40. Re-write each of these clauses to make their meaning clear to a twenty-first-century learner in Year 7.

2. Analyse the Universal Declaration of Human Rights (1948) and the European Convention on Human Rights (1950). Identify the sections in these documents that contain principles similar to those in clauses 39 and 40 of the Magna Carta.

3. Watch a short video on *The importance of the Magna Carta*. Using evidence from the video evaluate the viewpoint that "*The Magna Carta is an interesting historical document but has no relevance for the modern world*" (maximum 200 words). **http://www.bbc.co.uk/news/uk-11745856**

# Human rights today

## Key learning

Study the main provisions of: the UN Universal Declaration on Human Rights; the European Convention on Human Rights; the United Nations Convention on the Rights of the Child and the 1998 Human Rights Act. Understand their importance in protecting rights, equalities and freedoms. Evaluate the actions of governments across the world in protecting rights, equalities and freedoms.

Human rights declarations and conventions have all built upon the Magna Carta's key principle that laws should be fair and must apply equally to everyone.

The basis of human rights is respect for each person's life and dignity. Human rights do not have to be bought, earned or inherited. They belong to all of us simply because we are human. Each of us has the responsibility to protect and promote human rights for everyone.

Over 80 million people were killed and many others became **refugees** during the Second World War (1939–45). As a result, world leaders were determined to prevent further conflict. They also agreed that people's rights should be safeguarded in whichever country they lived. The United Nations was founded in 1945 to promote cooperation between nations.

## Universal Declaration of Human Rights 1948

One of the United Nations' first tasks after the Second World War was to draw up a Universal Declaration of Human Rights. This set out the basic human rights, equalities and freedoms to which everyone should be entitled. While the UN doesn't have the power to make governments turn its declarations into law, the 1948 Declaration does help us to evaluate the human rights record of every government across the world.

Article 1 of the Declaration states that:

'All human beings are born free and equal in dignity and rights. They are endowed with reason and conscience and should act towards one another in a spirit of brotherhood.'

The other 29 Articles from the Declaration include:

- Everyone has a right to life, liberty and security. (Article 2)
- No one shall be subject to torture or degrading treatment or punishment. (Article 5)
- All are equal before the law. (Article 7)
- Everyone has a right to seek and enjoy **asylum** from persecution in other countries. (Article 14)
- Marriage shall be entered into only with the free and full consent of the intending spouses. (Article 16)
- Everyone has the right to freedom of opinion and expression. (Article 19)
- Everyone has a right to education. (Article 26)

**Refugee** Someone who seeks protection in another country because of danger or discrimination at home.

**Asylum** Protection provided by a state for someone who has had to leave their own country as a political refugee.

## The United Nations Convention on the Rights of the Child 1990

In 1989, world leaders decided that children needed their own special convention. It was agreed that people under eighteen-years-old often need special care and protection that adults do not. The result was the United Nations Convention on the Rights of the Child.

The Convention encourages world governments to see children as human beings with distinct and special rights to: health and care, protection, participation in their society, and education and play.

To date, 194 countries have signed up to the Convention and are bound to it by international law. Every five years, governments provide the United Nations with a report on how effectively they are upholding the rights contained in the Convention. The UN Committee on the Rights of the Child monitors progress and holds governments to account if children's rights are under threat. However, the UN Committee does not have the power to punish governments for making poor progress.

**The right to life, health and care**

- Every child has the right to life.
- All children have a right to good health and good quality health care. All children should have clean water, nutritious food and a clean environment so they stay healthy. Governments should help families who cannot afford to provide a decent standard of living for their children.
- Children who are disabled, either mentally or physically, have a right to special care and education so they can lead full and independent lives.
- Children should not be separated from their parents unless it is for their own good.
- If parents decide to live apart, children have the right to stay in contact with both parents.
- Families who live in different countries have the right to get back together and live in the same place.

**Figure 1.9** Every child has the right to life, health and care. A health worker vaccinates a child against measles at the Binkolo community health centre in Sierra Leone

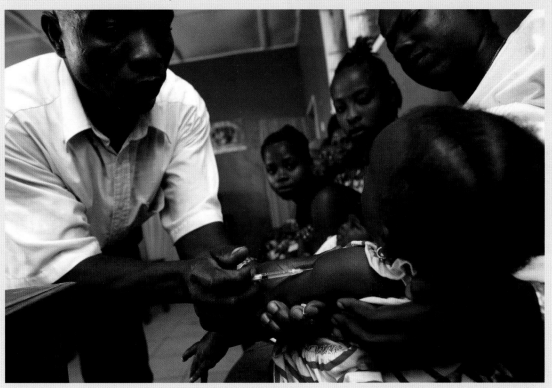

## The right to protection

- Governments should protect all children from violence, abuse and neglect.
- Children under the age of sixteen should not take a direct part in any war or conflict.
- Children who are refugees or asylum seekers have the right to special protection and have the same rights as children who were born in that country.
- Children should not be allowed to do work that is dangerous, might make them ill, or stops them going to school.
- Children have a right to be protected from dangerous drugs, and from the business of making or selling drugs.
- No child should be punished in a way that humiliates or hurts them.

**Figure 1.10** Children who are refugees have the right to special protection. Eight-year-old Fatima and her family were refugees from civil war in Syria. Many Syrians fled to neighbouring Lebanon where some have been taken in by Lebanese families to share their homes

## The right to participate and freedom of expression

All children have the right to:

- give their opinion when adults are making a decision that will affect them, and adults should take the child's opinion seriously
- find out things, and say what they think through speaking, writing, drawing, etc., unless it interferes with other people's rights
- think and believe what they want, and to practise their religion
- meet, make friends with, and join clubs with other children
- privacy
- information from TV, radio, newspapers and the internet. (These media should provide information that children can understand.)

## The right to education and play

- All children have the right to an education which should:
    - develop their personality, talents and mental and physical abilities
    - encourage respect for parents, and their own and other cultures
    - prepare them to live responsibly and peacefully in a free society
    - encourage respect for the natural environment.
- All children have the right to relax and play, and to join a wide range of activities.

## Activities

1. Study the summaries of children's rights from The United Nations Convention on the Rights of the Child on pages 11 and 12. Select rights that seem most urgent for children in the United Kingdom today. Explain your choices and describe any rights that you think should be added to the Convention.

2. Study the measures taken by the UK Government to improve children's online safety. Use information from this section and from the Online Safety Act 2016 to help you. List any additional measures you think the Government should take.

3. Analyse the Universal Declaration of Human Rights or the UN Convention on the Rights of the Child.
    a) Describe the duties all countries have towards refugees from war and conflict.
    b) Apply your knowledge to evaluate how far European countries have met their obligations to recent refugees from countries such as Syria, Iraq and Libya.

4. Design a presentation for younger learners to help them know about and understand the Universal Declaration of Human Rights or the UN Convention on the Rights of the Child. Ask for their ideas on how to build a better 'human rights culture' in your school and present these ideas to your head teacher or principal.

**Website**
The United Nations Children's Fund's site includes a full copy of the Convention together with news of international and national programmes to extend children's rights: **http://www.unicef.org/crc/**

# CASE STUDY

## Government acts to ensure children's rights are protected in the UK

Every five years the UK Government reviews its performance on children's rights against the articles in the UN Convention on the Rights of the Child. Part of the 2014 review considered the effect of widespread internet use for young people's rights and their safety.

The review found that there were around 50,000 UK adults involved in the downloading or sharing of indecent images of children. 4,500 reports of a child being bullied online had been received and 473,000 six to seventeen-year-olds were found to be visiting an adult website each month.

As a signatory to the Convention, the Government had a legal duty to respond to:

Article 17—States shall recognise the importance of mass media, and shall ensure access to material from a diverse range of national and international sources. However, State Parties shall also 'encourage the development of appropriate guidelines for the protection of the child from information and material injurious to his or her well-being.'

Article 34—States shall take all appropriate measures to protect children from sexual exploitation and sexual abuse, including involvement in sexual practices and in pornographic materials.

Although the Government had already taken steps to improve young people's online safety, in 2015 they placed the Online Safety Bill before Parliament for debate. This required internet service providers to improve children's online safety and became law through an Act of Parliament in 2016.

**Figure 1.11** UK children are vulnerable to adult exploitation on the internet

# The European Convention on Human Rights (ECHR) 1950

The **Council of Europe** built on the Universal Declaration of Human Rights to produce the European Convention on Human Rights (ECHR) in 1950.

### Article 1

## Introduction

This states that all countries signing up to the Convention have a duty to ensure that everyone within their borders has the following rights and freedoms.

### Article 2

## Right to life

Everyone has the right to have their life protected by law. Taking a life is acceptable only when it is absolutely necessary, for example in self-defence or to protect the life of someone else.

### Article 3

## Prohibition of torture

Everyone has the right not to be tortured or suffer inhuman or degrading punishment.

### Article 4

## Prohibition of slavery and forced labour

No one shall be held in slavery or be required to perform forced labour. This right does not apply to work related to military, prison or community service.

### Article 5

## Right to liberty and security

Everyone has the right not to be detained and deprived of their liberty, unless it is within the law and the correct legal procedures are followed. Everyone who is arrested shall be informed of the reason for the arrest in a language they can understand.

### Article 6

## Right to a fair trial

Everyone has the right to a fair trial within a reasonable period of time. Everyone charged with a criminal offence shall be presumed innocent until proved guilty.

### Article 7

## No punishment without law

No one should be found guilty of an offence that was not a crime at the time it took place; nor should they receive a heavier punishment than was applicable when the offence was committed.

### Article 8

## Right to respect for a person's private and family life

Everyone has the right to respect for their private and family life, their home, and their correspondence; although this right may be interfered with in certain circumstances, for example in the prevention of crime.

### Article 9

## Freedom of thought, conscience and religion

Everyone is free to hold whatever views and beliefs they wish – but their right to express or display these beliefs can be restricted in certain circumstances.

### Article 10

## Freedom of expression

Everyone has the freedom to express their opinion – but this may be limited for certain reasons, such as for the protection of public safety or the rights of others.

## Article 11
### Freedom of assembly and association
Everyone has the right to get together with other people in a peaceful way; this includes the right to form and join a trade union. No restrictions can be placed on this, unless it is for reasons laid down in law – such as national security or public safety.

## Article 12
### Right to marry
Men and women have the right to marry and have a family – but are bound by the laws covering whom people may or may not marry and where marriage may take place.

## Article 13
### A legal remedy
All states signing this Convention must provide an effective way for people to challenge public bodies or officials whom they believe have unlawfully deprived them of their rights or freedoms under this Convention.

## Article 14
### Prohibition of discrimination
Everyone is entitled to the rights and freedoms set out in the Convention without discrimination on any grounds, such as sex, race, colour, language, religion, political opinion, national or social origin, birth or other status.

**Council of Europe**   An organisation of forty-seven European states, founded in 1949, which protects human rights through international agreement. All members of the Council of Europe have signed up to the European Convention on Human Rights. The Council of Europe should not be confused with the European Council, which is a policy-making body of the European Union (EU). (See Chapter 12 for more details.)

*Rights to the freedoms in articles 8–11 may be restricted, where necessary, for reasons such as public safety, protecting the rights of others or preventing crimes.*

*The following protocols have been added to the Convention since it was first agreed in 1950.*

## Protocol 1 Article 1
### Protection of property
No one shall be deprived of their possessions, except in very limited circumstances. These allow, for example, the State to take money for the payment of taxes or confiscate goods which are unlawful or pose some kind of danger.

## Article 2
### Right to education
No one shall be denied the right to education. The State must respect the rights of parents to ensure that their child's education follows their own religious and philosophical beliefs.

## Article 3
### Right to free elections
Elections for government must be free and fair and must take place by secret ballot.

## Protocol 6 Articles 1 & 2
### Abolition of the death penalty
No one shall be condemned to death or executed. However, a state may make provision for the death penalty in its law at times of war or imminent threat of war.

**Website**
Find a copy of The European Convention on Human Rights here: **http://www.echr.coe.int/Documents/Convention_ENG.pdf**

The ECHR gives European citizens the following legal rights:

- life, liberty and security of the person
- to marry and have a family
- a fair trial in civil and criminal matters
- the right of appeal in criminal matters
- to vote and be a candidate in elections (subject to national age laws)
- freedom of thought, conscience and religion
- education
- freedom of expression
- freedom of movement
- freedom of assembly and association
- property or peaceful enjoyment of possessions.

The following are prohibited:

- torture and inhuman or degrading treatment or punishment
- the death penalty
- slavery and forced labour
- discrimination in the enjoyment of rights included in the ECHR
- expelling citizens of the country or preventing them from returning after travel overseas.

European citizens can appeal to the **European Court of Human Rights (ECtHR)** if they feel that laws in their own country have not protected their rights, discriminated against them or failed to safeguard their personal freedom.

People complaining that their rights have been ignored by their government have brought a wide range of cases to the ECtHR. These include:

- torture and ill treatment of prisoners
- discrimination against gay people
- lack of a fair trial within a reasonable time
- telephone tapping
- parents' rights when children are taken into care.

Governments have been required to take action following ECtHR judgements. For example:

- Turkey cut the maximum duration of police custody.
- Holland changed its law on the detention of patients with mental illnesses.
- Belgium changed its laws on homeless people.
- The UK banned the physical punishment of children by their teachers.

**European Court of Human Rights (ECtHR)** A court based in Strasbourg (France) which decides on cases in which it is claimed there has been a breach of the European Convention on Human Rights. The Council of Europe's member governments must accept the decisions of the court.

## The Human Rights Act 1998

By passing the Human Rights Bill, the UK Parliament brought nearly all the rights from the European Convention on Human Rights into UK law. All public bodies such as the police, schools, hospitals and armed forces must make sure they respect the rights contained in the Human Rights Act. If they do not, they can be taken to court.

**Website**
The Equality and Human Rights Commission's guide to the Human Rights Act is detailed but clear. A full copy of the Act is available at: **http://www.equalityhumanrights.com/your-rights/human-rights/what-are-human-rights/human-rights-act**

## Activities

1. Evaluate the viewpoint that – '*We shouldn't protect the human rights of criminals because they have broken the law.*' (This could be debated in class.)

2. Study the ECHR summary on pages 14 to 15 (You may also wish to refer to a full version of the Convention at **http://www.echr.coe.int/Documents/Convention_ENG.pdf**)
   a) Select six rights or prohibitions which you think are most important to you as a young person and arrange these in priority order.
   b) Justify your selection to other learners and review your decisions in the light of their comments.
   c) Finalise your list and explain your choices.

3. Compare the ECHR with the Universal Declaration of Human Rights.
   a) Record any differences in what they say and how they work.
   b) Check this with your teacher.
   c) Evaluate the viewpoint that – '*We don't need the ECHR as we already have the Universal Declaration of Human Rights.*'

4. In 2014 the ECtHR ruled that the UK's ban on prisoners being able to vote was unlawful.
   a) Research this case.
   b) Describe what happened.
   c) Explain why the ECtHR ruled that the UK's ban on prisoners voting was unlawful.
   d) Describe the UK Government's reaction.
   e) State and explain your own views on this case.

5. Research a recent case of a human rights abuse. (You will be able to find examples on the Human Rights Watch website **http://www.hrw.org/**. Human Rights Watch is a pressure group that draws attention to human rights issues.)
   a) Describe what's been happening.
   b) Explain which human rights are being abused.
   c) Describe any action by pressure groups, political parties or international organisations to stop the abuse.
   d) State and explain what you think is likely to happen next.

## The Human Rights Act – frequently asked questions

Q Does the Human Rights Act give people total freedom to do what they like?

A No. People can only enjoy their rights as long they do not restrict other people's freedoms. People have freedom of speech but must not encourage racial or religious hatred. If they do this, the police can take action against them.

Q If we have the Human Rights Act, is there any point in having other laws?

A The Human Rights Act provides a framework for many of our laws, but it is still up to Parliament to decide what should happen within this framework. The Human Rights Act states that all people should have the right to vote but it does not fix a particular voting age. It is up to each country's Parliament to decide.

Q Does everyone have a right to freedom?

A No. There are rules to allow freedom to be taken away from: criminals; people who may be planning to commit a criminal offence; people with infectious diseases and people trying to enter a country illegally.

Q If we have the Human Rights Act, why is there still heated debate about issues such as abortion and euthanasia?

A Sometimes rights clash. The right to life may clash with people's right to make choices. There are also debates about when life starts and when it stops. Abortions are not usually allowed after the 24th week of pregnancy in the UK because life is said to have started at that point. Euthanasia is illegal in the UK but legal in countries such as Switzerland and Australia.

Q Why do some MPs want to replace the Human Rights Act with a British Bill of Rights?

A Some MPs disapprove of the Human Rights Act being tied so closely to the European Convention on Human Rights. This allows the European Court of Human Rights to overrule the British Government on issues such as the right of prisoners to vote and the removal of terrorist suspects. A British Bill of Rights would make it more likely that the European Court of Human Rights would take account of decisions made in the UK Parliament.

# How effective are the Universal Declaration of Human Rights and ECHR at protecting human rights?

The United Nations' Universal Declaration of Human Rights and the ECHR have had a considerable influence on law across the world, in Europe and in the United Kingdom. People's rights enjoy a high level of protection as a result.

Unfortunately, there are many examples of people's rights being violated.

- Freedom of expression and democratic rights are restricted in China.
- There is widespread use of the death penalty outside Europe.
- Gay people are discriminated against in Russia.
- In 2014, the Syrian government was found to be causing civilian casualties by using chemical weapons near people's homes.

In the UK, there are claims that people's human rights are restricted unreasonably because of governments' fear of terrorism. Liberty, the human rights **pressure group**, continues to raise particular concerns about UK anti-terrorism law. The Government argues that it is necessary and reasonable to prevent terrorism by having laws that restrict some people's freedom and permit the checking of phone and internet records.

> **Pressure group** a group of people who share similar views on an issue and who advocate their case to elected representatives.

**Figure 1.12** Protest in favour of more democratic rights. Hong Kong, China

## Liberty's statement on anti-terrorism law and human rights

Human rights law requires the State to take steps to protect the right to life – which includes measures to prevent terrorism.

However, any measures taken against terrorism must be reasonable and not undermine our democratic values.

Yet, all too often, the risk of terrorism has been used as the basis for eroding our human rights and civil liberties:

- After the terrorist attack on New York's World Trade Center in 2001, emergency laws were passed to detain foreign nationals who were suspected of being terrorists. They could be detained for an unlimited period at a maximum security prison despite never being charged with any offence.
- To fit in with human rights law, indefinite detention was scrapped in 2005. In 2015, suspected terrorists could be placed under close supervision while remaining at home.
- Rights to free speech have been restricted and non-violent groups have been outlawed.
- The police, immigration officers or customs officers have powers to stop, search and hold individuals at ports, airports and international rail stations. They do not need any reason to suspect the person has any involvement in terrorism – or any other criminal activity. Anyone can be stopped but these powers are invariably used in a discriminatory fashion, with stops based on stereotype rather than genuine suspicion.
- Most recently, the Government has passed the Counter-Terrorism and Security Act 2015, which again contains a raft of proposals as unsafe as they are unfair – including powers to:
  - take away people's passports
  - exclude people from the UK
  - track and store data on people's conversations, contacts and movements.
- We believe that terrorism can, and must, be fought within the rule of law and the human rights framework. Repression and injustice, and the criminalisation of non-violent speech and protest, make us less safe; not more. They also undermine the values that separate us from the terrorist – the very values we should be fighting to protect.

(Adapted from 'Countering terrorism', Liberty: **www.liberty-human-rights.org.uk/human-rights/countering-terrorism**)

**Figure 1.13** Fear of terrorism has led to support for restrictions on freedom throughout the world

There are countries across the world where human rights have much less priority than in the UK. A pressure group, Amnesty, was founded in 1961 to highlight human rights abuses worldwide. Amnesty was founded by lawyer Peter Benenson, after he read about two Portuguese students who had been sentenced to seven years in prison for raising their glasses in a toast to freedom.

Amnesty remains an active pressure group with thousands of supporters, many of whom take action to help protect human rights. They do this in the following ways:

- writing letters and sending e-mails to leading politicians in protest about unfair treatment of individuals
- publicising the cases of people who have been unfairly imprisoned
- organising protests against particular governments
- persuading people not to go on holiday to or trade with the countries where human rights are restricted.

Amnesty's work has shown that human rights violation is a widespread problem.

## Activities

10. Take either the Government's or Liberty's position on the anti-terrorism debate. Using information from page 18 and your own research, list the main points for your chosen side of this argument. Debate your position with someone who has the alternative view. Decide whether there is any possibility of compromise and describe what compromises could be made.

11. Study Amnesty's logo. Using the information on Amnesty's website to help you **http://www.amnesty.org.uk/**, explain the links between the logo's design and the pressure group's aims.

12. Using information from Amnesty's website **http://www.amnesty.org.uk/**, describe the methods used by Amnesty to persuade governments to improve human rights. Evaluate how far these methods have been successful.

# The right to representation

## Key learning

Study and understand the right to representation including the role and history of trade unions and employers' associations. Evaluate the effectiveness of these organisations in supporting and representing their members.

## Legal representation

People often find it difficult to stand up for their own rights. This may be as a result of lack of knowledge or experience, low levels of confidence, or a feeling that fighting an injustice could lead to further trouble. This can be a particular problem for vulnerable groups such as children, the elderly or disabled people.

Since 1836, defendants have been entitled to legal representation in British courts. Young people under sixteen should normally have a parent or other 'appropriate adult' with them if interviewed by the police. Vulnerable adults are entitled to 'appropriate adult' support too.

All people arrested by the police have the right to legal advice and representation. Relying on the advice and support of a representative able to speak on their behalf makes it more likely that people will receive a fair trial in line with Article 6 of the Human Rights Act.

**Figure 1.14** Young people under 16 have the right to adult support if arrested

However, in 2015, a government report showed that people arrested by the police were often not getting the support to which they were legally entitled.

## Activities

1.  Study the information on the report, There to Help in the next column. Explain why it is important for young people or those from vulnerable groups to get the support of an 'appropriate adult' when arrested. (Try to include at least three reasons in your explanation.)

2.  Explain why the Home Secretary was concerned about what the report had revealed. Use the term 'justice' in your answer.

## Website

Find the executive summary of NAAN's report, There to Help, at: **http://www.appropriateadult.org.uk/images/pdf/2015_theretohelp_summary.pdf**

Go to NAAN's website to view TV news coverage of the report's launch in March 2015: **http://www.appropriateadult.org.uk/index.php/news/9-public-articles/154-theretohelp**

## Vulnerable people in police custody left without support says charity's report

There was widespread concern in March 2015 when the charity, National Appropriate Adult Network (NAAN), reported that up to a quarter of a million mentally ill adults were not being supported by an 'appropriate adult' while in police custody.

'Appropriate adults' are trained volunteers who can support vulnerable people arrested by the police by helping with basic communication with welfare, and offering advice on legal rights and welfare. The police first used 'appropriate adult' schemes in the 1980s following numerous miscarriages of justice involving vulnerable people. Everyone working in the legal and justice system agree that mentally ill people and those with learning disabilities, disabling brain injuries or autistic spectrum disorders find police custody particularly confusing, disturbing and frightening. There is very widespread agreement that justice may not be achieved for vulnerable adults unless they are supported by a trained person used to dealing with police procedures.

NAAN's report revealed that there were no active 'appropriate adult' schemes in some parts of the UK. Even where schemes existed, police reported that it was difficult to get hold of suitable volunteers to support vulnerable adults at weekends or at night – just those times when support was most needed. Moreover, one in every three police sergeants surveyed for the report had received no training to help them decide if an arrested person was 'vulnerable' and in need of independent support. In the most extreme cases, police officers admitted asking untrained adults to help out just so a police interview could go ahead.

The NAAN report, There to Help, used the police's own data to show that 'appropriate adults' were being used in only around 45,000 police detentions and voluntary interviews despite there being around 280,000 such events involving mentally vulnerable adults.

Home Secretary, Theresa May, agreed that the report's revelations were of considerable concern and promised to study its recommendations carefully.

## Website

This official UK Government website sets out the latest details of people's rights when arrested by the police: **https://www.gov.uk/arrested-your-rights**

### The development of trade unions in the UK

Between the late-eighteenth and mid-nineteenth centuries, Britain changed from a society where most people worked on the land and lived in the countryside to a nation where the majority worked in factories and lived in rapidly expanding towns.

This process of industrialisation (often known as 'the industrial revolution') was made possible by the use of new sources of energy – first water, then coal.

The disruption to society caused by industrialisation was made worse by twenty-two years of war with France (1793–1815) and huge rises in food prices. All this led to workers banding together to campaign for higher wages and better conditions. (At this time most working people did not have the right to vote.) The Government banned such 'combinations' fearing that they might lead to a revolution similar to the one in France.

The Government relaxed the Combination Acts in 1824 and **trade unions** developed rapidly. However, it was not until the Trade Union Act of 1871 that trade unions were given legal protection. The Government had recognised that working people had the right to support each other's interests in the workplace and to elect representatives to speak with employers on their behalf.

Following campaigns throughout most of the nineteenth century, most men (but no women) were given the right to vote in 1884. This prompted the unions to form their own political party (the Labour Party) to get their representatives elected to Parliament. Twenty-nine Labour candidates were elected to Parliament in the general election of 1906.

**Figure 1.15** The plaque below is from the village of Tolpuddle in Dorset. It commemorates six farmworkers who attempted to form a trade union in 1834. Their actions were illegal at the time and all six were sentenced to transportation to Australia.

Trade unions developed throughout the twentieth century, often playing an important part in influencing government decisions. By the end of the century, governments were making laws to reduce trade union power. This trend has continued and, by 2015, the Government had made it more difficult for unions to organise strike action. Over the last twenty-five years, trade union membership has fallen and is now concentrated in public sector employment such as the health service, transport and education. Today people are more likely to be employed in small workplaces. This can make it more difficult for employees to organise trade union activity.

> **Trade Union** An organisation of workers who join together to achieve common aims such as better pay and improved working conditions. Trade union leaders bargain with employers on behalf of union members.

## How trade unions and professional associations support and represent their members

Groups of employees set up trade unions to protect their rights and campaign for fair wages. If people are members of a trade union and have been treated unfairly by employers, they can ask their union for advice and help.

Professional associations aim to safeguard the interests of people engaged in a particular profession. For example, the British Medical Association promotes doctors' interests and helps to ensure that people practicing medicine have appropriate qualifications.

Trade union representatives and some professional associations negotiate with employers over pay and conditions for their members. Trade union leaders also discuss employment issues with members of the Government so as to gain better rights for all employees.

If an employer needs to make workers redundant, trade unions must be consulted so that they can make representations on behalf of the affected workers and perhaps suggest alternatives to job losses.

Some trade unions support and donate money to the Labour Party. Many Labour MPs in Parliament are supported by particular trade unions. This helps give trade unions influence in Parliament.

> ### Website
> The Trade Union Congress (TUC) website lists many of the major trade unions in the UK. It includes a history of trade unions, reasons for joining a trade union and news of current campaigns: **https://www.tuc.org.uk/britains-unions**

## Supporting members – some services provided by trade unions and professional associations

As well as legal advice, trade unions and professional associations provide a wide range of services to their members.

These include:

- Representation at work: a trade union or professional association official will accompany and advise people who need to discuss a complaint or disciplinary matter with their boss.
- Education and training: most trade unions and professional associations run training courses to help their members learn new skills. Some trade unions even help members financially if they want to go to university.
- A benevolent fund: most trade unions and many professional associations can offer financial help to their members if they have a major life crisis.

### Support to members provided by the Unite trade union

Unite is dedicated to serving the best interests of its members and will seek to improve their standard of living and the quality of their lives through effective relationships with employers and government.

Our structure means we can represent your interests effectively in your workplace, no matter what industrial sector you work in.

Members of Unite are entitled to a range of legal and member services with representation services covering a range of issues, both inside and outside the workplace.

We can help with personal injury claims, employment matters, wills, conveyancing and many other legal issues.

You never know when you might need advice with a problem at work. So it's good to know Unite is here to help.

(Adapted from the website of the Unite Trade Union: **www.unitetheunion.org**)

### Aims of the British Medical Association

Our vision is a profession of valued doctors delivering the highest quality health service where all doctors:

- have strong representation and expert guidance, whenever and wherever they need it
- have their individual needs met through career-long support and professional development
- are championed by the BMA and their voices are sought, heard and acted upon
- can connect with each other as a professional community
- can influence the advancement of health and the profession.

(From the website of the British Medical Association: **www.bma.org.uk**)

## Evaluation: trade unions – good or bad?

Trade unions were set up to represent workers' interests but, with fewer members than at any time since 1940, are they still doing that today?

Consider the contrasting viewpoints below.

### Trade unions are good for workers, businesses and society

- Trade unions promote fair, safe and discrimination-free employment practices. This creates the conditions for strong employee loyalty, flexibility and productivity.
- Unions can work with governments to improve conditions for all workers.
- Workers in companies with a recognised trade union earn 10 per cent more than in a comparable non-unionised workplace.
- Union members never have to face problems alone. Unions have workplace representatives to advise, support and represent members on a wide range of workplace problems.
- There are fewer accidents in unionised workplaces. Union health and safety representatives have legal rights to raise concerns and to take action to prevent accidents from happening.

**Trade unions fail to support workers and have a negative impact on business and society**

- Trade unions produce higher wages (for the union members) at the expense of fewer jobs. They have failed to recruit workers in low-skilled, low-paid jobs and so can't represent their interests.
- Trade unions spend too much time on political campaigns and don't do enough to support their members in the workplace.
- Trade union representatives try to prevent the introduction of more efficient ways of working and so make it more difficult for businesses to succeed.
- Strikes cause needless disruption to the lives of ordinary people.
- Employees can buy legal insurance at less cost than a trade union membership fee. This pays for expert support in the event of employment problems.

**Activities**

3. List five reasons why people join trade unions or professional organisations. Discuss your list with other learners and make adjustments as necessary, placing your reasons in priority order. If possible, check your list with a member of a trade union or professional association. Ask them why they are a member. Describe how far they agree with your list.

4. Explain why people might <u>not</u> want to join a trade union or professional association.

5. Evaluate the viewpoint that 'trade unions cause more problems than they solve'.

## How employers' associations support and represent their members

Employees can join trade unions for advice and support. Employers also have organisations that they can join for a similar purpose.

Two of the largest and best-known employers' associations are the Federation of Small Businesses (FSB) and the Confederation of British Industry (CBI). The FSB and CBI are both able to offer legal advice to employers and have regular discussions with the Government to promote policies to help business. Both of these employers' associations are keen to limit the amount of tax paid by employers and to reduce the number of regulations affecting business.

## Supporting business – some services provided by employers' associations

Other services provided to their members by the FSB and CBI include providing:

- legal documents online to save employers time in drawing up policies, contracts and official letters
- financial advice to help with loans, overdrafts, leasing and insurance
- business support to help with such things as checking customers' ability to pay and selling products overseas.

### FSB and CBI campaigns

Like the trade unions, the FSB and CBI organise campaigns to promote the interests of business. The Conservative Party is often willing to support these campaigns and some businesses have made donations to support the Conservatives.

**Figure 1.16** Back Small Business has been one of the Federation of Small Businesses' main campaigns

Examples of campaigns include:

- Keep Trade Local (FSB, 2015) asked the Government and local authorities to cut car parking charges and reduce business rates to encourage small business growth in town centres.
- The CBI made representations to the Government in 2015 to enable businesses to continue recruiting skilled workers from overseas in spite of public concerns about high levels of immigration.

**FSB Legal Benefits Package**

As a right of membership, the FSB offers the following services:

- access to legal advice from qualified lawyers 24 hours per day, 365 days a year
- tax advice from specialists
- information and documentation on employment law, tax and commercial law through the FSB's members-only website
- insurance cover for legal fees.

(Adapted from the FSB website: **www.fsb.org.uk**)

## Activities

6. Visit either the Confederation of British Industry (CBI) or Federation of Small Businesses (FSB) website. Describe one of the campaigns they are running.

7. Write an email from an employee to their boss persuading them to join an employers' association.

## Other organisations supporting people's rights

People have established a wide range of pressure groups and member organisations to represent their particular interests. By working together in this way, people are more likely to be able to protect their rights and to get their voice heard. (See Chapter 9 for more details.)

Some pressure groups exist to protect and promote the rights of vulnerable groups. Examples include:

- Age UK – speaks for people who have reached later life
- MIND – provides advice and support to empower anyone experiencing a mental health problem
- National Society for the Prevention of Cruelty to Children (NSPCC) – protects vulnerable children.

## Activity

8. Choose a UK-based organisation that supports the rights of a vulnerable group. Prepare a presentation to:
   - Describe the organisation's aims and what it does.
   - Explain why the organisation is needed. (Mention the vulnerable group and which of their rights may be under threat.)
   - Describe some of the organisation's achievements.
   - Describe how people can support the organisation.

# CASE STUDY

## The NSPCC

The NSPCC, established in 1889, is a leading children's charity campaigning to end child abuse in the UK.

The NSPCC protects children's rights by: helping children who have been abused to rebuild their lives; protect those at risk; and find the best ways of preventing abuse from ever happening. The charity seeks to influence government policy on children's rights and child protection. In 2015, the NSPCC ran campaigns to promote online safety and to expose the evils of child trafficking.

Children and their families are supported through the NSPCC helpline and ChildLine. The NSPCC provides advice to parents on how best to protect their children online and what to do if their sons or daughters become involved in gangs.

The NSPCC's website (**nspcc.org.uk**) provides a wide range of additional information about the charity's aims and what it does.

**Figure 1.17** The NSPCC campaigns and takes action against child cruelty

# Rights in conflict

## Key learning

Analyse rights in local, national and global situations where there is conflict. Evaluate outcomes in cases where rights and responsibilities need to be balanced using local, national and global contexts.

## Rights in conflict – UK examples

### Safety and security *v* liberty, privacy and free speech

The statement from pressure group Liberty on page 18 shows how the right to safety and security can conflict with the rights to liberty, privacy and free speech. The UK Government has restricted liberty, privacy and free speech in order to more easily defend the country against terrorism and to safeguard the public from attack. Liberty argues that this has gone too far and is creating problems rather than solving them.

### Media freedom *v* privacy

Another UK example involves the potential conflict between media freedom and privacy. This is explored in Chapter 8.

## Rights in conflict – the Palestinian question

According to the Universal Declaration of Human Rights:

- Everyone has the right to life, liberty and security of person (Article 3).
- (1) Everyone has the right to own property alone as well as in association with others.
  (2) No one shall be arbitrarily deprived of his property (Article 17).

What happens, though, when two groups of people both believe that they have the right to live in the same area of land and cannot agree to share it? Put very simply, this is what has happened in Israel. The Israeli Government and the government of the Palestinian territories, known as the West Bank and the Gaza Strip, are engaged in violent conflict over rights to land ownership. Most Palestinian people living in Israel also feel hostile towards the Israeli Government. Each side feels that its rights are being infringed by the other.

**Figure 1.18** Al-Masara, Palestinian territories – 6 April 2012: A Palestinian man confronts Israeli soldiers in a protest against the construction of the separation barrier in the West Bank town of Al-Masara

## History of the Israel / Palestine conflict

For centuries, Jewish people had longed for their own country where they would be safe from discrimination and persecution. They wanted to build a Jewish state on land in the Middle East known as Palestine that had been the Biblical kingdom of Israel, the traditional home of Jewish people.

After the Holocaust, in which six million Jewish people were murdered by the Nazis, a United Nations agreement of 1947 granted the Jewish people a large part of Palestine. This land became known as Israel. Palestinian Arabs who already lived there felt that was unfair and didn't accept the new country.

In 1948, the two sides went to war. The Arabs were defeated and thousands of Palestinian refugees fled from what was now the new Jewish homeland to Gaza and to land on the West Bank of the River Jordan.

Figure 1.19 Israel, Palestinian territories and neighbouring countries

Conflict continued and new wars broke out. Each side claimed rights over the territory now occupied mainly by Jewish people.

In 2005, a group called Hamas won elections in Gaza and took control there. Although there is international support for a solution to Palestinian problems, much of the world sees Hamas as a terrorist organisation. Hamas refuses to recognise Israel as a nation and is prepared to use violence so that Palestinians can return to their former homes.

Since then, Israel has held Gaza under a blockade, which means it controls its borders and limits who can get in and out. This makes it impossible for the people of Gaza to live normal lives. Many lack proper food and accommodation. The United Nations is providing **humanitarian aid**.

Other countries, particularly the United States of America (USA), have tried to resolve the dispute between the Arabs and Israelis. Nothing has worked. Many people want Gaza and the West Bank to be turned into a new nation – Palestine. Israel will not agree to this unless its own security and right to exist are safeguarded. There are also concerns about finding a permanent home for millions of families descended from the original Palestinian refugees.

**Humanitarian aid**   Emergency help given directly to people in urgent need as a result of war, natural disaster, disease epidemic or famine. It is usually short-term help until governments and international agencies can step in with longer-term support.

## Website

A detailed and balanced history of the Israel / Palestine conflict, including a timeline and an analysis of some of the current issues: **http://www.trust.org/spotlight/Israeli-Palestinian-conflict/?tab=briefing**

## Activities

1. List the human rights likely to be under threat as a result of the Israeli/Palestinian conflict.
2. Using the information from the section above explain why the conflict between Israel and Palestine has become so difficult to resolve.

## Practice questions

In the OCR specification, this section will be assessed using objective test questions and questions needing a written response.

1. Which **one** document was first to include the principle of 'The **Rule of Law**'?
   A   the Convention of Medina
   B   the Magna Carta
   C   the Universal Declaration of Human Rights
   D   the Human Rights Act.                                    [1 mark]

2. From the list below choose **four** rights or freedoms that are included in the **European Convention of Human Rights**.
   A   To become a citizen of any European Union country.
   B   To be able to view unbiased media.
   C   To have full time education or training to the age of 18.
   D   To be free from slavery.
   E   To have access to medical treatment that is free at the point of use.
   F   To be free from government interception of your personal communications.
   G   To have life, liberty and personal security.
   H   To have access to play and leisure facilities.
   I    To be able to vote in any European country.
   J   To have a fair trial.
   K   To be able to use violence to defend yourself.
   L   To be able to express your thoughts and ideas.          [4 marks]

3. Which one of the definitions below best matches the term '**age of criminal responsibility**'?
   A   The age at which a young person must be tried in a youth court.
   B   The age below which a young person cannot be held accountable in law for his or her actions.
   C   A period of time, after the Second World War, when criminals behaved with greater responsibility to members of the public.
   D   The age at which a young person is responsible for defending themselves in court.                              [1 mark]

4. Which **one** of the options below best matches the **main role** of an employers' association?
   A   Works with its members to improve employees' pay and conditions.
   B   Campaigns to get its members elected to Parliament.
   C   Persuades politicians to support business.
   D   Fixes prices among its members so that everyone can make a fair profit.                                       [1 mark]

5. Explain why human rights sometimes conflict.           [4 marks]

# Chapter 2:
# The law

In this chapter, we explore the nature of rules and laws. We investigate how laws can protect our rights and interests, and help us to settle disputes. We go on to consider where our laws come from and the important principles that should be features of all our law. Finally we investigate why laws are different in different parts of the United Kingdom. This chapter on *The law* builds on Chapter 1, *Rights and responsibilities* and helps us prepare for Chapter 3, *The legal system*.

Learning the following key concepts and terms will make it easier to organise your thinking and communicate your ideas:
- rules and laws
- fairness and justice
- common law
- legislation
- case law and precedent
- judge-made law
- presumption of innocence
- equality before the law
- legal jurisdiction.

School rules are more likely to be written down than household rules. Teachers and learners like to be clear about expectations and so find some simple rules useful. For example, a rule about walking on the left in narrow corridors helps keep everyone safe. Most people are happy to respect such a rule as it helps them to reach their destination quickly and safely – avoiding embarrassing corridor collisions. Most schools with narrow corridors have such rules but, in other respects, each school's rules can be very different.

Rules also apply in workplaces, clubs and organisations. By breaking a rule, we are not usually breaking the law. Nevertheless rule-breaking often leads to punishment within households, schools or organisations.

Laws are different. They are rules that apply in all situations. Laws usually apply to everyone in society, apart from children who are not affected by laws until they reach a particular age. (See Chapter 1 for more details.) People who break the law are treated more consistently than would usually be the case for rule-breakers in households and schools.

## Rules, law and society

### Key learning
Study the differences between rules and laws, and understand how rules and laws help society to deal with complex problems of fairness, justice and discrimination, to protect rights and freedoms, maintain order and resolve conflicts.

## What's the difference between rules and laws?

Rules in homes and schools are designed to remind people about safe, considerate and acceptable behaviour. For example, some households have rules about keeping dogs and cats out of bedrooms. Other households are quite relaxed about pets on beds, but less happy about animals in the kitchen at meal times. Such rules are not usually written down and, from time to time, people may agree to change them.

### Activities

1. Identify the unwritten rules in your home.
   a) Describe two of these rules and explain their purpose.
   b) Describe what happens when these rules are broken.
   c) Evaluate how far the household rules are applied consistently and whether any punishments are fair.

2. Study the rules in your school or college.
   a) Identify the rules that you think are the most important.
   b) Explain your choice.
   c) Describe any changes you would make to school rules and justify your choices.
   d) Explain what you think makes a 'good' school rule.

3. Evaluate how consistently your school rules are enforced and how fairly punishments are applied. Discuss your feelings with other learners and your teacher. Consider presenting your findings to a senior member of staff.

### Website
The Ministry of Justice website explains important aspects of the law and legal system: **www.justice. gov.uk**

Figure 2.1 The KC stadium in Hull has rules banning football and rugby fans from taking certain items into the ground. Carrying some of these items would also be illegal. Which ones do you think they are?

- enabling people suspected of crime to defend themselves properly
- sentencing criminals so that their punishment fits their crime
- compensating victims of crime so that they are in the same position as before the crime took place.

Fairness involves making judgements that fit the circumstances of a particular case without being influenced by personal feelings or interests.

**Activity**

4. Statues or paintings representing 'Justice' can sometimes be seen in or outside law courts. 'Justice' is often shown blindfolded, and carrying a sword and set of scales or balances.

   Explain why 'Justice' is shown in this way. Use the terms 'justice' and 'fairness' in your answer.

Figure 2.2 Justice is blind

**Website**

Justice UK is a pressure group that campaigns for greater fairness and justice in the law and legal system. Their website signposts other useful sources of information on all aspects of justice: **www.justiceuk.org.uk/about.html**

## Why do we have laws?

The law regulates our behaviour. We might not agree with all laws but everyone is expected to obey every law. (This is known as the Rule of Law – see page 9.)

If we ignored laws that we did not like, then there would be no common code of behaviour. People would never know what to expect from other members of their community and they would find it difficult to trust others.

Law and order would break down if laws were applied to some people or groups but not to others. People would protest about such unfairness and lose respect for the police.

## Fairness and justice

For legal systems to be respected, they must be fair and just. What exactly do these concepts mean?

Justice and fairness are closely related terms that are often used interchangeably.

Justice means giving each person what he or she deserves. In law, this includes:

- protecting everyone from crime and criminals

# CASE STUDY

## Birmingham Six: 40th anniversary of pub bombings that led to 'one of the worst miscarriages of British justice'

The Birmingham Six were in prison for nearly seventeen years before they achieved justice in 1991.

Today is the 40-year anniversary of two pub bombings in 1974, which killed 21 people and injured 182, that led to the charges and unjust life sentences for the Birmingham Six.

Bombs planted in two Birmingham pubs blew up ten minutes apart and, although telephone warnings were sent to local newspapers six minutes before, the pubs were not evacuated in time.

Six Irish men were jailed in 1975 for 16 years before their convictions were quashed in what is considered to be one of the worst miscarriages of justice in British history. They had claimed that police forced them to sign confession documents by torturing them.

The six men walked away from the Old Bailey on 14 March 1991 having had their innocence proved with the help of journalist, MP and campaigner Chris Mullin.

Members of the Provisional Irish Republican Army (IRA) were believed to have been responsible for the bombings as they had carried out similar attacks in England since 1973, however the group never claimed responsibility for the pub incidents and no others have admitted responsibility.

Five of the Birmingham Six were arrested for their alleged involvement in the pub bombings while they were in Heysham, Lancashire, as they waited for a ferry to Northern Ireland to attend a funeral. The sixth man was arrested in Birmingham. Incorrect evidence and statements led them to receive a total of 21 life sentences each – one for every person who died in the blasts.

No police officers were prosecuted for the imprisonment of the men although Mr Hill, one of the six who co-founded the Miscarriages of Justice Organisation, won the right to NHS trauma counselling.

Ten years later, each of the six men received compensation between £840,000 and £1.2 million.

(Adapted from *The Independent*, 21 November 2014)

A law works best when

- most people know about the law, and agree with it
- the law is clear and easy to understand
- the law can be enforced easily and without discrimination
- punishments are clear and applied fairly.

## The purpose of law – protecting safety

Many laws are designed to protect our safety. Laws forbidding **homicide**, assault and burglary are examples of this. Over the last hundred years, people's lives have become far more complex. In response, Parliament has passed many new laws to protect health and safety. Such laws protect people on the roads, in workplaces, shops, restaurants and schools, and even in the home.

> **Homicide**  Homicide includes murder and manslaughter. A killing is classified as murder if the accused person is 'of sound mind' and intended to kill or cause serious harm to his or her victim. Manslaughter is a killing where there was no intention to cause death or where the accused person has a partial defence such as loss of control.

### Activities

5. Study the news item from *The Independent* about the Birmingham Six.
   a) Describe what happened.
   b) Explain why this case is often described as one of the worst miscarriages of justice in modern times.
   c) Describe any lessons that we should learn from the Birmingham Six case.

6. Carry out your own research to describe any criminal investigation or trial that was said to have been unjust or unfair (a miscarriage of justice). You can use an example from the UK or elsewhere and from any time period. You may also use an example from a book, stage play, film or computer game.

   Explain why people felt that there had been a lack of justice or fairness.

## The purpose of law – protecting rights, and promoting freedoms and equalities

During the second part of the twentieth century governments passed laws to protect people's rights, promote their freedoms and guarantee equalities by safeguarding people against **discrimination.** This trend has continued in the twenty-first century.

**Figure 2.3** Laws affect many parts of our lives. Study each of the pictures below and list some of the laws that might apply in each situation. Compare your list with those made by other learners. Discuss the different reasons for the laws on your lists.

Lucy at work          Lucy shopping          Lucy's night out

# CASE STUDY

## Law in action – police protect the public fighting organised crime in Bexley, London

A father and his two sons have been jailed for a total of over sixteen years after being convicted of a range of offences including possession of a shotgun, burglary and handling stolen goods.

On Tuesday, 25 August at the Inner London **Crown Court:**

- SP, aged 31, was sentenced to six years and three months imprisonment after pleading guilty to possession of a shot gun, residential burglary, supplying prescribed medicines and identification fraud.
- TP, aged 29, was sentenced to six years and three months imprisonment after pleading guilty to possession of a shotgun, residential burglary, handling stolen goods, supplying prescribed medicines and identification fraud.

- JP, aged 58, was sentenced to three years and eight months imprisonment after pleading guilty to handling stolen goods and identification fraud.

Their arrests were part of a two-year undercover police operation to dismantle organised criminal networks suspected of committing hundreds of offences including burglary, theft, fraud, motor vehicle crime, drug dealing, money laundering and violent crime.

A total of 73 people were arrested in connection with the operation, in March 2015, and 50 people have been convicted, with other trials to come. The total collective number of years sentenced is in excess of 100.

The operation was launched following a rise in crime, particularly burglary and theft, in the Bexley area. Detective Chief Inspector Gary Holmes, said: 'This organised criminal family network was clearly identified in our investigations. I am hoping that our investigation and the sentences they have been given will discourage them and others from committing further crimes in the future. Committing crime in Bexley does not pay and we will continue to target offenders who commit crime.'

(Extract adapted from the Metropolitan Police website, *'Father and sons jailed'*, 28 August 2015)

The two most recent laws to protect equalities in the UK are the Human Rights Act (1998) and the Equality Act (2010). (See Chapter 1 for more details of the Human Rights Act.)

**Crown Court**   The court used by the State or Crown for the trial of serious criminal offences. (See Chapter 3 for more details on the court system in England and Wales.)

**Discrimination**   Unfavourable treatment often based on prejudice. For example, it would be reasonable to choose the job applicant with the best driving skills for a job in a transport company. Choosing a man because of a misplaced belief that men make the best bus drivers, would be discrimination.

### Activity

7. Study the purpose of the law and the case study about organised crime in Bexley.
   a) Explain why it is important for the police to combat organised crime.
   b) Describe other actions you think the police should take to protect public safety.
   c) Discuss these suggestions with other learners.

## The Equality Act, 2010

The Equality Act is designed to protect people against discrimination in relation to any of nine specific characteristics:

- age
- disability
- gender reassignment
- marriage and civil partnership
- pregnancy and maternity
- race
- religion and belief
- sex
- sexual orientation.

Discrimination can be direct or indirect. Direct discrimination occurs when someone is treated less favourably because of a 'protected characteristic' listed above. Examples of less favourable treatment could include: deciding not to employ them; refusing them training; denying them a promotion; or giving them worse terms and conditions than other workers.

Indirect discrimination occurs when everyday decisions made in an organisation or business disadvantage people on the basis of protected characteristics. An example would be posting a job advert that required applicants to be 1.8 metres tall. Since the average height of men in the UK is 1.77 m and for women it is 1.62 m, it would be more likely that men could apply for the job. This would be an example of indirect gender discrimination.

**Figure 2.4** Under the Equality Act of 2010, it is against the law to treat a person less favourably because of their sex

In the case of disability – one of the 'characteristics' protected by the Equality Act – employers and service providers have a legal duty to make reasonable adjustments to their workplaces to overcome barriers experienced by disabled people.

Employers also have a legal duty to make sure that their employees do not discriminate against a fellow worker because of a 'protected characteristic'. For example, it would be illegal for an employer to reject a job application from a man because the business's female workers wanted another woman to join their team.

The Equality Act also protects people with a 'protected characteristic' from harassment – being made to feel humiliated because of their age, race, religion, etc. For example, a worker would be subject to harassment if they received an email from a co-worker criticising their age. This would be even more serious if the email had been widely circulated.

**Figure 2.5** The Equality Act protects people from harassment because of age. Is this email harassment?

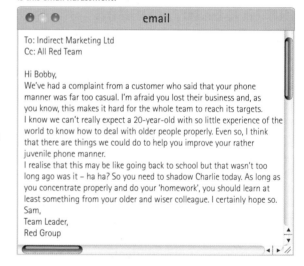

To: Indirect Marketing Ltd
Cc: All Red Team

Hi Bobby,
We've had a complaint from a customer who said that your phone manner was far too casual. I'm afraid you lost their business and, as you know, this makes it hard for the whole team to reach its targets. I know we can't really expect a 20-year-old with so little experience of the world to know how to deal with older people properly. Even so, I think that there are things we could do to help you improve your rather juvenile phone manner.
I realise that this may be like going back to school but that wasn't too long ago was it – ha ha? So you need to shadow Charlie today. As long as you concentrate properly and do your 'homework', you should learn at least something from your older and wiser colleague. I certainly hope so.
Sam,
Team Leader,
Red Group

**Figure 2.6** The harassment or victimisation of people with 'protected characteristics' is illegal under the Equality Act

**Figure 2.7** The Equality Act requires employers to make reasonable adjustments so that employees with disabilities can work as normally as possible

## Activities

8. The Equality Act gives employers the legal duty to make 'reasonable adjustments' to remove or reduce any substantial disadvantage faced by disabled workers which would not be faced by a non-disabled person. Describe the 'reasonable adjustments' that employers could make in the following situations.
   a) A man works in a call centre and uses a phone as part of his job. He develops a serious hearing impairment.
   b) A woman who is blind is given a job working with new colleagues in an unfamiliar part of the building.
   c) Factory workers are paid a bonus depending on the number of items they make. A disabled worker needs to have four short breaks during the day to deal with their condition and this reduces their output.
   d) A disabled employee has several short periods of sickness absence because of a permanent health condition. The employer is aware of the absences. The employer needs to make some workers redundant and decides to take the amount of their sickness absence into account.

9. Apply your knowledge and understanding of the Equality Act to each of the following cases. State and explain your judgements in each case.
   a) An employer allows a pregnant worker to have time off not just for ante-natal appointments (which is a legal requirement) but also to attend fitness classes for pregnant women at a nearby gym. The worker makes up the working hours lost while at the gym. A male worker also asks for time off to go to a gym and offers to make up the time. He argues that it would be unlawful to refuse his request. *Is he right?*
   b) A worker with a learning disability has a contract to work from 9 a.m. to 5.30 p.m. but wishes to change these hours. This is because the friend who accompanies him to work is no longer available before 9 a.m. but can help at 9.30 a.m. The employer says that it is important for everyone to turn up at 9 a.m. She claims that it is her legal right to enforce the contract. *Is she right?*
   c) An employer has a vacancy for someone to support women and girls who have been the victims of violence – usually caused by men. She decides that it will be lawful to advertise the job for women only. *Is she right?*
   d) An employer decides to provide his employees with company cars. Workers can qualify for a car as long as they have a full driving licence and are over 35 years of age. The employer has done this to keep insurance costs down and thinks these conditions are legal. *Is he right?*
   e) An employer needs enough staff for night shifts but has found it difficult to get volunteers from his workforce. He decides to change the shift arrangements for all workers so that everyone has the same number of late night shifts each month. Every worker is treated equally but one of the female workers claims that the shift changes are discriminatory. *Is she right?*

Workers also have legal protection from victimisation. Victimisation occurs if, having complained about discrimination or harassment, an employee is treated unfairly because they had complained.

### Website

For more details on the Equality Act and its impact on the workplace, access the appropriate Advisory, Conciliation and Arbitration Service (ACAS) guides and videos at: **www.acas.org.uk**

## Making a complaint under the Equality Act

The Equality Act is part of civil rather than criminal law (see page 40). This means that the police and the criminal courts are not involved. A person with a 'protected characteristic' must take action themselves if they have been discriminated against, harassed or victimised because of that characteristic.

*Study the complaint process on the right. It isn't necessary to follow each of the steps in turn. People who have been victims of discrimination have the right to take legal action straight away. However, employees usually try to resolve the problem informally or through mediation if they can.*

**Advisory, Conciliation and Arbitration Service (ACAS)** ACAS provides free and impartial information and advice to employers and employees on workplace relations and employment law. When things go wrong, ACAS offers conciliation to resolve workplace problems. They also provide training for employers to encourage better relationships in the workplace. ACAS is an independent organisation supported with funding from the Government.

**Citizens Advice** An independent charity that offers free, confidential and impartial advice to everyone on rights, responsibilities and the law. Citizens Advice is funded by donations and grants from public funds.

**Employment tribunal** Employment tribunals can hear cases brought by employees who think that their employer, a potential employer or a trade union has treated them unlawfully. Examples of unlawful treatment include unfair dismissal and unreasonable discrimination. A three-person independent panel will hear the claimant's case as well as that of the person or business against whom the claim is being made. (See Chapter 3 for more details on the court system in England and Wales.)

Keep a record of relevant events: include dates and times, and a description of what happened together with copies of any relevant paperwork, such as, letters, memos, emails, notes of meetings.

Seek information and advice from the **Advisory, Conciliation and Arbitration Service (ACAS)**, **Citizens Advice**, a trade union or a solicitor.

See the boss or supervisor to try to sort the problem out informally.

(Ask for the support of a work colleague or trade union representative at this stage or any of the stages below.)

Use the company's grievance procedure to make an official complaint.

Contact your trade union, professional association or ACAS to see whether they can resolve the matter through mediation.

Take legal action by taking the case to an **employment tribunal** for an independent judgement. This must be done within three months of the problem occurring. Before being able to lodge an employment tribunal claim, potential claimants must first notify ACAS of their intention to claim so that ACAS can offer the opportunity to resolve the issue using conciliation. (For more on tribunals, see page 65.)

### Websites

The Citizens Advice website offers information and advice on all aspects of the law and legal system (scroll to the bottom of their homepage for the appropriate links): **www.citizensadvice.org.uk**

For more information on employment tribunals, visit the GOV.UK website at: **www.gov.uk/employment-tribunals**

# CASE STUDY

## Law in action – Police disclosure of trivial offences is a breach of human rights – Supreme Court rules

In June 2014, the **Supreme Court** considered the following case:

## Background

The police issued warnings in 2002 to an eleven-year-old boy (T) for the theft of two bicycles. The warnings were disclosed by the police in 2008 when T, by now seventeen, applied for a part-time job with a football club possibly involving contact with children. They were disclosed again in 2010 when T applied for a place on a university course in sports studies which again might have involved contact with children. T had no other criminal record.

**Figure 2.8** What types of youth crime should be disclosed by police when college, universities and employers make their checks?

## T's claim

T's lawyers argued that a minor offence committed when eleven years-of-age did not affect T's suitability for adult employment or education even if he did come into contact with children. Disclosing his 2002 police warnings had violated T's right to respect for private life under Article 8 of the European Convention on Human Rights (ECHR).

## The Supreme Court's judgment

**Figure 2.9** The Supreme Court logo

The Supreme Court agreed with T and his lawyers. Supreme Court Justices ruled that it was unreasonable for the **State** to disclose all T's personal data and that there should be proper protection for citizens in line with Article 8 of the ECHR. Adults should not be haunted by relatively trivial offences committed in the past, particularly when they were children, as this would breach their human rights and could affect their employment prospects. As a result of the Supreme Court's judgment, the Government made changes to the 1997 Police Act. This brings UK law into line with Article 8 of the ECHR.

### Website

To find out more about the Supreme Court's role and the cases it has heard recently, go to its website: **www.supremecourt.uk**

### The purpose of law – settling disagreements

The law is also used as a way of settling disagreements. Judges are asked to decide who is right or wrong in disputes over such things as land ownership, money, employment and relationships.

**Supreme Court** The Supreme Court is the final court of appeal in the UK for civil cases, and for criminal cases from England, Wales and Northern Ireland but not Scotland. It hears cases of the greatest public or constitutional importance affecting the whole population. (See Chapter 3 for more details on the court system in England and Wales.)

**State** An organised political community under one government.

## Activities

10. Study the section on how the law should protect rights, and promote freedoms and equalities. Also analyse the case study on police disclosure of trivial offences before answering the questions below.

    a) Explain why the case study on the police disclosure of trivial offences shows that the law can sometimes be unjust and unfair.

    b) Describe how the Supreme Court put things right.

    c) State and explain which types of criminal offence you think should lead to a person being barred from working with children and vulnerable adults. Should such barring affect ex-offenders for life or for a fixed period?

    d) Check your responses to question 10c) by visiting the website of the *Government's Disclosure and Barring Service* DBS at: **https://www.gov.uk/government/organisations/disclosure-and-barring-service** and study the *DBS* referrals guide to relevant offences for England and Wales.

# CASE STUDY

## Law in action – customer claims against builder for poor work

### Background

Megan bought new kitchen units and found a self-employed builder to fit them. They agreed a price and the builder said installation would take him four days. Her builder agreed to install the units while she was out at work. She paid him half of the cost of the work once he started and agreed to pay the rest once he had finished.

Megan did not notice any problems until she got home from work on the fourth day. The new worktop was damaged and the doors did not fit. There was also a leak under the sink.

Megan tried to sort out the problem by getting the builder to meet her. The builder claimed that he had done his best but blamed Megan for 'buying such poor quality kitchen units'. He also said she must have caused the sink to leak herself. The builder asked to be paid the rest of his money but Megan refused.

### Megan's claim

Megan could not get the builder to agree to come back again, so she hired a new builder to replace the doors and worktop. He also fixed the sink.

Megan then issued a **small claim** in her local **County Court** against the first builder claiming:

- a refund of the money already paid to him

- the cost of buying and fitting new worktop and doors, and fixing the sink.

The builder issued a defence, saying that the units were not in good condition in the first place and issued a counterclaim for the money Megan hadn't paid him.

## The judgment

Megan could prove her case with photos of the poor work. She was also able to show the judge receipts for the replacement worktop and doors, and for the additional installation costs. The judge found that some of the first builder's work had been done well, but that it had been not been finished to a satisfactory standard under the Supply of Goods and Services Act.

The judge ruled in favour of Megan and ordered the builder to pay her for the extra cost of putting right his poor work. However, the judge also found that Megan was not entitled to a refund of the money she had already paid because some of the work had been good.

**Figure 2.10** Customers can use the small claims service of the County Court if they are not able to sort out problems with workpeople or traders

**Figure 2.11** The work of Magistrates' Courts, County Courts and tribunals are now sometimes brought together in one Justice Centre like this one in Aberystwyth, Wales

**Small Claim**  Claims of under £10,000 are known as 'small claims'. If you think someone owes you less than £10,000, you can present your case simply and informally.

**County Court**  County Courts deal with civil matters such as financial or housing disputes, family issues, personal injury and breach of contract. (See Chapter 3 for more details on the court system in England and Wales.)

## Activities

11. Study the section on how the law can help people settle disagreements. Also analyse the case study on Megan's dispute with her builder before answering the questions below.
    a) Using examples from Megan's case, explain why the County Court can be helpful to consumers.
    b) Describe the court's judgement in Megan's case and evaluate how far you think justice was achieved.

# Key legal principles

### Key learning
Study and understand the fundamental principles of law: the *presumption of innocence* and *equality before the law.*

## The presumption of innocence (innocent until proved guilty)

The first key principle of UK law is the presumption of innocence. People must be seen as innocent until they are proved to be guilty. So when a **defendant** is brought to court charged with a criminal offence, the **prosecution** must prove that the defendant is guilty. It is not the defendant's responsibility to prove that he or she is innocent.

A defendant does **not** have to:

● answer questions in a police interview
● provide a defence case statement (a document setting out the basics of their defence)
● give evidence at their trial
● provide an explanation for any of the issues raised by the prosecution
● answer questions asked by the prosecution.

However, **juries** are allowed to take a defendant's silence into consideration when reaching their verdict of 'guilty' or 'not guilty'. As a result, most defendants usually make some response to the charges against them.

New laws are sometimes brought in at times of national emergency. This happened after the terrorist attack on New York's World Trade Center in 2001. The Anti-Terrorism, Crime and Security Act allowed the imprisonment of terrorism suspects without trial.

**Defendant**  The person accused of an offence.

**Prosecution**  Prosecution lawyers work on behalf of the Crown and in cooperation with the police, to prove that the defendant is guilty. They produce evidence and call witnesses to support their case.

**Jury**  A group of ordinary people aged eighteen and over. In a Crown Court, the jury listens to arguments and evidence from the prosecution and the defence to decide whether the accused person is guilty or not guilty.

The imprisonment of terrorist suspects without trial can be said to undermine the principle that people should be seen to be innocent unless they are proved guilty. (See Chapter 1 for more details.)

The presumption of innocence can also be threatened if the police publicise arrests or identify people stopped for traffic offences.

# CASE STUDY

## Staffordshire Police withdraw their drink driving Twitter campaign

Over Christmas 2013, Staffordshire Police ran a social media campaign in which drivers were named on Twitter if they had been arrested and charged with drink-driving offences. Critics argued that the police campaign suggested drivers were guilty even though trials had not taken place. The motorists had been charged with an offence but it is against the ancient and fundamental right to a presumption of innocence to shame them before a court had found them guilty.

**Figure 2.12** The police now accept that they should not publish the names of people charged with drunken driving before a court has convicted them.

The **Information Commissioner's Office (ICO)** received a complaint and spoke to Staffordshire Police. The ICO's concern was that naming people who have only been charged alongside the hashtag 'drink driver' strongly implies a presumption of guilt. The ICO felt that the police campaign wasn't consistent with the **Data Protection Act**. The police withdrew the campaign accepting that they should not be implying guilt before conviction.

**Information Commissioner's Office (ICO)** An independent regulator sponsored by the Ministry of Justice that reports directly to Parliament on data protection and privacy issues. Part of the ICO's role is to make sure the Data Protection Act is fully implemented.

**Data Protection Act** The Data Protection Act (1998, revised in 2015) controls how personal information is used by organisations, businesses or governments. Everyone responsible for using personal data must follow strict rules called 'data protection principles'. For example, they must make sure the information is used fairly and lawfully.

## Activities

1. Study the section on the presumption of innocence and the case study about Staffordshire Police's twitter campaign.
   a) Describe the police's campaign.
   b) Explain why the Information Commissioners Office objected.
2. In 2014, the BBC announced that police had searched the house of a celebrity as part of their investigation into a sex offence. The BBC also showed a video of the police operation which appeared on a television news broadcast watched by millions. No arrests were made and the celebrity who was away at the time, said the allegation was completely false.

   Explain why publicity given to arrests of suspects and searches of their property can threaten the principles on which English law is based.

## Equality before the law

The right to equality before the law (as part of the right to a fair trial) is part of Article 7 of the Universal Declaration of Human Rights. It is also included in the Magna Carta. (See Chapter 1 for more details.)

The principle of equality before the law means that:

- All people should receive a fair, public hearing.
- Cases should be heard by competent, independent and impartial persons in courts established by law.
- Defendants should have time to prepare their case and should be tried without delay.
- Defendants are entitled to legal representation which should be provided by the State through **legal aid** if the defendant cannot pay.
- Defendants should be able to understand what is being said in court and should have the right to an interpreter if they need one.

- Defendants have the right to attend court and question witnesses.
- Any judgement should be made public (except in special circumstances where it is necessary to respect children's confidentiality).
- Defendants should have the right to appeal to a higher court.

**Legal aid**   In order to make sure that people with low incomes can have access to justice, the Government provides financial assistance. This enables people to receive independent legal support in criminal cases as well as in civil cases if their problems are serious.

**Solicitor**   A member of the legal profession qualified to deal with property transfers, the drawing up of wills and other legal matters. A solicitor may also instruct barristers and represent clients in some courts.

**Work to rule**   By working to rule, employees work strictly according to the rules of their contract, refusing to do any work outside their job description and for which they are not being paid. This reduces the amount of work completed.

### Activities

3.  Study the section on equality before the law and the news story on the 'legal aid crisis' below.
    a)  Describe the solicitors' campaign.
    b)  Explain why the solicitors were angry with the Ministry of Justice and how this is connected with the principle of equality before the law.

4.  Prepare a presentation for younger learners to help them understand the importance of the two key principles of English law – the presumption of innocence and equality before the law. Use the concepts of justice and fairness in your presentation.

**Barrister**   A qualified member of the legal profession who is a specialist at representing their clients in court.

**Magistrates' Court**   A court through which all criminal cases pass. Serious cases are sent to the Crown Court for trial. Minor criminal matters are tried in the Magistrates' Court. (See Chapter 3 for more details on the court system in England and Wales.)

# CASE STUDY
## Legal Aid Crisis

As **solicitors** prepare for crisis talks with government ministers over cuts to legal aid fees, their ongoing **work to rule** is clogging up the legal system. And **barristers** are due to join the protest on Monday.

The justice system has never been famous for working quickly, but now it is facing a massive slow-down.

Solicitors across England and Wales have been refusing to work on any new case funded through legal aid in protest at a government decision to go ahead with a cut of 8.7 per cent in the fees they are paid.

As the protest enters its fourth week, police officers are struggling to find lawyers to attend interviews with suspects – there simply are not enough duty solicitors to go around.

**Magistrates' Courts** too are feeling the strain. A busy Magistrates' Court might have 50 people appearing in a day, but only one duty solicitor, meaning many are going without legal representation.

Defendant Jamal Madden told *Channel 4 News* his experience at Bradford Magistrates' Court had been 'terrible' due to the 'waiting and the not knowing'. Mr Madden said the lone duty solicitor had 'got too much on his hands', adding it had been 'the worst day of my life, to be honest with you'. Without seeing a lawyer he pleaded guilty to burglary and his case was sent to the Crown Court for sentencing.

The Ministry of Justice said in a statement: 'The changes we are making to criminal legal aid are designed to deliver value for money to taxpayers and do not impact on the availability of high quality legal advice to those who need it most. Although we recognise that the transition will be challenging for lawyers, these changes (to fees) will put the profession on a sustainable footing for the long term. We have already pledged that an independent review looking at the impact of the new arrangements will begin in July 2016.'

(Adapted from *Channel 4 News*, 22 July 2015)

# Civil law and criminal law

## Key learning

Study the key differences between criminal and civil law and apply this knowledge to classify specific examples.

## Civil law

Civil law covers disputes between individuals, groups of people or organisations. People use civil law if they are in dispute with a supplier over a faulty product or poor service. (See example of the poor kitchen installation on page 36.) Civil law also covers the types of dispute below:

- employment and other contracts or agreements
- unfair treatment at work
- cases of discrimination under the Equality Act (see page 32)
- land and property ownership
- inheritance
- divorce, separation, and child access and custody
- copyright and patents
- accident and injury
- negligence

**Figure 2.13** Divorce and separation disputes can be sorted out using civil law but it is often easier, quicker and less costly to settle differences using mediation if possible

- tax and benefits
- mental health
- immigration.

## Criminal law

Criminal law covers offences against the community as a whole. Parliament decides which types of behaviour should be criminal offences. Offences covered by criminal law usually fall into one of the categories below:

- Against the person such as: homicide; rape; robbery and assault.
- Against property such as: theft; burglary and fraud.
- Against the State or Crown such as: tax evasion; smuggling; misconduct in public office; terrorism; immigration offences and currency forgery.
- Participatory offences where a person has encouraged or assisted a criminal. This includes a type of assistance known as **joint enterprise**.

Some types of criminal offence do not fit neatly into the four main types above. These include: offences against children and vulnerable adults; drug offences; road traffic offences; offences against the environment and animals; keeping a dangerous dog; offences against the legal system; **public order offences** and **inchoate offences**.

**Joint enterprise**   The rule of joint enterprise or common purpose means that all participants in a crime can be held responsible for its outcomes. So if a gang attack someone and that person is wounded with a knife, all members of the gang may be charged with a serious offence if they actively assisted or encouraged the attack. (The Supreme Court made this reinterpretation of the law on joint enterprise in February 2016.)

**Public order offences**   People have rights to freedom of speech and freedom of assembly, but these rights need to be balanced against the rights of others to go about their daily lives without being obstructed or feeling threatened. Public order offences are offences that prevent people going about their normal business. Examples include rioting and violent disorder.

**Inchoate offences**   The police can arrest and charge people who are planning or intending to commit a crime. Even though there are no victims, criminal activity has taken place.

**Table 2.1** Civil and criminal law – the main differences

| | Civil law | Criminal law |
|---|---|---|
| Purpose | Settling disputes and compensating victims | Deterring and punishing people who offend against the community at large |
| Who investigates the problem? | The victim – usually assisted by a solicitor or other representative | The police |
| Who pays for all this? | The two parties in the case will need to pay their legal costs. Sometimes solicitors will agree **'no win, no fee'** with their client. Victims with low incomes may be able to claim legal aid. | The administration of criminal law is mainly funded by the State |
| Who takes the case to court? | The victim – usually assisted by a barrister | Usually the **Crown Prosecution Service (CPS)** |
| Which courts deal with the case? *(The Court system is complicated because it has grown up over hundreds of years. See Chapter 3 for more details.)* | County Court, Family Court or Tribunal (depending on the type of case) High Court | Magistrates' Court or Crown Court (depending on the seriousness of the offence) |
| Which courts deal with any appeal? | High Court Appeal Tribunal or Upper Tribunal Supreme Court | Court of Appeal Supreme Court |
| What happens to the victim? | *If they win*, they will receive compensation from the loser who may also be made to pay all or part of the victim's legal costs *If they lose*, they are likely to have to pay all or part of the winner's legal costs as well as their own | May be offered emotional support from the charity Victim Support The Court may order the offender to pay compensation to the victim Victims may also be able to claim compensation from the Criminal Injuries Compensation Authority To win 'damages' from the criminal, they will need to use civil law |
| What happens to the person in the wrong? | Compensates the winner and may also be ordered to pay the winner's legal costs | Punishments could include: <br>• community orders <br>• fines <br>• imprisonment |

**'No win no fee'** This is also called a 'provisional fee arrangement'. The lawyer agrees to charge a fee only if he or she wins the case.

**The Crown Prosecution Service** The CPS considers information provided by the police. CPS lawyers decide whether there is enough evidence to take a matter to court and whether doing so would be in the 'public interest'. The CPS works independently of the police to prepare cases for court and to organise the prosecution of alleged offenders. The CPS also provides information, assistance and support to victims and prosecution witnesses.

## Activities

1. Read extracts from Adama's message to a friend below. Make a note of all the possible law-related issues and decide which are criminal and which are civil matters.

> Signed for United yesterday. Over the moon – have a three-year deal and £60,000 a week. Been looking at flats to rent and like one near the river.
>
> So far so good but still unhappy with Lexi and her attitude about Grace – who's two years old already. I'll need to do something so I can see my daughter regularly.
>
> Have you heard about my argument with the road sign? Lost control and crunch. Large dent in new motor and the steering's not as good as it was. Must have dozed off – might have to pay for the sign! A mate in the trade will fix the dent quick and then I'll sell. Let the buyer beware.
>
> To make it worse, got a ticket for leaving the motor in a shoppers' car park 'til I could get it moved. Unfair. No shoppers at that time of night!
>
> My cheeky sister Rose is in trouble again – keeping the neighbours up all night with her wild parties. A guy disrespected her so she slapped him. He fell and hit his head. Hospital case.
>
> Talking of hospitals, my mum's treatment has been a nightmare this time. A* care for years, then the doctor didn't notice mum had skier's thumb. Now she's having to wait months for an operation and can't use her hand.
>
> How's the marriage plan going? Sure you still want me to be best man?

2. Adama wants to know whether it would be worth considering legal expenses insurance. Visit the Consumers' Association website **www.which.co.uk** to research the benefits of such insurance and advise Adama.

3. The law on joint enterprise was changed by a ruling of the Supreme Court on 18 February 2016 after judges considered the case of Ameen Jogee. Research the Jogee case and the court's decision. Explain how far you support the court's reinterpretation of the law on joint enterprise.

**Figure 2.14** People together in a gang risk being charged with a serious offence if they actively encourage or assist the main offender

**Figure 2.15** Following the Dangerous Dogs Act of 1991, it is a criminal offence in the UK to own dogs such as this Pit Bull Terrier

# The main sources of law

## Key learning

Study the main sources of law: common law, Parliamentary legislation, international law and case law (judge-made law) to understand how laws are made.

## Common law

The English legal system is founded on common law. Law in medieval times was based on decisions made by judges about what was right and wrong. From the twelfth century onwards, judges would travel around England bringing justice to people wanting to settle disputes. Their decisions were based on England's beliefs and traditions. So, for example, stealing from another person or causing them personal injury was thought by most people to be a threat to the peace and prosperity of an entire community. Judges made decisions about such issues as theft, murder and assault. These rulings were written down and then used by other judges. Through this gradual process of establishing precedent (courts setting out judgements for others to follow), laws became 'common' or recognised by everyone. Common law was largely judge-made law rather than law made by Parliament.

## Parliamentary legislation

Today most new laws in England and Wales are proposed by the Government and decided by Parliament. These laws are known as statute laws. For example, the Conservative Government of 2015 proposed **legislation** to encourage welfare claimants back into work. This kept a promise made by the Conservatives during the general election campaign.

Sometimes new laws are proposed by individual Members of Parliament (MPs). In 2015, Labour MP, Rob Marris, proposed the Assisted Dying Bill in the House of Commons. His Bill sought to change the law so that people with terminal illnesses could end their lives as long as they had medical supervision. The Bill was defeated by 330 votes to 118. (See Chapter 6 for more details on this legislative process.)

## International and European Law

When a country joins the European Union (EU), it allows most EU law to become part of its own national law. So UK law has been heavily influenced by laws made within the EU. For example, the UK Human Rights Act of 1998 is based on European law. (See Chapter 1 for more details.)

> **Legislation**   Acts or laws passed by a parliament or assembly.

As a member of the United Nations (UN), the UK is bound by a range of international laws and treaties on: human rights, environmental protection and relationships between nations. For example, the International Law of the Sea covers such things

**Figure 2.16** Laws to regulate matters of life and death have caused some of the most serious legal arguments of the last thirty years

as rights to navigation and ownership of resources on the seabed. Here again, UK law should reflect these international agreements. (See Chapter 12 for more details of the UN.)

## Case law or 'judge-made' law

Precedent is still a very important feature of English law. When a judge hears a case in court, he or she will refer to other similar cases from the past. In order for laws to be applied consistently or 'in common', the judge will follow the decision made by senior or equal ranking judges in these earlier cases. In February 2016 the Supreme Court reinterpreted the law on joint enterprise, judging that an incorrect precedent had been set in 1980 and that hundreds of people had been wrongly convicted for over thirty years.

Sometimes senior judges rule that past decisions do not fit with recent advances in technology or modern thinking. Judges may reinterpret the law to bring it up to date and so set a new precedent for other judges to follow. After setting a new precedent, judges may also recommend that Parliament reviews the law so as to bring it properly up to date. For example, the Consumer Rights Act of 2015 brought consumer law up to date by including laws on the purchase of digital content.

> **Website**
> For details of current legislation and about how laws are made, try Parliament's website: **http://www. parliament.uk/**

**The Tony Bland ruling – an example of case law**

## Background

Tony Bland, a young Liverpool fan, was crushed and suffered severe brain damage in the Hillsborough football stadium disaster of 1989. Although he was able to breathe normally, Tony needed to be fed through tubes and doctors felt that there was no chance of him regaining consciousness. Only a high level of medical care was keeping Tony alive.

## Submission to the Court

Tony Bland's doctors, supported by his family, asked the courts for consent to withdraw treatment so that Tony could die peacefully.

## Decision

The High Court and the House of Lords agreed that it would be lawful to withdraw the artificial nutrition and hydration that was keeping Tony alive. Treatment was stopped and Tony became the 96th victim of the Hillsborough disaster on 3 March 1993, aged 22, after being in a coma for nearly four years.

This was a 'landmark' case which set an important precedent. Judges ruled that it was lawful to withdraw treatment so that a person could die peacefully, but it remained unlawful for doctors to give a person treatment intended to kill them. This remains the legal position following Parliament's rejection of the Assisted Dying Bill in 2015.

## Activities

1. Design a slide or chart to show the sources of English law. Include the following:
   a) Four sections – each showing a different source of English law:

   | | |
   |---|---|
   | Common law | European and international law |
   | Parliamentary legislation | Case law |

   b) A centrepiece showing the chart's purpose:

   Sources of English law

   c) Descriptive sentences selected or adapted from the ones below and placed in the correct section:

   *Laws passed by Parliament after being proposed by the elected Government and sometimes also by MPs or members of the House of Lords.*

   *Laws made by judges as they interpret or adapt existing laws to fit new situations.*

   *Laws based on traditional ideas of right and wrong interpreted and recorded by judges as they travelled around the country to dispense justice.*

   *Laws based on the UK's treaties and agreements with other countries.*

   d) An example of a law from each source.
   e) A photograph or illustration to accompany each source similar to the ones in Figure 2.17 and placed in the correct section:

**Figure 2.17** Use these images or ones like them to complete your chart on the different sources of English law

European Court of Human Rights

## Activities

2. Study Tony Bland's case and carry out your own research to investigate other landmark rulings linked to the welfare of people who are very ill or wish to end their lives. Some important rulings include:
   - Doctor Nigel Cox, 1992
   - Annie Lindsell, 1997
   - Doctor Moor, 1998
   - Miss B, 2002
   - Tony Nicklinson, Paul Lamb and AM, 2014
   - Ms C, December 2015
     a) Analyse each of these rulings.
     b) Choose one that you think set the most important precedent.

   c) Choose one ruling that was very significant but did not lead to any adjustment to the law.
   d) Justify your choices.

3. The Assisted Dying Bill of 2015 proposed that terminally ill people capable of making their own decisions should have the right to assistance should they want to end their life.

   Carry out some further research on this issue using internet-based material from the time.
   a) Describe the main arguments made in favour of the Assisted Dying Bill.
   b) Describe the main arguments made against the Bill.
   c) Explain your own position. Should MPs have voted to change the law?

# The different legal jurisdictions of the UK

## Key learning
Study the different legal jurisdictions of the UK (England and Wales, Scotland and Northern Ireland) and understand the reasons for these differences.

The UK does not have a single legal system. This is because the UK is a political union of nations that were once independent.

The Kingdom of Great Britain was created in 1707 by bringing Scotland into partnership with England and Wales. Scotland had its own separate legal system at the time. It was decided that this would continue largely as it had been before the union with England and Wales.

The political union between Great Britain and Ireland in 1801 created the United Kingdom of Great Britain and Ireland but allowed Ireland to keep its separate courts. Today only the six northern Irish counties (known as Northern Ireland) remain part of the UK but Northern Ireland still has a different court system from that of England and Wales.

This means that England and Wales, Scotland, and Northern Ireland have separate **legal jurisdictions**.

**Legal jurisdiction** An area of land where a particular legal system has authority.

Scotland, with its separate parliament, and Northern Ireland, through its assembly, also have the power to pass their own laws. For example, the age of criminal responsibility is twelve-years-old in Scotland but ten in England, Wales and Northern Ireland. (See Chapter 1 for more details on the age of criminal responsibility.)

However, there are more similarities than differences in the laws of these separate jurisdictions. For example, employment law in all three jurisdictions is very much the same. On the other hand, there are major differences in family law.

## Website
A guide to Scottish Law can be found on the website of the Student Lawyer – an information source for students thinking of a career in law: **http://thestudentlawyer.com**

## Activity

1. Investigate and describe at least two differences or similarities between law in England and Wales, and law in Scotland. You could explore some of the following:
   - where Scottish law came from
   - how Scottish law is made
   - Scotland's criminal courts including the size of a jury
   - Scotland's civil courts
   - Scottish lawyers and their training.

## Northern Ireland

Until recently, Northern Ireland was bitterly divided between loyalists (people who want to remain part of the UK) and republicans (people who want Northern Ireland to leave the UK). The two sides now share power in the Northern Ireland Assembly. It has responsibility for education, planning and development, and public safety. The Assembly can pass its own laws and has its own court system.

## Scotland

An independent country until 1707, Scotland has its own parliament with the power to pass its own laws. Scotland's legal system is largely separate from the rest of the United Kingdom, but the UK Supreme Court does act as the highest court for appeals in Scottish cases and a source of precedent for all Scotland's courts to follow. In 2014 Scottish people voted to remain part of the UK. However, with the Scottish National Party as an important political force in the country, Scotland may eventually break away from the rest of the UK. If this happens, the UK Supreme Court may lose its power to establish precedent for legal judgements in Scotland.

## Wales

An independent country until 1543, Wales has its own language. This almost died out in the 1960s, but has become more popular since. The Welsh Assembly, formed in 1998, has responsibility for: planning; environment, culture and sport; education; health; and transport. The Assembly has made changes to the law to fit Welsh circumstances but Wales still shares its legal jurisdiction with England.

**Devolution of power** The transfer of some decision-making to local control.

## England

England does not have its own assembly but, in 2015, the Government was considering a greater **devolution of power** to the English regions. Everything that affects England is decided through the United Kingdom Parliament.

In addition, the UK Parliament makes decisions about systems of government, taxation, economic policy and defence for the whole of the UK. England and Wales have a common legal jurisdiction.

## Practice questions

In the OCR specification, this section will be assessed using objective test questions and questions needing a written response.

1.  A male employer interviews a female candidate for a job on a sales team. She is 55 years old. Which one of the employer's actions would be **illegal**?
    A  Asking her different questions to those asked of a male candidate.
    B  Asking her to take maths and English tests linked to the demands of a job.
    C  After an excellent interview, rejecting her application because of a poor reference.
    D  After an excellent interview, rejecting her because younger employees wanted a team mate of their own age.　　[1 mark]

2.  Which one legal issue would usually be dealt with by the **County Court**?
    A  An assault linked to a dispute about property.
    B  An employee stealing food from a café where he worked.
    C  A contract dispute between an employer and employee.
    D  A customer who had been over-charged on their mobile phone contract.　　[1 mark]

**Study** the **Source** in the next column and answer questions 3 and 4 that follow.

3.  Choose one option to show **who would decide** the case in the source in next column.
    A  the Football Association (FA)
    B  the Equality and Human Rights Commission
    C  a Magistrates' Court
    D  an employment tribunal.　　[1 mark]

4.  Choose one correct **outcome** for the case in the source in the next column.
    A  Maggie has been forced out and must get her job back. This is a case of harassment.
    B  Maggie must get her job back. This is a case of direct discrimination and disabled people have full legal protection from losing their job.
    C  Maggie cannot claim unfair discrimination because it is sometimes dangerous for a disabled person to attend a football match.
    D  Maggie can be dismissed if her behaviour at work does not fit in with the new aims of the company.　　[1 mark]

5.  Explain why laws are needed.　　[4 marks]

## Source
## Leading football reporter claims discrimination

*Maggie Lambert, an experienced football journalist, has been sacked from her job with a television company. Maggie says that she has been a victim of unfair discrimination because she needs to use a mobility scooter. She claims that her career is 'in ruins' and that she may never get another job.*

*Maggie is supported by several players and team managers, some of whom are very close friends. Brian Maloney, the retired Ireland international said, 'Maggie was one of the lads really and always very fair'. However, Brian admitted that some players hated the way she mocked them for mistakes on the pitch and also that she could be 'rude but funny with it'.*

*Television company bosses claim to have 'acted within the law'. They added, 'Sadly Ms Lambert's football reporting is twenty years out of date. Our viewers want a different style that fits in with our company's new aims. We've made reasonable adjustments for her disability by asking her to report only from grounds with ramps and lifts but we can't put up with her rudeness any longer.'*

*Maggie Lambert thinks the television company are just making excuses and that it's her disability that's the real problem. She decides to take legal action.*

# Chapter 3:
# The legal system

This chapter on *The legal system* builds on learning from Chapter 1, *Rights and responsibilities* and from Chapter 2, *The law*.

In this chapter, we explore the ways in which the law is administered and enforced, and assess how far this achieves justice and fairness. We go on to study how best to manage and respond to crime.

Learning the following key concepts and terms will make it easier to organise your thinking and communicate your ideas:

- legal representative
- judge
- tribunal
- juror
- sanction
- retribution
- reform
- rehabilitation.

# How the legal and justice system works in England and Wales

## Key learning

Study the operation of the justice system in England and Wales to understand the distinct roles of: the police, judges and legal representatives. Know about how the criminal and civil court and tribunal systems work, and understand the other ways of settling disputes. Apply this knowledge and understanding to particular cases. Compare the youth justice system with adult systems.

Study and understand the responsibilities and roles of citizens in the legal system as a juror, magistrate, special constable, Police and Crime Commissioner, and member of a tribunal hearing.

## The role and powers of the police

### The purpose of the police

In the *State of Policing*, its annual assessment of policing in England and Wales for 2013/14, **Her Majesty's Inspectorate of Constabulary (HMIC)** sums up the police's purpose as follows:

*'The first duty of the state is the protection of its people. (The police) hold not only a special position of power in society, but also one of trust.*

*With those positions go high expectations; these are expectations not only of integrity and honour, but of efficiency and effectiveness in dealing with the causes and the consequences of crime.*

*People need to be safe, and to know and feel that they are safe. If they become victims of crime, they need to know that they will be believed, that they will be properly treated, and that wherever practicable those who have harmed them will be pursued and brought to justice.*

*The public's expectations depend on the police having the capabilities to deal with crime efficiently and effectively, and having strong leadership to police with integrity and honour.'*

*(HMIC)*

> **Her Majesty's Inspectorate of Constabulary (HMIC)**
> An organisation independent of government that has responsibility for monitoring standards in police forces and reporting to the public.

**Figure 3.1** Even though police responsibilities are very different from 200 years ago, the police's purpose is largely unchanged

## Website
Find the location of police forces in the UK and link to their websites via: **www.police.uk/forces**

### History of the UK police service

The UK police service began in Scotland when the City of Glasgow Police was founded in 1800. This was the UK's first professional force. It was not until 1829 that Sir Robert Peel, Home Secretary in Lord Liverpool's Conservative Government, proposed that London should have its own permanent, paid police officers to protect the capital.

Peel's Metropolitan Police Force, dressed in blue coats and top hats, began to patrol the streets of London in September 1829. Their uniform was chosen so that police officers could not be mistaken for soldiers. People were suspicious of the army and Peel wanted police officers to get the public on their side. He thought that by building trust, people would help the police to fight crime.

The County Police Act of 1839 led to each county and most large towns having their own police force.

Her Majesty's Inspectorate of Constabulary (HMIC) was established in 1856 to inspect police forces and to report on how well the police were doing their job. This is a role HMIC still has today. HMIC is independent of the Government.

## Website
The Metropolitan Police website contains information on police history, the work of the police, police careers and crime: **http://content.met.police.uk**

## Police rights and responsibilities

In the UK legal system, the police:

- keep people safe and prevent crime
- investigate crime
- arrest and charge suspects
- collect evidence
- brief the Crown Prosecution Service (CPS)
- give evidence in criminal courts.

The police need to carry out their duties fairly and justly. For these reasons, police work is regulated by codes of behaviour and laws. When people know what to expect from the police and feel confident of fair treatment, police work will be more effective. Police officers are trained to know their responsibilities as well as their rights.

## Website
To find out more about how the Crown Prosecution Service helps to achieve justice go to: **http://cps.gov.uk**

### Police responsibilities

- uphold the law, protect human life and keep the peace
- record any offence brought to their attention
- be polite and treat people with respect
- tell people their name and the station at which they are based
- obey the law themselves
- follow all the codes of practice for dealing with citizens
- inform citizens of their rights when stopped, searched, arrested or charged
- make accurate statements as witnesses in court
- use reasonable force only as a last resort
- avoid any form of discrimination.

### Police rights

- expect cooperation from citizens
- stop anyone in a public place and ask them to account for their actions
- stop and search people who they reasonably suspect may have committed or be about to commit a crime
- arrest someone who is committing a criminal offence, has committed an offence or is about to do so
- use reasonable force to stop, search or arrest people
- enter premises without permission to save life, or to deal with or prevent a crime
- seize property if they think it may have been stolen or if it is evidence linked to a crime
- charge someone with committing a criminal offence if there is enough evidence
- detain someone for up to 24 hours without charge.

### Citizens' responsibilities

- obey the law
- not to obstruct the police
- not to attempt to destroy evidence
- cooperate with legal advisers.

## Citizens' rights

- fair treatment, according to the law and without discrimination
- receive an explanation before any search is carried out
- receive the names and contact details of officers carrying out searches
- to be searched in private by an officer of the same sex if the search involves more than removing outer clothing such as a coat or jacket
- be asked for permission by the police to search property unless a search warrant has been issued
- receive a reason if arrested
- when arrested, not to be interviewed until taken to a police station
- be advised about rights and cautioned before a formal interview
- inform someone if arrested
- receive food, have breaks and receive medical help while with the police
- receive legal advice if arrested
- have an 'appropriate adult', usually a parent, present at the interview if under 18 or with learning difficulties
- be able to read the police codes of practice
- remain silent or to refuse to answer some questions
- read, check and sign or withdraw any statement made to the police
- not usually be detained for more than 24 hours without being charged
- receive an official custody record when released.

## Activities

1. Study police responsibilities and the challenges they face.
   a) List the skills needed by a successful police officer.
   b) List the personal qualities he/she will need.
   c) Compare your lists with those of other learners.
   d) Adjust your lists and rank the skills and personal qualities in order of priority, placing the most important ones at the top.
   e) Write a paragraph (maximum 100 words) for a police recruiting campaign describing the type of person who would make an ideal police officer.

2. Sir Richard Mayne, Joint Commissioner of the Metropolitan Police in 1829, described the role of the police as follows:

   *'The primary object of an efficient police is the prevention of crime: the next that of detection and punishment of offenders if crime is committed. To these ends all the efforts of police must be directed.'*

   Study this section and Sir Richard's description above.
   a) Re-write Sir Richard's description to make it fit the police's role today.
   b) Compare Sir Richard's description with your own.

3. The police do not prosecute alleged offenders. Explain why it is important for a separate, independent organisation (the CPS) to do this work.

## Activities

4. Police forces sometimes produce small laminated cards to give to arrested people. The card contains a clear statement of the person's rights.
   a) Check whether your local police force uses such a card or has a statement of citizens' rights on their website.
   **Either**
   b) Amend your police force's card or online statement to make it more suitable for a person with limited levels of literacy in English.
   **or**
   c) Design a card that would be helpful to an arrested sixteen-year-old with average reading ability.

## Police challenges today

- Dealing with changing patterns of crime.
  - Crimes such as theft, burglary and robbery have decreased but sexual offences, human trafficking and slavery are increasing.
  - Crimes such as fraud can now be committed on a massive scale, at speed, from overseas and by offenders unknown to the victim.
  - Changes in the types of crime being committed reflect changes in technology. Modern criminals are more likely to be using a computer to hack into people's bank accounts than a crowbar to open a safe.

- Supporting vulnerable people.
  - People are living longer and, as they get older, they are often more vulnerable to exploitation. People with mental health problems are more likely to be cared for in the community than in the

## Citizens' rights and responsibilities when stopped, searched, arrested and charged by the police

The police have an important responsibility to advise people of their rights when stopped, searched, arrested and charged. To ensure fairness and justice, young people aged sixteen or younger and vulnerable adults have a right to additional levels of support.

**Figure 3.2** Police officers need to keep the public on their side

past. The police now have a major role supporting health and social service teams as they respond to the needs of mentally disturbed people.

- Managing limited funds.
  - In a world of cost reductions for all public services, the UK's forty-five police forces must manage resources very carefully.
- Responding to higher levels of public scrutiny.
  - The police are more accountable than ever before. Police forces are required to explain their actions to their elected Police and Crime Commissioner, the general public, *HMIC*, the **Independent Police Complaints Commission (IPPC)** and the media.

**Figure 3.3** Sussex Police have a sponsorship agreement with a car dealership. This helps to achieve better value from a limited budget

### Activity

5. Study this section. List all the ways in which the Government encourages people to have confidence in the police. Explain why public confidence is vital to the success of police work.

## Citizen action

### Working as a special constable

The special constabulary is a force of unpaid, trained volunteers who work with and support their local police.

'Specials', as special constables are known, come from all walks of life. They all volunteer for a minimum of four hours a week and are an important link between the regular (full-time) police and the local community. People who work as special constables usually have another paid job outside the police service and come from a wide range of backgrounds.

Once special constables have completed their training, they have the same powers as regular officers and wear a similar uniform.

People become special constables for different reasons, including to:

- give something back to their community
- learn new skills and gain valuable experience
- enjoy a new personal challenge
- gain experience of the police force before applying to join as a regular officer.

**Qualifications needed to become a special constable**

- no formal educational qualifications are needed, but applicants must pass a literacy test
- a clear personal record without criminal convictions or police cautions
- the physical and mental abilities to perform police duties (but there are no minimum or maximum height requirements)
- citizenship of a country in the **European Economic Area**, including the UK, or indefinite leave to remain as a UK resident
- positive security clearance and reference checks.

**Independent Police Complaints Commission (IPPC)** A public organisation independent of the Government and the police. The IPPC is responsible for dealing with complaints made against police forces in England and Wales.

**European Economic Area (EEA)** A free-trade area created in 1994 by an agreement between the European Free Trade Association (EFTA) (excluding Switzerland) and the European Union (EU). Citizens of each EEA country have the right to work in any other EEA country.

## A special constable's duties

Special constables patrol their community and take part in crime prevention initiatives. They sometimes also help to deal with major incidents in support of regular police officers.

**Figure 3.4** Special constables' duties

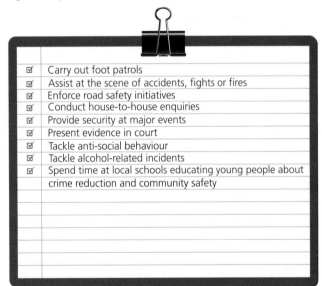

|   |   |
|---|---|
| ☑ | Carry out foot patrols |
| ☑ | Assist at the scene of accidents, fights or fires |
| ☑ | Enforce road safety initiatives |
| ☑ | Conduct house-to-house enquiries |
| ☑ | Provide security at major events |
| ☑ | Present evidence in court |
| ☑ | Tackle anti-social behaviour |
| ☑ | Tackle alcohol-related incidents |
| ☑ | Spend time at local schools educating young people about crime reduction and community safety |

## Activities

1. Special constables have different jobs in different police forces. Check your local police force's website and record special constables' main activities.

2. Study this section and at least one of the recommended websites. List the three most important reasons for someone becoming a special constable.

3. Explain why communities benefit from special constables working alongside regular police officers.

## Citizen action

# Keeping the police accountable: the work of Police and Crime Commissioners

Police and Crime Commissioners (PCCs) are elected representatives, often nominated by the main political parties, whose job is to make sure the police are answerable to the communities they serve.

PCCs aim to cut crime and deliver an effective police service that meets the needs of the whole community efficiently.

PCCs are responsible for working with local chief constables and their team of senior officers to decide:

- how the area is policed
- how the police budget should be spent
- the amount of council tax that should be charged for the police
- the type of information residents should receive about what the local police are doing.

PCC elections are held every four years. Everyone aged eighteen or over has the right to vote. In the first PCC elections (2012), only 15.1 per cent of people voted. Many electors didn't know what a PCC was and most had heard little about the election candidates. Voter turnout increased to 27% in 2016.

**Figure 3.5** PCCs often keep in touch with the public through newsletters and social media

Once elected, a PCC works full-time in the role and appoints a small staff team to help. PCCs do not become part of their local police force. They remain independent and have the power to remove the chief constable if agreed policing targets are not met.

PCCs spend much of their time visiting different parts of their area consulting residents about crime and policing issues. People can contact their local PCC to make a suggestion or to complain about local policing.

During 2016, PCCs began to take responsibility for local fire and rescue services. Transferring control of fire services from local authorities to PCCs aims to increase efficiency, save money and encourage greater cooperation between these two emergency services.

## Website

Find out more about PCCs' roles and responsibilities by visiting their association's website at: **www.apccs. police.uk/role-of-the-pcc/** from where you can also find your local PCC.

## Activity

1. Relatively few people have voted in PCC elections so far. Study the section on page 52 and write a blog post to persuade your family and friends to vote in the next PCC election.

    Your piece should contain:
    a) details of what a PCC does
    b) reasons to vote.

## The role of legal representatives

People in trouble with the police or making a claim through the civil justice system are likely to need legal advice. (People have a right to free legal advice if they are questioned at a police station.)

In criminal cases, trained lawyers prepare cases. Lawyers work on behalf of the Crown to prosecute the accused person or seek to defend the accused person against the charges brought against them.

In civil cases, lawyers support either the person making the claim (claimant) or the person opposing the claim (respondent).

Solicitors usually help prepare cases but may also represent their clients in the lower courts. Barristers, often assisted by solicitors, usually represent clients in the higher courts.

Citizens wanting professional legal representation usually go to a solicitor but it is also possible to go directly to a barrister.

Citizens needing legal advice often find it useful to start by visiting websites of organisations such as Citizens Advice or Which? (The Consumers' Association). Citizens have

a right to receive legal aid to cover their legal expenses in some cases ( for further details of legal aid see page 39).

Citizens have the right to represent themselves as defendants in a criminal case, and as claimants or respondents in a civil case.

## Websites

The GOV.UK website provides up-to-date information about rights to legal representation and legal aid: **https://www.gov.uk**

The Law Society is the independent professional body for solicitors. Their website includes details of solicitors' work and common legal issues where a solicitor's support might be useful: **http://www. lawsociety.org.uk**

**Figure 3.6** Solicitors offer a wide range of legal services

## Why should criminals have lawyers?

Lawyers working on criminal cases are often asked why they are willing to defend people charged with criminal offences.

Without legal representation for accused people, our criminal justice system would be very unjust. For justice to be done, defendants should have the right to legal advice and assistance.

**A defence lawyer's responsibilities in a criminal case**

- support their client during police interviews
- gather information about the crime, or alleged crime, looking for anything that could assist their client's case
- study the charges made against their client in detail
- interview any possible defence witnesses and prepare them for a court appearance
- advise their client whether they should plead guilty to the charge (or to a lesser offence) or to plead innocence
- arrange for their client to be represented in court
- discuss the case with their client as it progresses through the court advising a change of plea if necessary
- if their client is found guilty, argue on their behalf for a reasonable punishment.

Not everyone who faces criminal charges is guilty. If those accused of committing a crime did not get legal support, there would be many more innocent people in prison. Without skilled legal advice and representation, defendants might struggle to put their case across convincingly. Juries have to make their decisions on the basis of the evidence heard in court. Jurors are unlikely to believe a defence case that is poorly argued.

## Website

An interesting and detailed site covering the whole of the legal and justice system. The site includes some of the latest court judgements and advice for people opting to represent themselves in court: **https://www.judiciary.gov.uk/**

## Activities

2. Select three of the most important reasons why legal advice and representation are helpful to a citizen facing criminal charges or needing to respond to a civil claim. Use the term 'justice' in your list of points.

3. Explain why it is important for criminal defence lawyers to keep their personal feelings out of the cases on which they work.

4. A friend aged fifteen has been arrested and is on their way to the police station. Send a text message to your friend's parents to let them know about your friend's rights to support and legal advice. (Visit the GOV.UK website **https://www.gov.uk** to search for information about support and legal advice at a police station.)

5. Research the qualifications and training needed for anyone interested in a career as a legal secretary, solicitors' clerk, solicitor or barrister.

## The different types of criminal court and how they work

Once the police have arrested and charged a suspect, and the Crown Prosecution Service has prepared the case, the accused person (defendant) will face trial in a criminal court. (For information on a defendant's rights in court, see page 38.)

## Magistrates' Courts

Criminal cases start in the Magistrates' Court. The less serious cases may be tried and sentenced there, especially if the accused person (defendant) pleads guilty. Magistrates are trained people who listen to the evidence and decide how to deal with the defendant. Magistrates usually sit as a 'bench' of three.

**Sentences a Magistrates' Court can give**

A Magistrates' Court can give punishments including:

- up to six months in prison (or up to twelve months in total for more than one offence)
- a fine generally of up to £5,000
- a community sentence, such as unpaid work in the community.

The court can also give a combination of punishments – for example, a fine and unpaid work in the community.

If the court decides a sentence should be for longer than six months, it passes the case to the Crown Court for sentencing.

## Crown Courts

Magistrates send more serious offences, such as robbery, to the Crown Court for trial. In the Crown Court, a judge and jury will listen to the evidence. The jury decides whether the defendant is guilty or not guilty. They must do this before being told about any past crimes carried out by the defendant. The judge advises the jury on points of law, makes sure the trial is fair and decides the sentence. He or she takes the defendant's other offences (if any) into account. (See Chapter 2, page 31, for an example of the type of case heard in a Crown Court.)

**Figure 3.7** Who's who in a Magistrates' Court

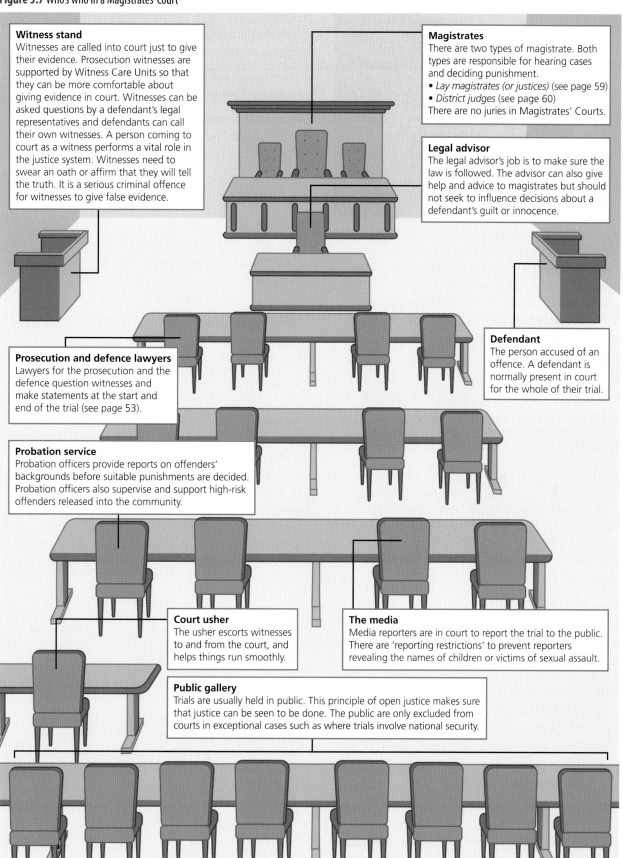

**Witness stand**
Witnesses are called into court just to give their evidence. Prosecution witnesses are supported by Witness Care Units so that they can be more comfortable about giving evidence in court. Witnesses can be asked questions by a defendant's legal representatives and defendants can call their own witnesses. A person coming to court as a witness performs a vital role in the justice system. Witnesses need to swear an oath or affirm that they will tell the truth. It is a serious criminal offence for witnesses to give false evidence.

**Magistrates**
There are two types of magistrate. Both types are responsible for hearing cases and deciding punishment.
• *Lay magistrates (or justices)* (see page 59)
• *District judges* (see page 60)
There are no juries in Magistrates' Courts.

**Legal advisor**
The legal advisor's job is to make sure the law is followed. The advisor can also give help and advice to magistrates but should not seek to influence decisions about a defendant's guilt or innocence.

**Prosecution and defence lawyers**
Lawyers for the prosecution and the defence question witnesses and make statements at the start and end of the trial (see page 53).

**Defendant**
The person accused of an offence. A defendant is normally present in court for the whole of their trial.

**Probation service**
Probation officers provide reports on offenders' backgrounds before suitable punishments are decided. Probation officers also supervise and support high-risk offenders released into the community.

**Court usher**
The usher escorts witnesses to and from the court, and helps things run smoothly.

**The media**
Media reporters are in court to report the trial to the public. There are 'reporting restrictions' to prevent reporters revealing the names of children or victims of sexual assault.

**Public gallery**
Trials are usually held in public. This principle of open justice makes sure that justice can be seen to be done. The public are only excluded from courts in exceptional cases such as where trials involve national security.

**Figure 3.8** Most cities and some larger towns have Crown Courts

A Crown Court is organised in a very similar way to a Magistrates' Court. A judge sits in place of the magistrate or magistrates and there is space for the twelve-person jury opposite the witness stand. The defendant's place is usually in front of the public gallery. It is sometimes known as the 'dock' and has direct access to cells below the court.

### Victims' rights

Victims do not have a central role in criminal proceedings. The Crown takes responsibility for the prosecution and so victims have no right to legal representation in court. However, if they are witnesses, victims have all the rights of a court witness, including the right to support. In 2013, victims were given the additional right to state how they had been affected by the crime – physically, emotionally, psychologically, financially or in any other way. This is known as a victim impact statement.

## Appeals

Defendants unhappy with the decisions made in a Magistrates' Court are able to appeal to a Crown Court.

Appeals from the Crown Court generally go to the Court of Appeal.

## Youth justice

Young people under eighteen have the right to special support in the justice system. During a police interview, they are entitled to be accompanied by a parent or other responsible adult. If convicted, they are not normally sent to an adult prison.

Courts have a legal duty to safeguard the welfare of all young people and to prevent them reoffending. As a result, the youth justice system emphasises **restorative justice** and **rehabilitation** rather than **retribution**.

Most young people have their cases heard in a youth court but serious offenders can be sent for trial in a Crown Court. A youth court deals with issues such as: theft and burglary; anti-social behaviour and drug offences.

A youth court is a special type of Magistrates' Court for people aged between ten and seventeen.

Either three magistrates or a district judge 'sit' in a youth court. There is no jury in a youth court. Parents or carers must accompany young people under sixteen.

A youth court can give a range of sentences including:

- community sentences
- Detention and Training Orders carried out in secure centres for young people as an alternative to prison.

### How youth courts are different from adult courts

Youth courts are less formal than adult courts:

- defendants are called by their first name
- the magistrates or judge, lawyers and court staff usually sit on the same level as the defendant
- lawyers and court officials do not wear wigs, gowns or uniforms
- parents or carers sit with the defendant and can contribute to the discussions
- members of the public are not allowed in to the court (unless they get permission)
- **Youth Offending Team (YOT)** workers attend the hearing rather than probation officers.

**Restorative justice**   The offender makes peace with the victim and makes up for any loss or damage.

**Rehabilitation**   Helping an offender to fit back into the community. This may include treatment for alcohol or drug problems, help getting a job or assistance with housing.

**Retribution**   Making sure that an offender is punished in a way that satisfies the victim, and his or her family and friends. The criminal is 'made to suffer' for what they have done.

**Youth Offending Team (YOT)**   Youth offending teams work with young offenders and supervise any community sentences. They look into the background of a young person and try to help them stay away from crime.

**Figure 3.9** Room layout for a youth court hearing

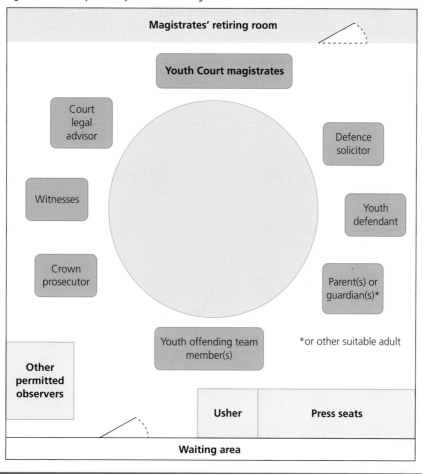

## Websites

For a simple official government guide to courts, tribunals and sentencing try: **https://www.gov.uk/browse/justice/courts-sentencing-tribunals**

The Crown Prosecution Service website offers useful information for witnesses and victims: **http://www.cps.gov.uk**

The Courts and Tribunals Judiciary website provides detailed information on every aspect of the court system from the history of court dress to judicial careers. It also includes a detailed chart showing how the court system works: **https://www.judiciary.gov.uk**

# Citizen action

## Being a lay magistrate

Most magistrates are lay magistrates (also called Justices of the Peace). Lay magistrates are unpaid volunteers from a wide range of backgrounds and occupations. They may be retired or unemployed. Magistrates do not have legal qualifications but do receive training.

Magistrates must be able to listen to all sides of a case and use their common sense to contribute to fair and reasonable decisions.

Lay magistrates usually sit in a group of three. One magistrate will have been trained to lead a discussion to resolve the case. Magistrates decide whether the defendant is guilty and what punishment to impose. They deal with a range of minor and straightforward criminal cases such as theft, criminal damage, public disorder and motoring offences. Magistrates also 'sit' in youth and family courts.

## Activities

1. Consider the following cases. Link each one with appropriate criminal courts:
   a) an allegation of robbery against a thirty-year-old
   b) a seventeen-year-old accused of a drugs offence
   c) a sixteen-year-old accused of rape
   d) a sixty-year-old accused of shoplifting
   e) a forty-year-old wishing to appeal against a Crown Court guilty verdict for attempted murder.

2. Visit the Justice website and find the *You be the judge* section at: **http://www.ybtj.justice.gov.uk/**.

   Consider at least two of the criminal cases from the website. Give your sentence and answer the questions below.
   a) A judge or magistrate will take <u>aggravating factors</u> into account when deciding a sentence. Define this term and give an example.
   b) A judge or magistrate will also take <u>mitigating factors</u> into account when deciding a sentence. Define this term and give an example.
   c) Judges and magistrates take other issues into account when deciding the sentence. Some possible issues are listed in the table alongside. For each:
      - State how the sentence may be affected.
      - Explain reasons for this.
        (The first row has been completed for you.)

3. List at least four differences between a Magistrates' Court and a Crown Court.

4. Youth courts are said to be 'less formal' than Magistrates' Courts or Crown Courts.
   a) State three ways in which youth courts are 'less formal' than adult courts.
   b) Explain why less formality makes it more likely that the youth courts achieve fairness and justice.

   c) Describe any disadvantages of youth courts being less formal than adult courts.

| Factors | Likely effect on the sentence | Explanation |
|---|---|---|
| It was the third time the offender had been convicted for assault in four years. | Longer | The offender has not learned his or her lesson from previous punishments so something more severe is needed. The community needs protection from this person. |
| The defendant makes an immediate plea of guilty. | | |
| The defendant is of 'previous good character'. It is their first offence. | | |
| The defendant shows no regret for his actions and continues to blame his victim during the court case. | | |

**Figure 3.10** Magistrates' Court

## Website

You be the judge (or magistrate). An interactive site where you can have a go at passing sentences in real cases. Includes video about the workings of a Magistrates' Court: **http://www.ybtj.justice.gov.uk/**

The GOV.UK website includes a summary of what magistrates do and a section on how to apply: **https://www.gov.uk/become-magistrate/what-magistrates-do**

The Magistrates Association website includes further information about what magistrates do and how to become a magistrate: **https://magistrates-association.org.uk/**

The Citizenship Foundation run mock trial competitions for school students: **http://www.citizenshipfoundation.org.uk/main/page.php?435**

## Magistrates – fact check

- Magistrates are also called Justices of the Peace and are allowed to use the initials JP after their name.
- Magistrates can be appointed at eighteen-years-old and must retire at seventy.
- Roughly equal numbers of men and women are magistrates.
- Most magistrates are in court for the equivalent of eighteen days per year with two additional days for training.
- Magistrates with a job are entitled to time off for their duties.
- Magistrates are unpaid, but may claim expenses and allowances so as not to lose out.
- Magistrates are not legally qualified but have a legal advisor in court for support.
- Magistrates refer to sentencing guidelines and case law before making decisions.

**Figure 3.11** Can you be a magistrate?

# Health
Can you
- hear clearly, with or without a hearing aid?
- sit and concentrate for long periods of time?

# Personal qualities
Are you
- aware of social issues?
- mature?
- reliable?
- committed to serving the community?

Do you
- understand people?

Can you
- understand documents?
- follow evidence?
- communicate effectively?
- think logically?
- weigh up arguments?
- reach a fair decision?

# Good character
It's unlikely you'll be taken on if you have been:
- found guilty of a serious crime
- found guilty of a number of minor offences
- banned from driving in the past 5 to 10 years
- declared bankrupt

**Conflicts of interest**
You can't be a magistrate if you work in a job where there could be a conflict of interest – for example if you are a police officer.

## Activities

5. Ask your teacher if it would be possible to invite a local magistrate to visit your class. Design questions to ask about their work and record their answers.
6. Do you think that you would make a good magistrate? Review the qualities magistrates need. List the qualities you already have and the ones you may need to work on. Which learners in your group do you think would make good magistrates?
7. Consider the work magistrates do. Describe what you think would be the most stressful parts of the job and which parts of the job would require most training.
8. Explain why police officers are not allowed to become magistrates. (Use the term 'conflict of interest' in your answer and explain what it means.)
9. Magistrates could be, for instance, plumbers, teachers, bar staff, garage mechanics or sales staff. They could also be retired or unemployed. Explain why it is important that magistrates come from a variety of different backgrounds.

# Judges' roles and powers

Judges interpret and uphold the law. They are legally trained, experienced lawyers who are able to make sure that court cases are heard fairly and outcomes are just. Lawyers apply to become judges. Their applications are dealt with by the Judicial Appointments Commission, an independent group of people, drawn mainly from the legal profession. (See Chapter 6 for more details of the judges' role in the British Constitution.)

**Figure 3.12** Experienced lawyers can apply to become judges

Judges are expected to apply statutory law and previous case law to the facts of each case.

Judges decide punishments in criminal courts and outcomes in most civil cases. They also keep order in court.

Judges in a Crown Court do not decide whether defendants are guilty or innocent – that is the jury's responsibility. However, a Crown Court judge is able to advise and support a jury on points of law.

District judges hear the more complex cases in Magistrates' Courts, but will also work in County Courts hearing civil cases, and may also deal with some family law cases as long as they are qualified to do so. District judges will move around a 'circuit' of County Courts hearing mostly civil and family cases. They usually make their rulings alone.

The most experienced judges hear serious criminal cases or important civil cases in the High Court where they may also rule on criminal appeals.

As we found out in Chapter 2, judges do not pass laws; that's Parliament's job. However, we also learned that judges interpret existing laws so that they fit particularly unusual cases or are more suitable for modern conditions. In this way, senior judges' decisions set precedents that are followed in lower courts.

## Websites

You be the judge. An interactive site where you can have a go at passing sentences for real cases. Includes video about the workings of a Crown Court: **http://www.ybtj.justice.gov.uk/**

Find out more about what judges do and which judge sits in which type of court by referring to the Courts and Tribunals Judiciary website at: **www.judiciary.gov.uk/about-the-judiciary/who-are-the-judiciary/judicial-roles/judges/**

## Activities

10. Study this section on judges and the section on being a magistrate (pages 57 to 60).
    Decide where to place the descriptions below.
    (Descriptions can be placed in one column on the chart or in both columns or left out.)
    I.   usually decides sentences alone
    II.  is supported by a legal adviser
    III. has substantial legal training and experience
    IV.  sitting in court takes up most of their time
    V.   decides whether defendants are guilty or not guilty
    VI.  deals with criminal cases
    VII. retires at sixty five years old
    VIII. gives advice on points of law

| Lay magistrate | Judge in Crown Court |
| --- | --- |
|  |  |
|  |  |
|  |  |
|  |  |

11. From the list below, select the activities for which judges have responsibility.
    I.   putting together evidence for the court to hear
    II.  hearing more complex cases in Magistrates' Courts
    III. deciding whether or not Crown Court defendants are guilty
    IV.  making statute law
    V.   appointing other judges
    VI.  applying case law
    VII. keeping order in court
    VIII. discussing evidence with the jury to help them with their verdict

12. Find out more about the work of the Judicial Appointments Commission from their website: **https://jac.judiciary.gov.uk/**
    a) Describe the qualities needed to become a judge.
    b) Describe the selection process.
    c) Give lawyers three top tips for success in the selection process.

# Citizen action

## Serving on a jury

Trial by jury can be traced back to the Magna Carta of 1215 which stated that a citizen has a right to 'the lawful judgment of his peers'.

Any citizen aged eighteen to seventy can serve on a jury. Each year 200,000 people are chosen to perform this **civic duty**. Names are randomly selected by computer. This ensures that jurors are fully representative of their community. People chosen for jury service have a legal responsibility to serve.

Most juries are used in the Crown Court, but some civil cases are also decided by jury. These include cases involving damage to a person's character or reputation.

Jury trials account for less than 1 per cent of all criminal trials because most cases are dealt with in a Magistrates' Court. Of those cases that do go to the Crown Court; two out of every three defendants plead guilty.

**Civic Duty**   The responsibilities a citizen has to their community.

## What do jurors do?

Jurors' decisions are critically important for individual defendants. These decisions also affect the community as a whole. Serving on a jury is one of the most important civic duties that anyone can perform.

Jury service normally lasts for two weeks. Jurors may hear more than one case in that time. Employers are required by law to give jurors time off work unless this would have a very damaging effect on their business. Jurors are paid expenses and compensated for loss of earnings.

**Figure 3.13** In English and Welsh Crown Courts a jury of twelve people hear all the evidence before deciding the defendant's guilt or innocence

In a criminal trial, a twelve-person jury listens to the evidence and then decides whether or not the defendant is guilty. Juries do not decide the punishment; that's the judge's job.

Jurors say nothing whilst in the court room, but they can take notes. After hearing the evidence, jurors discuss the facts of the case amongst themselves to decide their verdict. They do this secretly in a secluded room. Jurors are allowed no communication with anyone outside the room, and any technology that may interfere with the secrecy of the jury, such as phones or tablet computers, is removed until a verdict is reached.

### The juror's oath

People serving on a jury must make an oath or non-religious affirmation before the trial starts.

The affirmation – *I do solemnly, sincerely and truly declare and affirm that I will faithfully try the defendant and give a true verdict according to the evidence.*

Jurors are reminded that all defendants are innocent until proved guilty.

*'Important – It is an offence for anyone to attempt to interfere with or intimidate a juror in any case before the Crown Court. If anyone approaches you about a case you must tell a court official or police officer at once so that the matter can be reported to the trial judge.'*

(Extract from *Your Guide to Jury Service*, HM Courts and Tribunals Service, 2015.)

### Website

Further information for people summoned to serve on a jury is available at: **www.gov.uk/jury-service/ overview**

### Activities

1.  If possible, find someone who has served on a jury – parent/carer, older relative or friend, teacher. Ask them to describe their experience but *do not* ask about their private jury room discussions as these must remain confidential.

2.  An eighteen-year-old friend complains about being summoned for jury service. They argue that it would be better for judges to decide guilt or innocence. Persuade them that jury service is an important civic duty. Include the following in your argument:
    a)  the origins of jury service
    b)  the advantages of jury trial for justice and fairness
    c)  an explanation of why decisions made by juries affect the whole community and not just individual defendants.

# Civil Courts

Although some civil cases are heard in Magistrates' Courts, most are dealt with by County Courts, family courts or tribunals. (For more information on tribunals, see page 65.)

## County Courts

There are numerous County Courts or 'small claims courts' covering England and Wales. These deal with civil matters such as financial or housing disputes, family issues, personal injury and breach of contract. Most cases are brought by people attempting to recover debts or trying to gain reasonable compensation for a breach of contract, for example, replacement or repair of a faulty item. (See Chapter 2, page 36 for an example of such a case.)

For small claims (with a value of £10,000 or less) court proceedings can take place using written evidence online without the need to attend a hearing. The court charges a fee for issuing a claim – the amount depends on the size of the claim. The respondent is sent a copy of the claim, giving them a chance to oppose it or to reach a settlement out of court. Most claims are settled by respondents before a court hearing. If a case does go to court, both parties (claimant and respondent) will need to present their case to a judge.

### Website

The GOV.UK website provides information on how to make a small claim in a County Court and sets out the scale of fees: **https://www.gov.uk/make-court-claim-for-money/overview**

### Mediation services

Sometimes people just need an impartial, calm person to help them sort out their dispute fairly. In such cases, a mediation service can be quicker and cheaper than going to court. The Ministry of Justice's Civil Mediation Service puts claimants in touch with people trained to help settle disputes. Mediation can take place by phone if both parties agree and may take less than an hour.

### Website

The GOV.UK Justice website enables people to contact a local civil mediation adviser and specifies the fees for using this service: **http://www.civilmediation.justice.gov.uk/**

**Figure 3.14** Small claims can sometimes be settled through mediation using a phone and computer from home. Some court cases can also be settled through a telephone conference

If there is a hearing, claimants and respondents can:

- represent themselves
- pay for a barrister or solicitor to represent them
- ask someone such as a relative or an advice worker to speak on their behalf – the court needs to grant permission for this form of representation.

Small claims hearings are usually held in the judge's room or a court room at a County Court. They are less formal than criminal proceedings. People sit together around a table. The judge will try to make a fair judgement by drawing out relevant information from both parties. Telephone conference calls, involving the judge, claimant and respondent, are often used as alternatives to court hearings. After the hearing, the judge explains their decision in a letter (also known as a judgment) which is sent to the claimant and the respondent. The letter also describes the action that each party must take.

If the claimant wins, they can ask the court to collect any payments from the respondent using court bailiffs if necessary. If the debt is not paid within seven days, the bailiff will visit the respondent's home or business, to see if anything can be sold to pay the debt.

# Making a small claim over faulty goods – four simple steps

### STEP 1 Letter or email to complain

Sometimes all that is needed is a properly written complaint. State clearly why you are unhappy and describe the remedy you think would be fair (including payment of your losses and expenses). End with what will happen if you do not get a reply. (Businesses usually give information on their websites about how to complain or will provide copies of their complaint procedure.)

### STEP 2 Alternative Dispute Resolution (ADR)

If you have been unable to settle with the business, you can use an Alternative Dispute Resolution (ADR) scheme instead of court action. ADR schemes use a mediator or **ombudsman** to help you and the business reach a solution. You may have to pay a fee for using the scheme, but this is usually refunded if you are successful.

### STEP 3 Small Claims Court

If you cannot agree, the only option left is to use the Small Claims Court. Complete the claim form and pay the court fee. The court will encourage you both to negotiate an agreement. If this isn't possible, the court will arrange a hearing. At the hearing, you and your opponent will have a fair chance to explain your position. The judge will decide a fair remedy and inform all parties in writing.

### STEP 4 Remedy or compensation

If your claim is successful, you should receive the agreed money or remedy. If the respondent does not do what has been agreed or ordered by the court, the judgement can be enforced.

**Ombudsman** An independent service that provides dispute resolution for businesses supplying services in areas such as communications, energy, property, law, financial services and copyright licensing.

## Websites

The Which? (Consumer Association) website provides clear and detailed advice about how to use the law to resolve consumer problems: **http://www.which.co.uk/consumer-rights/**

The Consumer Ombudsman website includes details of how it can help with claims: **http://www.consumer-ombudsman.org/**

## Family law courts

Family matters are dealt with in the Family Division of the High Court, by district judges in County Courts and in specialist Magistrates' Courts known as Family Proceedings Courts.

The various types of Family Court deal with issues such as:

- some aspects of domestic violence where a person needs protecting from their abuser
- divorce
- financial support for children after divorce or relationship breakdown
- disputes between parents over the upbringing of children
- adoption (to give full legal parental rights and duties to the adoptive parents).

These are all 'private law cases' in which matters are brought to court by a person seeking a judgement in their favour.

Family courts also hear 'public law cases' where a local authority or the NSPCC (see page 24) are seeking a court judgement to protect children.

## Activity

3. Explain why it is better to try mediation in civil disputes than to take a case to court.

## Activities

4. You buy a jacket from a well-known high street fashion chain. You hang the jacket up in a cupboard at home for two weeks, then wear it for a night out. When you get home, you notice that the collar has faded. It was clearly faulty when you bought it, but the store manager refuses to replace it or refund your money even though you point out that the Consumer Rights Act gives you thirty days from the date of purchase to reject a faulty item. The manager claims that you must have caused the jacket to fade by leaving it in the sun.

   Write an email or letter of complaint. Use the template below to help you.

5. State two reasons why it is important to have a separate legal division in civil law to resolve family matters.

**Figure 3.15** Template for a complaint

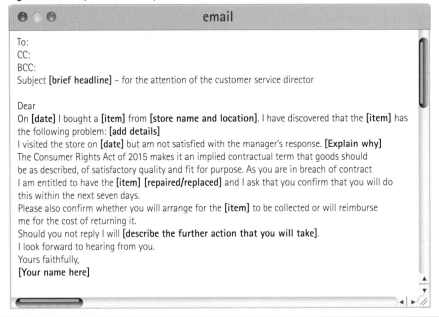

To:
CC:
BCC:
Subject **[brief headline]** – for the attention of the customer service director

Dear
On **[date]** I bought a **[item]** from **[store name and location]**. I have discovered that the **[item]** has the following problem: **[add details]**
I visited the store on **[date]** but am not satisfied with the manager's response. **[Explain why]**
The Consumer Rights Act of 2015 makes it an implied contractual term that goods should be as described, of satisfactory quality and fit for purpose. As you are in breach of contract I am entitled to have the **[item]** **[repaired/replaced]** and I ask that you confirm that you will do this within the next seven days.
Please also confirm whether you will arrange for the **[item]** to be collected or will reimburse me for the cost of returning it.
Should you not reply I will **[describe the further action that you will take]**.
I look forward to hearing from you.
Yours faithfully,
**[Your name here]**

### Domestic violence and forced marriage

Courts can intervene in cases of family abuse.

Two types of order can be granted:

- a non-molestation order, which can either prohibit particular behaviour or general molestation
- an occupation order, which can define or regulate rights of occupation of the home.

Anyone breaching a non-molestation order can be arrested and taken through the criminal justice system.

Family Courts can order the removal of a suspected abuser from their home.

Fifteen designated County Courts also have powers to prevent forced marriages, and to offer protection to victims who might have already been forced into a marriage. Any assault is a matter for the police and the criminal courts.

**Figure 3.16** Forced marriage has been a criminal offence since 2014 and County Courts can use civil law to protect people at risk

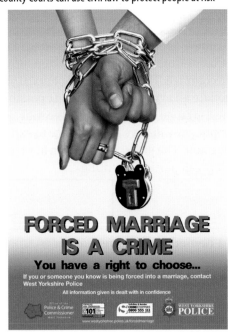

**FORCED MARRIAGE IS A CRIME**
You have a right to choose...
If you or someone you know is being forced into a marriage, contact West Yorkshire Police
All information given is dealt with in confidence

# CASE STUDY
## Forced Marriage Case (based on real events)

After hearing that she would be taken to Pakistan and shot if she refused to marry a man chosen by her parents, a teenage girl went to her local police station for help. Still wearing her pyjamas, the upset sixteen-year-old told police that she was being made to marry a man she had only met once.

Following the girl's appeal for help, the County Court used a 'protection order' preventing one of her relatives from arranging the child's marriage either in the UK or abroad. The order also prohibited any harassment of the sixteen-year old and prevented the relative from encouraging others to force the girl to marry. The orders were backed by powers of arrest.

Later the child applied to the court for the protection orders to be lifted, claiming that she wanted to travel abroad to see a sick relative. The judge was suspicious and felt that relatives had made the sixteen-year-old ask for the orders to be removed. The protection order remained in place.

Even though the court had insisted that its permission would be needed before the girl could marry, relatives went ahead with their plans and an expensive wedding took place in the UK.

As a result, two of the girl's relatives were taken to court charged with the criminal offence of conspiring to force a girl to marry against her will. One of the girl's relatives claimed that she didn't fully understand the protection orders but this was contested by the prosecution.

### Activities

6. Study the case study on forced marriage above.
   a) Describe the rulings made by the County Court.
   b) Explain why these rulings were made.
   c) Describe the charges against the two relatives.
   d) State whether the charges would be heard in a civil court or criminal court.
   e) One of the women claimed not to have known about the details of the County Court order. Explain whether this is likely to lead to greater leniency when the case is tried.
   f) State whether forced marriage is a criminal or civil offence giving reasons for your answer.

## Tribunals

Around one hundred and thirty different types of tribunal deal with approximately one million cases per year – more than in any other part of the justice system. Tribunals resolve disputes connected with such issues as employment, immigration, mental health and criminal injury.

Tribunals are an informal and relatively quick way of settling disputes. Tribunal members are lay people with the particular knowledge and experience needed to make fair decisions. A tribunal panel usually has three members, one of whom will be a chairperson with legal training.

As tribunals are part of the civil justice system, they do share some features of a normal court of law. For instance, in most cases, claimants and respondents are asked to give evidence under oath. Lying can be viewed as **perjury** (a criminal offence) and punished through a criminal court.

**Perjury** When a person who has taken an oath as a witness, or their interpreter, deliberately makes a false statement in a court or tribunal.

### Website

The Courts and Tribunals Service website includes details of all the types of tribunal that sit in England and Wales as well as information about how they work: **http://www.justice.gov.uk/tribunals**

## Appeals

Upper tribunals can hear appeals against the decisions of local tribunals. Appeals are heard by experienced judges.

Appeals against decisions of a County Court are held in the High Court. Permission to appeal is only given if there is a chance that the verdict was wrong or if the trial was unfair because correct procedures were not followed.

### Activities

7. Describe the purpose of tribunals.
8. Explain why there are so many different types of tribunal.
9. State two ways in which tribunals are different from ordinary courts.

**Figure 3.17** A tribunal panel tries to help both sides reach agreement

## Citizen action

### Membership of a tribunal

Most tribunal hearings are chaired by legally qualified tribunal judges but they often sit with two people (members) who are not lawyers but who do have practical and specialist knowhow to help them decide a case. For example, an employment tribunal may include one member with employer experience and one member with employee experience.

Members listen to the evidence, and may question both sides in the dispute (claimant and respondent) as well as any witnesses. Tribunal members take an equal part in making decisions but are advised on points of law by the legally qualified chairman.

Members must have experience or background knowledge relevant to the work of the tribunal on which they sit. Tribunals advertise for new specialist members. People who apply need to have the right skills and knowledge to make fair and just decisions.

Members are almost all paid a fee and are expected to work at least fifteen days a year. Unless they have recently retired from full-time work, most members also have a regular job. Members usually serve for five years and then can have their appointment renewed if they have been reliable and effective.

### Website

Find out more about the service provided by the Tribunals Service at the Courts and Tribunals Judiciary website: **www.judiciary.gov.uk**

### Activities

10. Explain why tribunal members with no legal qualifications or experience are still able to make a useful contribution to decisions.
11. List the qualities needed by an effective tribunal member.

## Citizens in the legal and justice system

### Key learning

Evaluate the effectiveness of citizens' roles in the legal system.

## How effective are citizens in the legal and justice system?

We have seen that ordinary people can fill important positions in the legal and justice system as:

- special constables
- Police and Crime Commissioners
- magistrates
- jurors
- tribunal members.

There has been particular concern about citizens' role in jury trials. Can ordinary people make good jurors? Do jury trials lead to unjust outcomes?

## Are juries fair?

Even though juries decide less than one per cent of all criminal cases in England and Wales, defendants in these cases are charged with the most serious criminal offences and face considerable loss of liberty. It is very important for jury decision-making to be fair so that people can have confidence in the criminal justice system. Opinion polls show strong public support for jury trials, but there are questions about whether juries act fairly.

The Ministry of Justice explored this question by commissioning an independent study into over 68,000 jury verdicts across all Crown Courts in England and Wales and involving 1,000 jurors.

The Ministry of Justice study, *Are juries fair?*, considered some concerns about jury trials:

**Q  Do all-white juries discriminate against black and minority ethnic (BME) defendants?**

**A**  Many people think that all-white juries discriminate against BME defendants, but the research found this was untrue. BME defendants are not more likely than white defendants to be found guilty by largely white juries. White defendants accused of racially motivated crimes are just as likely to be found guilty by all-white juries as by racially mixed juries.

**Q  Are juries less likely to convict defendants accused of serious offences such as murder and rape?**

**A**  There were no major differences in jury conviction rates based on the severity of the offence (defined by maximum sentence). Some people believe that juries are more likely to find an alleged rapist not guilty than guilty. Juries actually convict more often than they acquit in rape cases. Other serious offences (attempted murder, manslaughter, GBH) have lower jury conviction rates than rape.

Figure 3.18 Jury conviction rates by severity of offence

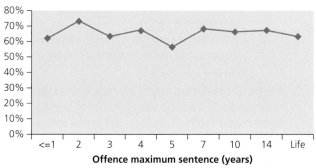

**Q  Do verdicts vary between courts?**

**A**  Differences exist in jury conviction rates between Crown Courts, but it is a myth that juries rarely convict at certain courts. All courts have a jury conviction rate of 53 per cent or higher. More research is needed about why courts in some parts of the country are more likely to convict. This could be linked to the quality of police evidence, the skills of prosecuting barristers or public attitudes to crime and justice in some parts of the country.

Figure 3.19 Age groups who fully understood oral instructions on the law

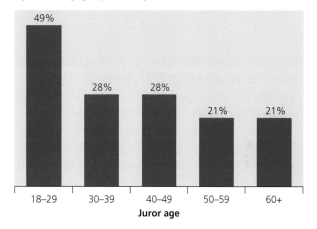

**Q  Do jurors understand judges' guidance on points of law?**

**A**  Judges often ask jurors to consider particular questions or points of law when making their verdict. Younger jurors (aged 18–29) were more likely to fully understand what the judge had told them. Only 21 per cent of jurors over 60 understood the judge's guidance.

Jurors also told researchers that they would like more guidance on how best to conduct their discussions in the jury room.

**Q  Are jurors influenced by media coverage of the crime at the time it took place?**

**A**  A trial usually takes place several months after the crime took place. Most jurors' memory of any media coverage had faded in this time. For those who did remember what they had read or seen, most said that it had not influenced their view of the defendant's guilt or innocence. Most of the remainder said the media reports had left them with the impression of guilt rather than innocence.

**Figure 3.20** Emphasis jurors recalled in media coverage

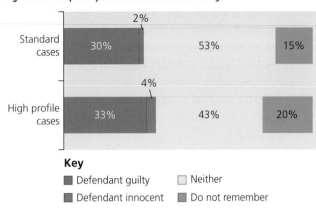

**Key**
- ■ Defendant guilty
- ■ Defendant innocent
- □ Neither
- ■ Do not remember

**Q  Do jurors search the internet during the case in ways that might affect their verdict?**

**A**  38 per cent of jurors in high-profile cases used the internet to read coverage of their trial or to research details about the defendant. It might be expected that younger jurors would be more likely to look for information on the internet, but the research found that most jurors who said they looked for information on the internet (68 per cent) were over 30 years of age.

Overall findings:

- Juries are efficient. They reach a verdict more than 99 per cent of the time.
- Juries appear to decide cases on the evidence and the law.
- Juries convict on almost two-thirds (64 per cent) of all charges presented to them.

## Website

Find the Ministry of Justice's full report *Are juries fair?* on their website at: **http://www.justice.gov.uk/ downloads/publications/research-and-analysis/ moj-research/are-juries-fair-research.pdf**

## Activities

1. Study extracts from the study *Are juries fair?*
   a) List three major concerns people had about juries before the study took place.
   b) Describe what the research found in response to each concern.

2. Using evidence from the study, respond to the argument that only people over the age of forty should serve on juries

### Juror jailed for researching trial on internet

In 2013, Mr K was found guilty of contempt of court for using the internet to research the case he was hearing as a Crown Court juror. He was punished with a two-month prison sentence.

Mr K was serving on a jury hearing a fraud case, but the trial had to be stopped when his offence was discovered. The judge had warned jurors not to use the internet to research details of the case.

Sentencing Mr K, judges said: 'We are sure he knew that conducting research on the internet was an interference with the administration of justice.'

Later, the Attorney General said: 'Jurors who use the internet to research a case undermine justice. It creates a risk that the defendant will be convicted or acquitted, not on the evidence, but on unchallenged and untested material discovered by the juror.'

**Figure 3.21** Jurors must not research details of their trial.

## Activities

3. Explain why judges instruct jurors not to use the internet to research details of their trial.

4. Evaluate the arguments for and against leaving the justice system to the professionals.
   a) Add any points of your own to those made in Figure 3.22 on page 69.
   b) List points for and against in priority order and justify your 'top' choices.
   c) Summarise your own point of view, supporting it with points and evidence from this chapter, and from your own research.

5. Review all the 'Citizen action' sections in this chapter so far. Describe the ways you might like to become involved as a citizen in the legal and justice system.

**Figure 3.22** Arguments for and against leaving the justice system to the professionals

## Advantages of leaving the justice system to the professionals

Lawyers are properly trained over many years. They know the law. Ordinary people do not. What they know comes from unrealistic crime programmes on television.

Professionals are experienced. It's their job. They work on legal issues every day and know their way around the system. If the professionals do make mistakes, people can always appeal against verdicts.

Judges are less likely to worry about their verdicts, feel intimidated or become emotional. They can usually tell if a defendant or witness is lying.

Ordinary people have busy lives. You can't expect people to do jury service well alongside their other commitments. The public's elected representatives in Parliament can make sure the system is just and fair.

## Advantages of involving citizens in the justice system

The justice system should reflect the standards and values of the general public. Lawyers are often out of touch with the lives of ordinary people.

By getting involved, citizens can find out more about how the justice system really works.

Citizens can evaluate whether the law is being applied justly and fairly, see things that professionals might miss and expose injustices.

Citizens have the freshness and insights of those who are new to the system and have not become case-hardened or cynical like some professional lawyers.

# Managing crime

## Key learning

Study the factors affecting crime rates in society. Consider the different causes of crime and evaluate strategies to reduce it.

## How much crime is there?

It is not possible to be sure about how much crime there is. The police record crimes that come to their attention. Unfortunately many crimes are not reported and, in some cases of fraud, people may not even realise that they have been victims of crime.

The Crime Survey of England and Wales gives perhaps the best indication of changing crime patterns by asking people whether they have been victims of crime. Survey results can be compared with those from previous years to find out which crimes are increasing and which are falling.

UK crime is falling overall as it is in other European countries. However, criminal behaviour is also changing, giving the police new challenges. (For more information, see page 50.)

Careful analysis of the crime figures also shows that, while some types of crime are falling, other types are increasing.

**Table 3.1 Changing patterns of crime** – using data from police recorded crime and from the Crime Survey of England and Wales, 2015

| Offences | Percentage change from 2005 | | Reasons |
|---|---|---|---|
| Robbery | −64%* | | Less alcohol consumption and drug addiction amongst young people. There is also some evidence that the removal of lead additives from petrol has led to less violent behaviour generally. |
| Possession of weapons | −46% | | |
| Violence with injury | −41% | | |
| Violence without injury | −59% | | |
| Burglary of homes | −26% | | Homes and cars are more secure. Stolen household items have relatively little value and can be traced more easily. |
| Burglary of businesses | −40% | | |
| Vehicle theft | −50% | | |
| Criminal damage | −46% | | Smart phone and tablet ownership has given young people more to do. Greater likelihood of being caught acts as a deterrent. |
| Shoplifting | +16% | | People's incomes have fallen and so more are tempted to steal from shops for the things they want. |
| Fraud | +43% | | There are greater online opportunities for fraud. It is difficult for the police to detect fraud, so more people are trying it. |
| Rape | +109% | | Easier access to pornography on the internet is leading to more violence against women. People are also more likely to report rapes because they have greater confidence that the police and courts will deal with cases effectively. Both these factors help to explain the increase. |
| Other sexual offences | +26% | | The police have become more successful at detecting sex offenders by monitoring online activity. People are also more likely to report sex offences than in the past. |
| **All crime** | −34% (estimated) | | Crime fell by one third overall from 2005 to 2015 but there was a 6% increase in recorded crime in the year to September 2015. |

(*This means that there were 64 per cent fewer cases of robbery in 2015 than in 2005.)

---

**Activities**

1. Study Table 3.1 and identify the correct statements from the list below:
    i. Crime may have fallen overall, but it is increasing in all the key areas such as rape, robbery and burglary.
    ii. Crime has fallen significantly since 2005, but we should be concerned about the increases in fraud and rape.
    iii. Crime decreases are all about better policing. As the police get better at detecting particular types of offence, crime rates should fall.
    iv. Cuts in police numbers are likely to lead to increases in all types of crime.
    v. More crime is moving online making it more difficult to bring offenders to justice.
    vi. Reasons for changes in crime rates are sometimes complex. More research is needed for some of the changes.

2. Use the website **http://www.crimerates.co.uk** to find out about crime rates in your area. Compare this data with information about another part of the country.
    a) Describe the main differences.
    b) Explain possible reasons for these differences.

## Websites

For more statistics on UK crime go to: **https://www.gov.uk/government/collections/crime-statistics**

Compare crime rates in different parts of the UK using: **http://www.crimerates.co.uk**

The BBC's Newsnight debate considers why violent crime may be decreasing: **https://www.youtube.com/watch?v=nIUmaqL7qEo**

# What causes crime and how can we reduce it?

## Causes of crime

Social scientists agree that the causes of crime are complex but disagree about which causes are the most important.

## Reducing crime

Most politicians agree that a variety of measures are needed to reduce crime.

Nevertheless, there are two main ways of approaching the issue depending on what you believe to be the main causes of crime.

Governments tend to use a mix of these two approaches. Nevertheless, Conservative governments have tended towards the view that criminal behaviour is a matter of personal choice whereas Labour governments have focused more on social conditions.

**Figure 3.23** Causes of crime

**Poverty**

People who see themselves as poor compared to other members of their society are more likely to steal than those who consider themselves to be well off.

**The normalisation of criminal behaviour**

Some people come to think that certain types of negative behaviour are socially acceptable. For example, men are more likely to commit sexual offences if they view women as inferior – a view that may have been reinforced by the media.

**Upbringing and socialisation**

Children are more likely to turn to crime if they are brought up in families where adults show little respect for other people, are inconsistent, have no work or are violent. Gang culture also creates the conditions where individuals are more likely to engage in crime.

**Alcohol and drugs**

People are more likely to take risks and be aggressive if they are influenced by alcohol and drugs. Drug addicts often fund their habit through crime.

**Low levels of social integration and control**

Young people sometimes commit crime because they aren't integrated into society as well as most adults. Adults may have a partner, children, a steady job and rent to pay. These commitments cause adults to avoid the risk of engaging in crime.

**Frustration (strain theory)**

Most people know what it means to be successful in their society but not everyone has the same opportunities or abilities to achieve their goals. If people cannot meet their aspirations by using legal methods, they may attempt to achieve success through crime instead.

**Table 3.2** Viewpoints and preferred strategies for reducing crime

| Viewpoint on the causes of crime | Preferred crime reduction strategies |
|---|---|
| • Crime is mainly a matter of personal choice. Poverty and poor examples set by parents do not automatically lead to criminal behaviour. Many people overcome these problems but others may need help to do so. | • Make sure rules are clear and that there is a high risk of getting caught.<br>• Make punishments more severe.<br>• Help people overcome alcohol and drug dependency and psychological disorders.<br>• Make sure everyone has good educational opportunities.<br>• Outlaw discrimination. |
| • Crime is caused mainly by social conditions. Too many people are on the edge of society; unemployed or with low-wage jobs and in poor housing. These conditions encourage people to turn to crime. | • Improve housing conditions.<br>• Tackle child poverty by increasing welfare support for poor families.<br>• Create more apprenticeships and jobs.<br>• Provide better opportunities for young people from poorer areas. |

## Websites

The History Learning Site contains a useful explanation of why women commit fewer crimes than men: **http://www.historylearningsite.co.uk/sociology/crime-and-deviance/who-commits-crime/**

Science Daily contains some complex but interesting research on the social reasons why people commit crime and how governments should respond: **http://www.sciencedaily.com/releases/2013/10/131010091555.htm**

The Huffington Post website includes a link to a video in which Professor Stephen Pinker discusses why violent crime is falling: **http://www.huffingtonpost.co.uk/2014/04/23/newsnight-why-is-violent-crime-decreasing_n_5202742.html**

## Activities

3. Explain why politicians may disagree about how best to respond to crime.
4. Study this section and carry out some of your own research on the causes of crime.
   a) Describe what you believe to be the main causes of crime.
   b) Discuss your findings with other learners.
   c) Identify three further steps you think the Government should take to reduce crime.
   d) Explain the reasons for your choices.

# Responding to crime

## Key learning

Study the nature and purpose of different sanctions for different criminal offences. Evaluate the effect of different sanctions on offenders and their families, victims and their families, and wider society.

## Dealing with criminals

### Imprisonment

Imprisonment is the most severe sentence courts can impose. Prison sentences are reserved for the most serious crimes such as murder or rape, and for criminals who repeatedly offend.

There are about 80,000 people in prison across the UK. Less than 4,000 are women. The average sentence is around fifteen months.

**Figure 3.24** Prisoners by age in June 2013 (England and Wales)

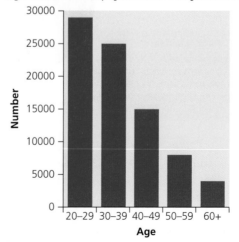

Adapted from Ministry of Justice data

## Why are people imprisoned?

**Table 3.3** Sentenced prisoners by type of prisoner and offence – June 2015 (England and Wales). All figures are percentages (%). Adapted from Ministry of Justice data

| Offence | All prisoners (%) | Adult male (%) | All female (%) | Male aged 15–17 (%) | Male aged 18–20 (%) |
|---|---|---|---|---|---|
| Violence against the person | 27 | 27 | 28 | 25 | 25 |
| Sexual offences | 17 | 17 | 3 | 8 | 8 |
| Robbery | 11 | 11 | 9 | 23 | 21 |
| Burglary | 10 | 10 | 7 | 11 | 15 |
| Theft and 'handling' | 6 | 6 | 16 | 6 | 6 |
| Fraud and forgery | 2 | 2 | 6 | 0 | 1 |
| Drugs offences | 14 | 13 | 13 | 9 | 15 |
| Motoring offences | 1 | 1 | 1 | 0 | 2 |
| Other offences | 11 | 10 | 15 | 16 | 9 |
| No data | 1 | 1 | 1 | 0 | 1 |

### Prisoner facts

- 26 per cent of prisoners are from ethnic minority groups or are of mixed race. (12 per cent of the UK population belong to an ethnic minority group or are mixed race.)
- 20–30 percent of all offenders have learning or other difficulties that make it difficult for them to deal with police, courts or prisons.
- 24 per cent of prisoners had lived with foster parents or in a children's home, or had been taken into care at some point when they were a child.
- 29 per cent of prisoners had experienced emotional, physical or sexual abuse as a child. (53 per cent of women prisoners had experienced such abuse.)
- 41 per cent of prisoners had observed violence at home as a child.
- 37 per cent of prisoners had a family member who had been found guilty of a criminal offence.
- 59 per cent of prisoners reported regularly playing truant and 42 per cent had been permanently excluded from school.

- 61 per cent of prisoners stated that they were single when they came into custody.
- Around one-half of prisoners reported being in paid employment at some time in the year before custody. However, 13 per cent reported never having had a job.
- Almost two-thirds (64 per cent) of prisoners had been in receipt of benefits at some point in the twelve months before coming into custody.
- 47 per cent of prisoners held no academic qualifications.
- 15 per cent of prisoners reported being homeless before custody.
- 64 per cent of prisoners had taken class A drugs and 22 per cent had drunk alcohol every day in the four week before custody.

(The Prison Reform Trust)

Prison is seen as a good way of making it clear to criminals that their offences are unacceptable and will not be tolerated. This is known as retribution. Prison also gives citizens some protection from criminals. Nevertheless prison is not always very effective at helping to reduce crime in the long term. Over 60 per cent of ex-prisoners commit another crime after their release.

Pressure groups such as the Howard League for Penal Reform think that imprisonment usually fails to **reform**

**Reform** An offender is reformed if they begin to understand the impact of their behaviour on others and make sure their actions support rather than harm other people.

## Activities

1. Study the information in this section on the prison population and rewrite the paragraph below so that it is correct.

   *The UK's total prison population is around 30,000 of which just under half are women. People aged forty and over are more likely to be in prison than younger people. Prisoners tend to be a normal cross-section of society. Most have a partner, educational qualifications and have experienced a well-balanced home life. Around 12 per cent of prisoners belong to an ethnic minority group or are mixed race – the same as in the general population.*

2. Summarise the purpose of imprisonment.

3. Study the data in Table 3.3 on page 73
   a) State the main reasons for the imprisonment of males aged 20 or younger.
   b) Compare the reasons for the imprisonment of men and women.

4. Study the information on **prisoner facts** and all the other information in this section.
   a) Prepare some proposals that might help reduce the number of people in prison.
   b) Compare your ideas with those of other learners.
   c) Change your list as necessary.

and rehabilitate offenders. The Howard League campaigns for more effective ways of steering people away from crime. In particular, they think that more people who have committed less serious crimes should be made to put things right. They should support their victim in some way or carry out community service (this is known as restorative justice).

### Alternatives to prison

There is general agreement that prison is the right place for people who are a serious threat to the public. However, there are alternative ways of dealing with less dangerous criminals. Some of these options are described in the table below. Courts can use a mix of these methods.

**Figure 3.25** Community service is often used as an alternative to prison

**Table 3.4** Alternatives to prison

| Restorative justice | This usually includes face-to-face contact between the offender and their victim. The offender hears about the impact of their crime and apologises to the victim. The offender may also compensate the victim in some way. |
|---|---|
| Community sentences | Community sentences include between 40 and 300 hours of unpaid work for the community's benefit such as removing graffiti or clearing litter. Community sentences may also include measures to help people stay out of trouble. These measures might include treatment for alcohol or drug dependency. |
| Electronic monitoring or 'tagging' | The offender must stay away from certain areas and/or be at home at certain times (usually at night). |
| Fine | Courts may ask offenders to pay a fine as an alternative to prison. |
| Suspended sentence | A prison sentence that the offender will not need to serve if they stay out of trouble for a set period of time. The offender gets support to help them stay out of trouble. |

# Supporting victims of crime and protecting society

## Supporting victims

Victims are often very severely affected by crime. Physical injury or loss of property can have a huge impact on a crime victim and their families. People are also affected psychologically.

- Rape victims sometimes find it difficult to trust other people or to have satisfying sexual relationships.
- People whose homes are burgled sometimes can't bear to live there anymore.
- People who have been assaulted often no longer want to go out.

### Activities

5. Study the Howard League for Prison Reform website and describe their proposals for reducing the prison population.

   Prepare a report of no more than 200 words recommending action to reduce prisoner numbers in the long term.

6. Match the correct purpose with each of the punishments in the table below.

| Punishments | Purpose |
|---|---|
| Unpaid work in the community | Reform |
| Imprisonment | Rehabilitation |
| The offender hears about the impact of their crime and apologises to the victim | Retribution |

7. Use the information in this section and further research of your own to summarise the reasons why it is necessary to imprison some offenders.

8. Find out more about restorative justice. Recommend its use for particular offenders and types of offence. Explain why it would not be suitable for some types of offence.

9. Describe the types of support that victims of crime might need.

10. Explain why hate crime may have a particularly negative impact on victims.

11. Analyse the website of one organisation that aims to support victims of crime. Describe any work done by the organisation that is likely to be particularly helpful for crime victims.

### The effect of hate crime on victims

#### What is hate crime?

Hate crime is a crime against you, your friends, your family or your property because of your actual or presumed sexual orientation, transgender identity, disability, race or religion.

Hate crimes can take many forms, such as: physical and verbal attacks; vandalism and graffiti; cyber bullying; abusive text messaging and hate mail; offensive signs or gestures and threatening behaviour.

#### Effects on victims

Hate crime affects the individual in every area of their life, work, school and home. People who experience such crime may feel guilty, humiliated and too embarrassed to complain. Stress may lead to emotional symptoms such as a loss of self-confidence and self-esteem. More serious physical and mental health problems may develop, not only for the victim, but also for their whole family.

#### Don't let them get away with it

Hate crime is committed by people who do not care how much they hurt their victims. If they go unchallenged, they will continue to put others in danger. Report it so they can be caught before others suffer.

(Adapted from the Stop the Hate website: **http://www.stopthehate.org.uk/**)

There are several national organisations that provide support for crime victims. One of the most prominent is Victim Support. Victim Support is a charity that provides confidential emotional support and practical advice to victims of different types of crime.

## Protecting society

Governments are spending more time and money protecting society against crime. It is far more effective to prevent crime and to stop people from offending, than to deal with crime once it has happened.

Four developments over the last twenty years have been especially useful in assisting the police and acting as a deterrent to potential offenders.

### Closed Circuit Television Cameras (CCTV)

Town centres, sports stadia, shopping centres, and main roads and motorways are just some of the places that are monitored continuously by CCTV. Many homes and businesses are also protected. CCTV makes it likely that property crimes, assaults and motoring offences will be recorded. CCTV evidence is increasingly important when suspects are prosecuted.

## Monitoring mobile phones and internet use

Mobile phones reveal their owners' location and movements as well as records of messages received and sent. Mobile phone records often provide important evidence for the police. The Government's intelligence services monitor people's use of electronic devices to identify possible conspiracy. This enables the police to disrupt terrorism and other potentially serious criminal offences.

## Deoxyribonucleic acid (DNA) evidence

Each cell of our bodies contains a 'genetic fingerprint' that can help to identify us. Hairs, flakes from skin, blood, saliva and other bodily fluids left at a crime scene can match the offence to a particular individual. The National DNA Database provides police with the most effective tool for the prevention and detection of crime since the development of fingerprint analysis over 100 years ago.

Since 1998, more than 300,000 crimes have been detected with the help of the DNA database which holds samples from over five million people, 80 per cent of whom are men.

## Improved security

Car theft and burglary are far less common thanks to more complex security. Cashless payment, fingertip or iris identification, property marking and tracking systems have all acted as a deterrent to potential offenders.

Several organisations exist to prevent crime and deter criminal behaviour. These include:

**Figure 3.26** CCTV cameras are one of four factors that have helped to cut crime over the last 20 years

### National Crime Agency (NCA)

The NCA was set up by the Government in 2014 to disrupt new types of organised crime. NCA has units to deal with cyber-crime, fraud, illegal immigration and child exploitation.

### Crimestoppers

A national charity that encourages people to make contact anonymously to report crimes that have taken place or are being planned. This can be done without fear of intimidation or possible retaliation. Crimestoppers also gives people information and advice to help them keep safe and prevent crime.

### Child Exploitation and Online Protection Centre (CEOP)

CEOP is part of the Government's National Crime Agency (NCA). CEOP protects children from harm online and offline, directly through NCA-led operations and by working with local and international agencies. CEOP provides advice to families and schools about how to reduce the risk of online exploitation.

### The Forced Marriage Unit (FMU)

The Government's Forced Marriage Unit operates a public helpline to provide advice and support to victims of forced marriage as well as to professionals dealing with cases. FMU gives simple safety advice, helps victims prevent their unwanted spouse moving to the UK ('reluctant sponsor' cases), and, in extreme circumstances, rescues victims held against their will overseas.

**Websites**

More information on the work of the National Crime Agency can be found on its website: **http://www.nationalcrimeagency.gov.uk/**

Find out about Crimestoppers' role in helping to prevent crime and bring criminals to justice at: **https://crimestoppers-uk.org/**

CEOP's website gives details of its work to prevent the exploitation of young people online and offline: **http://www.ceop.police.uk/**

Use the Government's official information website (GOV.UK) to search for more information on the National DNA Database and the Forced Marriage Unit: **https://www.gov.uk/**

Victim Support. Supports victims of all types of crime: **https://www.victimsupport.org.uk/**

Disrespect nobody. This site links to a range of organisations that can help victims of different forms of sexual and domestic abuse: **https://www.disrespectnobody.co.uk/**

**Activities**

12. Explain why it is no longer enough for a police force to rely on regular patrols to deter potential criminals and on 'tip offs' from local people to catch offenders.

13. Explain why modern crime prevention and detection methods have raised concerns from human rights groups. In your answer, you should:
    a) Describe the policing methods that human rights groups have concerns about.
    b) Explain why they are concerned.

14. By exploring the relevant websites or social media, analyse the objectives and methods of Crimestoppers, CEOP, the Forced Marriage Unit or any other UK organisation that aims to protect the public from crime and its effects.
    Design a multi-media presentation for younger learners to introduce them to the organisation and describe how they might use its services.

## Practice questions

In the OCR specification, this section will be assessed using objective test questions and questions needing a written response. Study the Source and answer questions 1 and 2 below.

1. Choose one correct option to show who can be charged with a **criminal offence** in this case.
   - A  only Evie
   - B  only Alisha
   - C  both Evie and Alisha
   - D  neither Evie nor Alisha. [1 mark]

2. Study the statement and reason below carefully. Choose option **A**, **B**, **C** or **D** to show whether each part (statement and reason) is true or false.

   **Statement** – Evie and Alisha have a legal responsibility not to obstruct the police

   **Reason** – because, if they obstruct the police, they will not get independent legal representation.
   - A  The statement and the reason are both true, and the reason is a correct explanation of the statement.
   - B  The statement and the reason are both true, but the reason is not a correct explanation of the statement.
   - C  The statement and reason are both false.
   - D  The statement is true but the reason is false. [1 mark]

3. Which one of the following is the best description of a **lay magistrate**?
   - A  people with a university degree in law
   - B  local representative of the legal profession
   - C  elected police officers
   - D  members of the public without direct legal experience. [1 mark]

4. Which one of the statements below is correct for a person **under 18**?
   - A  Must have a parent, guardian or carer present when arrested by the police.
   - B  Must have a parent, guardian or carer present when questioned by the police.
   - C  Must be charged and released back into their parents' care within 12 hours of being arrested.
   - D  Must receive independent legal advice before arrest takes place. [1 mark]

5. Oppose the viewpoint that prison is the best place for criminals. [8 marks]

## Source

### Teenagers in trouble with police

*Evie (aged 14) takes a jacket from her classroom because she is cold. She plans to put it back the next day.*

*She meets Alisha (aged 18) that night.*

*Alisha insists on buying the jacket, even though she knows it doesn't belong to Evie. Evie gives Alisha the jacket but refuses the money.*

*Later the police arrest both girls. Alisha gives the police a false name and address.*

# Chapter 4:
# Democracy, elections and voting in the UK

This chapter on *Democracy, elections and voting in the UK* lays the foundation for further study of *National, local, regional and devolved government* in Chapter 5 and *The British constitution* in Chapter 6. In Chapter 10, *Politics beyond the UK*, the UK's representative democracy is compared with political systems in Switzerland and China.

In this chapter we explore the ways in which decision-making takes place in the UK's representative democracy.

Learning the following key concepts and terms will make it easier to organise your thinking and communicate your ideas:

- classical democracy and representative democracy
- candidate
- inclusive franchise and pluralism
- free elections
- secret ballot
- political party
- party policy and manifesto
- fixed-term parliament
- constituency
- rule of law, personal freedom, tolerance, respect for diversity and equal opportunity
- first-past-the-post election, proportional representation and referendum.

# How democracy works

## Key learning

Study the differences between classical democracy and representative democracy. Understand the key features of representative democracy in the UK and their relevance to Article 21 of the Universal Declaration of Human Rights. Understand how British democracy is underpinned by key values. Know that Members of Parliament represent constituencies, and know who can and cannot vote in UK parliamentary elections. Investigate the roles and responsibilities of citizens in British democracy.

## Classical democracy and representative democracy

Democracy means 'rule of the people'. Each person with voting rights has a say in decision-making. Decisions in some early democracies were made at frequent meetings of all citizens. These simple systems of government evolved into the democracies that most of the world's people experience today.

### Classical democracy

The earliest democracy in the world began in Athens, now the capital city of Greece, over 2,500 years ago. Athens was one of several Greek states. Many of these states also adopted democracy as a way of making decisions.

Only adult male citizens who owned land or their own houses had the right to vote. Women could be citizens but had no political rights. Most of the work in Athens was done by slaves or foreign workers. Neither group could be citizens or have voting rights.

Athenian citizens held regular meetings at the Assembly to vote on issues ranging from war to the regulation of ferry boats. This system of government with its frequent and direct voting by citizens is known as classical democracy.

**Figure 4.1** In a classical democracy citizens vote on issues directly rather than electing representatives to vote on their behalf

79

A problem for these classical democracies was that it became inconvenient for men to attend such frequent assembly meetings. So most democracies asked citizens to choose representatives who would attend meetings and vote on behalf of everyone else. Nevertheless, all citizens could participate directly when there was a really important vote.

Different Greek states used different methods to choose representatives. Athens used a lottery in which men drawing winning tickets would serve for one year in the Athenian parliament known as the Council of 500. This system became known as representative democracy.

## Representative democracy

Representative democracies now use elections to choose those men and women who will represent all citizens. Representatives in the UK Parliament are known as **Members of Parliament (MPs)**. They are elected by those UK citizens who have the right to vote.

Almost anyone can stand as an election **candidate**. Candidates campaign to get as many votes as possible from the other citizens. At first, most candidates were popular or important people in their communities. As populations grew and communications improved, candidates with similar views formed **political parties**. This made it easier for voters to decide who to vote for. Voters may not have met the parliamentary candidates standing for election in their **constituency** but they can decide which political party they prefer and vote for the candidate representing that party.

Even in representative democracies, some decisions are thought to be too important to be left to representatives. Over the past few decades the UK governments have used a **referendum** (a type of **direct democracy**) to decide each of the following:

- continued membership of the European Union (1975)
- greater powers for Scotland and Wales (1997)
- power sharing in Northern Ireland (1998)
- changing the UK voting system (2011)
- law-making powers for Wales (2011)
- Scottish independence (2014)
- UK membership of the European Union (2016).

**Members of the UK Parliament (MPs)**
Successful candidates who represent their constituency in Parliament.

**Candidate**   A person who asks people to vote for him/her as their representative.

**Political party**   A group of people with similar ideas who campaign together to win elections.

**Constituency**   An area of the country with around 60,000 voters. Each of the UK constituencies elects one representative to Parliament.

**Referendum**   A vote in which all electors are able to decide a single issue.

**Direct democracy**   A system of decision-making in which all electors have the right to vote on the most important issues.

*"Everyone has the right to take part in the government of his country, directly or through freely chosen representatives… The will of the people shall be the basis of the authority of government; this will shall be expressed in periodic and genuine elections which shall be by universal and equal suffrage [the right to vote in political elections], and shall be held by secret vote or by equivalent free voting procedures."*
Article 21, Universal Declaration of Human Rights, 1948

### Activities

1. 'Electronic communication enables us to return to the decision-making of classical times by using direct democracy.'
   a) State three features of classical democracy.
   b) Explain why electronic communication would allow direct democracy to be used as an alternative to representative democracy.
   c) Suggest three advantages and three disadvantages of introducing more direct democracy.

# Features of democratic government in the UK

## An inclusive franchise

If a democracy is to live up to its definition of 'rule by the people', it's important for everyone to be included: a principle known as **pluralism**.

In the UK, the right to vote was extended during the nineteenth and twentieth centuries. The **franchise** for UK Parliamentary elections (general elections) includes most people over the age of eighteen who are:

- citizens of the UK or the Republic of Ireland or qualifying Commonwealth countries
- and on the **electoral register**.

UK citizens living overseas can also vote, as long as they have not been away from home for more than fifteen years.

People not allowed to vote in UK general elections are:

- members of the House of Lords
- citizens of EU countries living in the UK
- convicted prisoners
- anyone with a registered mental incapacity
- anyone found guilty within the previous five years of corrupt or illegal practices in connection with an election.

Recently there have been discussions about reducing the voting age (see page 8) and about whether prisoners deserve voting rights.

**Pluralism**   A system of decision-making in which all groups are included.

**Franchise**   The right to vote for representatives.

**Electoral register**   A list of all those people who are entitled to vote and have applied to do so.

## Regular, free and fair elections

**Figure 4.2** A polling station

Citizens must be able to vote regularly so that representatives can be changed and new policies supported. UK general elections are held every five years. If elections were held too often, representatives and governments would have too little time to properly plan, implement, evaluate and adjust their decisions.

Elections can only be described as 'free and fair' if each citizen has the right to be an election candidate. In the UK, any citizen can be an election candidate as long as they are able to persuade ten registered electors from the constituency to sign a candidate nomination form. The candidates also need to pay a deposit of £500. (This is returned as long as they receive at least 5 per cent of the total votes cast.)

Candidates and political parties have balanced access to the media according to rules that media representatives draw up independently of the Government. There are also rules to:

- limit the amount of money candidates can spend on their election campaign
- prevent candidates from deliberately misleading voters
- forbid bribes
- safeguard voting arrangements; for example by prohibiting candidates from going into a polling booth with a voter.

Figure 4.3 William Hogarth's 1755 painting shows electors voting by publicly declaring their vote.

## A secret ballot

Secret voting was brought in by the Ballot Act of 1872. Before then, voting took place in public. This allowed candidates and their representatives to put pressure on people to vote 'the right way' as in Hogarth's painting above. Now voters are able to make their decision in private and their vote is confidential.

## A choice of candidates and political parties

In a democracy, it is important that citizens can choose from parties and candidates representing a range of different views. An elector can then vote for a party or candidate with views closest to their own. This would be more difficult if all the candidates in an election represented one political party.

There are five main political parties that campaign across the UK as well as additional parties in Scotland, Wales and Northern Ireland. (For more details of these parties, see pages 86 to 89)

## Activities

2. Explain why a secret ballot is so important in democratic elections.
3. Design a simple diagram to show how to become a candidate in a parliamentary election.

Figure 4.4 A choice of parties and candidates is necessary for democracy to work effectively.

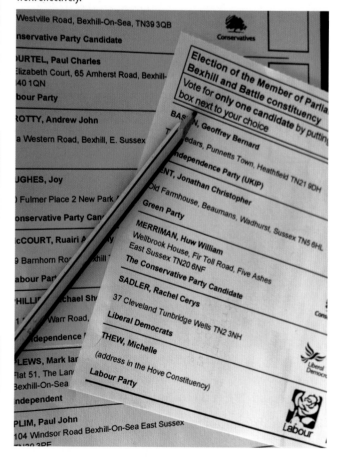

### Extending the franchise

**1832** Act of Parliament gives voting rights to the richest 15 per cent of men.

**1838–48** A pressure group (The Chartists) campaign for all men to have the vote.

**1859** Liberal Party formed. It promises to extend voting rights.

**1871** Workers gain the right to set up trade unions.

**1884** Vote extended to wealthiest 60 per cent of men over twenty-one.

**1897–1918** Women campaign for the right to vote.

**1906** Labour Party founded. It campaigns for all adults to have the vote.

**Figure 4.5** Some women were prepared to break the law to gain the right to vote

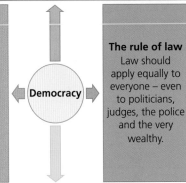

**1914–18** First World War. Women prove they can do 'mens' jobs'.

**1918** All men over twenty-one gain the right to vote. So do women over the age of thirty.

**1928** Women gain the right to vote at twenty-one.

**1969** Voting age cut from twenty-one to eighteen.

**2014** Scottish sixteen-year-olds vote in the referendum on Scottish independence.

**2015** Voting age cut to sixteen for elections to the Scottish Parliament and Scottish local authorities but, in December, Parliament rejects a proposal that United Kingdom 16-year-olds should be allowed to vote in the 2016 European elections.

## Supporting democratic government

Democracy can only work if everyone has an equal say in how the country is run.

UK citizens generally support four key values that underpin effective democratic government and **civil liberties**. Without widespread public support for these values, democracy would be under threat.

**Civil liberties** Rights such as freedom of speech that are granted to all citizens by law.

**Figure 4.6** For democracy to work it must be supported by four key values

**Personal freedom**
Everyone should be free to put forward their ideas, stand for election and criticise the government. Artists, playwrights and writers should be free to express new ideas and criticise established thinking. A free media should help to communicate ideas, expose any political corruption and hold elected representatives to account.

**Tolerance and respect for diversity**
A person's race, gender, culture, religion, political beliefs and sexual orientation should be respected by everyone else. All people's opinions and ideas should be listened to as long as they don't encourage hatred or discrimination against others.

**Democracy**

**The rule of law**
Law should apply equally to everyone – even to politicians, judges, the police and the very wealthy.

**Equal opportunity**
Everyone should have the same chances to participate in decision-making, to protest and to become a representative.

### Activity

4. Explain why democracy would be impossible without the four key values of: personal freedom; tolerance and respect for diversity; equal opportunity and the rule of law.

## Citizen action

### Citizens' roles and responsibilities in a democracy

There are different ways in which citizens can contribute to UK democracy. This chapter considers: voting; joining a political party and being an election candidate. Chapter 9 explores other ways that citizens can influence decision-making and hold their representatives to account.

Around one-third of people on the electoral register do not bother to vote in elections for the UK Parliament. It is thought that well over one million people aren't even on the electoral register. These are matters of considerable concern to politicians who realise that, for democracy to work, as many people as possible need to be involved.

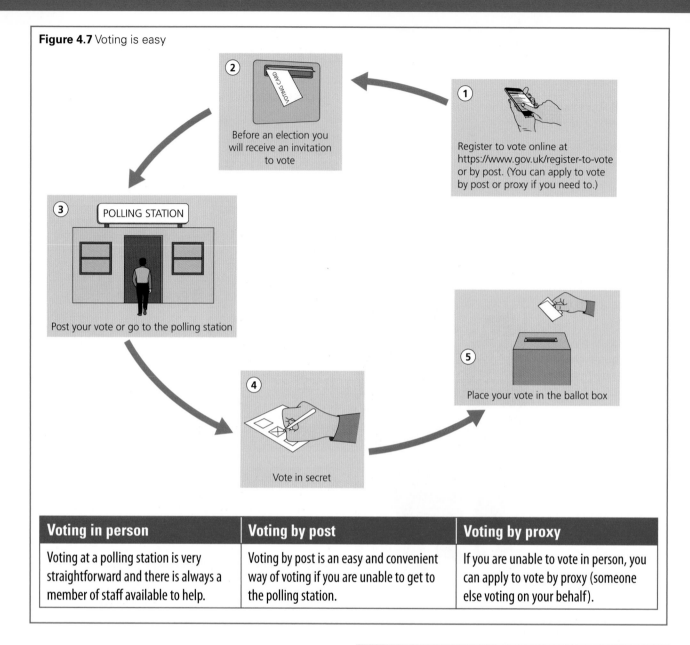

**Figure 4.7** Voting is easy

1. Register to vote online at https://www.gov.uk/register-to-vote or by post. (You can apply to vote by post or proxy if you need to.)

2. Before an election you will receive an invitation to vote

3. POLLING STATION
Post your vote or go to the polling station

4. Vote in secret

5. Place your vote in the ballot box

| Voting in person | Voting by post | Voting by proxy |
|---|---|---|
| Voting at a polling station is very straightforward and there is always a member of staff available to help. | Voting by post is an easy and convenient way of voting if you are unable to get to the polling station. | If you are unable to vote in person, you can apply to vote by proxy (someone else voting on your behalf). |

## Being a candidate

To get more fully involved, people over eighteen can be candidates in an election. It is not necessary to belong to a political party to be an election candidate. Those candidates who are elected then represent their **local authority ward** or parliamentary constituency. Successful candidates should try to represent all citizens; not just those who voted for them. (See page 80 for more details.)

**Local authority ward**  Just as the UK is divided into constituencies, so local authorities are divided into wards. Electors in each ward vote for candidates to represent them at the local authority's council meetings.

(See page 80 for more details.)

### Activities

5. A friend tells you that they are not going to vote because it's too complicated and not important anyway. Make a case against their point of view and support your case with evidence.

6. Find out more about the work of your local MP by visiting their website or following them on social media. MPs or Members of the House of Lords are often willing to speak to citizenship students in school. Ask if your teacher can help arrange a visit.

## Joining a political party

Election candidates often belong to a political party. People who join a political party meet with other party members to come up with proposals to improve the local community or the country as a whole. There are several political parties in the UK and most people are able to find one that matches their views. (See pages 86 to 89.)

**Figure 4.8** Candidates do not have to belong to a political party

People who join political parties can have a say in deciding their party's ideas and viewpoints. They can contribute to the party's policies and influence the **election manifesto**.

Members of political parties can:

- attend meetings of the party to decide on policies and campaigns
- help raise money to support the party
- prepare online and offline messages for electors
- visit electors to persuade them to vote for party's candidates

- campaign on local or national issues
- help to choose candidates for elections
- represent their party as a candidate in an election.

**Election manifesto** A document written by members of a political party which states what the party aims to do if it gets into power.

**Figure 4.9** Leaflets like these are written and delivered by political party members

There have been concerns about declining party membership but during 2015 almost all UK political parties reported membership growth. For example, Labour Party membership increased when members were given a greater say in choosing a leader.

### Websites

The Electoral Commission provides details of the rules for election campaigns, clear guidance for people thinking of being candidates and help for anyone registering to vote: **http://www.electoralcommission.org.uk/**

Part of the Electoral Commission site also contains guidance on how to join the electoral register and about voting in general: **http://www.aboutmyvote.co.uk/**

Parliament's website includes a short video about getting involved in elections: **http://www.parliament.uk/get-involved/elections/**

Find your MP by entering your postcode: **http://www.parliament.uk/mps-lords-and-offices/mps**

# UK political parties

## Political parties campaigning across the UK

### Key learning
Study the UK's major political parties, and their philosophical and political differences.

Five major political parties campaign across England Wales and Scotland. (For more on each party's policies, see Chapter 7.)

| The Conservative Party | Conservatives |
|---|---|
| Background | Founded in 1834 from the former Tory Party.<br><br>The dominant party of the twentieth century, competing with Labour for power.<br><br>By the general election in 2020, the Conservatives will have played a leading part in government for half of the 21st century to that point. (Includes being part of a coalition government with the Liberal Democrats from 2010 to 2015.)<br><br>Famous Conservatives include Winston Churchill and Margaret Thatcher. |
| Policies | Encourages people to be independent and believes that private companies should have a leading role in running public services such as transport, health and education. Seeks to reduce spending on welfare benefits and public services so that taxes can be cut.<br><br>Split on European Union (EU) membership, but supports strong defence (including upgraded nuclear weapons). |
| Main supporters | Most landowners and business owners.<br><br>People living in rural constituencies, and the towns and cities of southern England and the Midlands. More popular with older voters. |
| MPs and share of the vote (2015 general election) | 330 MPs<br>37 per cent of the total vote |
| Membership | 150,000 members (2014 figures)<br>Full members pay £25. (£5 if under 23) |
| Website | **https://www.conservatives.com/** |

| The Green Party | Green Party |
|---|---|
| Background | Founded as the People Party in 1972 by a group of friends concerned about the effects of population growth on the planet.<br><br>Became known as the Green Party in 1985 and had candidates elected to the European Parliament in 1999.<br><br>The first Green Party MP was elected to Parliament in 2010. |
| Policies | Encourages personal freedom and **sustainable development**. Wants more decision-making to take place at local level and to return public services to public ownership.<br><br>Favours non-violent solutions to conflict and so would scrap the UK's nuclear weapons. Would seek to change the EU and give priority to sustainable development across Europe. |
| Main supporters | Supporters are from all backgrounds, but are mainly young.<br><br>Support is concentrated in those cities and towns where the party has campaigned successfully. |
| MPs and share of the vote (2015 general election) | 1 MP (Caroline Lucas representing the Brighton Pavilion constituency)<br>4 per cent of the total vote |
| Membership | 66,000 (October 2015)<br>Full members pay £31. (£5 for students) |
| Website | **https://policy.greenparty.org.uk/** |

**Sustainable development**   Meeting today's human needs while making sure future generations will also be able to meet their needs.

| The Labour Party | Labour |
|---|---|
| Background | Formed by the trade unions to get working people elected as MPs. Founded in 1900 and formed a **minority government** in 1924. Competed with the Conservatives for power during the twentieth century and was dominant from 1997 to 2010. Famous Labour people include Clement Atlee and Tony Blair. |
| Policies | Seeks to reduce inequality and create jobs by increasing spending on welfare benefits and public services. This would be paid for by raising taxes for wealthier people. Wants public services to be **nationalised** rather than run by private companies. Supports EU membership but split on whether the UK should have nuclear weapons. |
| Main supporters | Trade union members and their leaders. People living in London, and the larger towns and cities of northern England and Wales. Popular with people working in public services, with black and minority ethnic voters, and with young people. |
| MPs and share of the vote (2015 general election) | 232 MPs 30 per cent of the total vote |
| Membership | 370,000 (October 2015) Full members pay £46. (£1 for students) |
| Website | **http://www.labour.org.uk/** |

| The Liberal Democrats | Liberal Democrats |
|---|---|
| Background | The Liberal Party was founded in 1859. The Liberals were one of the two dominant parties in the UK until the 1920s when Labour became stronger. In 1988, the Liberals merged with the Social Democratic Party to form the Liberal Democrats. The Liberals formed a **coalition government** with the Conservatives from 2010 to 2015. It was the first time they had been in government for almost a hundred years. Famous Liberals include Lloyd George and William Beveridge. |
| Policies | Favour more choice and competition than Labour, but would regulate business more than the Conservatives. They support higher taxation and would spend this on improving public services. Support greater freedom from censorship and oppose surveillance by the Government. Strongly support EU membership but would not upgrade the UK's nuclear weapons. |
| Main supporters | Supported by people from a range of backgrounds. Support has been strongest in western England and in suburban areas. |
| MPs and share of the vote (2015 general election) | 8 MPs 8 per cent of the total vote |
| Membership | 81,000 (September 2015) Full members are asked to pay £70. (£1 for students) |
| Website | **http://www.libdems.org.uk/** |

**Minority government**  A government usually made up of MPs from the largest political party in Parliament but one that doesn't command a majority. Minority governments can be outvoted by all the other MPs voting against the Government. A minority government can only pass laws if some MPs from other political parties are prepared to provide support.

**Nationalised**  Nationalised businesses are owned and run by the State on behalf of the people. In 2015, the Labour Party developed a plan to nationalise the railways rather than leave rail transport in the hands of independent companies.

**Coalition government**  If no single political party has a majority of MPs in Parliament, two or more parties can co operate to form a government together. This happened in 2010 when a coalition of Conservative and Liberal Democrat MPs had a parliamentary majority.

| The United Kingdom Independence Party (UKIP) |  |
|---|---|
| Background | UKIP traces its origins back to 1991 when a university lecturer decided to campaign for the UK to leave the EU. <br><br> UKIP won the largest number of votes in the 2014 European elections and 24 UKIP representatives were elected to the European Parliament. <br><br> Most famous politician – Nigel Farage. |
| Policies | Leave the EU and improve trade links with the rest of the world. Reduce immigration, and promote British values and traditions. <br><br> UKIP has a similar view to the Conservatives on the economy, taxes and public services. |
| Main supporters | Support has proved strongest in the coastal areas of southern and eastern England. <br><br> Popular with older voters of white British heritage. |
| MPs and share of the vote (2015 general election) | 1 MP (Douglas Carswell representing the Clacton constituency) <br><br> 13 per cent of the total vote |
| Membership | 42,000 (January 2015) <br><br> Full members pay £30. (£2 for people under 22) |
| Website | **http://www.ukip.org/** |

# Political parties in Scotland, Wales and Northern Ireland

## Scotland

By 2015, the Scottish National Party (SNP) had become the leading political party in Scotland, winning 56 of the 59 Scottish seats in the UK Parliament. It also forms the Scottish Government within Scotland's parliament.

The SNP wants Scotland to be independent from the rest of the UK. It favours: higher levels of public spending paid for from taxation, Scotland's membership of the EU and scrapping nuclear weapons.

## Wales

Plaid Cymru, the Party of Wales, wants independence for Wales. Plaid Cymru has similar policies to the SNP but so far has not enjoyed great success in Wales. It won three seats in the UK Parliament at the 2015 general election. Labour is the largest party in Wales and controls the Welsh Government.

## Northern Ireland

Northern Ireland has its own political parties, most of which either support continued union with the UK or campaign for an Irish republic. Until peace talks in 1997, extremists on each side of this debate resorted to violence and terrorism. Since then, disagreements have been dealt with through debate and negotiation. Elections are keenly contested. Up to now, **unionist** parties have gained more seats in the UK Parliament than **nationalist** parties. Both sides share power in the Northern Ireland Assembly, but relationships are often difficult and government sometimes breaks down.

**Unionist** An individual or political party supportive of the union of England, Wales, Scotland and Northern Ireland in one United Kingdom.

**Nationalist** An individual or political party supportive of the idea that the nations of England, Wales and Scotland should be independent states, and that there should be a republic for the whole of Ireland.

## Activities

1. Choose a famous person from one of the UK's political parties.
   a) Describe their main achievements.
   b) Explain why they remain famous today.
2. The information about the main political parties was written after the 2015 general election.
   a) Study the results of recent elections, by-elections and opinion polls.
   b) Identify political parties that are becoming more or less popular than they were in 2015.
   c) Explain the reasons for these changes in their popularity.
3. Study the policies and statements of the main UK political parties using their websites to find out more about their ideas.
   a) Select a political party that you would be most likely to vote for at the next election.
   b) Explain the reasons for your choice.
   c) Ask your teacher to help organise a mock election or a 'Question Time' debate so that you can discuss the party's ideas in more depth with other learners.
4. Some of the main political parties in Scotland, Wales and Northern Ireland campaign for independence from the UK.
   State three reasons why they support independence.

# Key features of UK electoral systems

## Key learning

Study the key features of electoral systems used within the UK including those used in elections for the European Parliament. Evaluate the systems through understanding their possible advantages and disadvantages, and their impact on election outcomes.

Different elections systems are used across the UK. The general election for the UK Parliament uses a first-past-the-post system where the person with the most votes is declared the winner. This system is also used in English and Welsh local authority elections.

Different types of proportional representation are also used in UK elections.

These include the following systems:

- closed party list
- additional member
- single transferable vote.

Proportional representation means that the number of representatives elected is more likely to match (be in proportion to) the number of people who voted for them.

## First-past-the-post (UK general elections)

A general election for the UK Parliament takes place once every five years. Electors in each of the UK's constituencies vote for one candidate only. The candidate with the most votes becomes that constituency's Member of Parliament.

Table 4.1 Advantages and disadvantages of first-past-the-post

| Advantages | Disadvantages |
|---|---|
| Simple to understand | A candidate can be elected with support from less than half the voters |
| Easy to organise | Voters may feel their vote is 'wasted' if they vote for a party candidate who has little chance of winning |
| More likely to lead to a majority government | Can produce a government that over 60 per cent of voters do not support |
| People have a single representative in Parliament and so know who to contact with constituency issues | Voters may feel unrepresented if their MP belongs to a political party they do not like |

Table 4.2 2015 general election result for the Cambridge constituency

| Candidate | Party | Votes | Percentage of votes cast |
|---|---|---|---|
| Daniel Zeichner | Labour | 18,646 | 36% |
| Julian Huppert | Liberal Democrat | 18,047 | 34.9% |
| Chamali Fernando | Conservative | 8,117 | 15.7% |
| Rupert Read | Green | 4,109 | 7.9% |
| Patrick O'Flynn | UKIP | 2,668 | 5.2% |
| Keith Garrett | Rebooting Democracy | 187 | 0.4% |

62.1 per cent of electors voted

## Activities

1. Analyse the election result for the Cambridge constituency in 2015.
   a) Voting for the Conservatives, UKIP, Green Party or Rebooting Democracy might be described as a 'wasted vote'. Explain how far you agree.
   b) What strategy might the Labour or Liberal Democrat candidate use to give them a better chance of winning the seat in the next general election?

# CASE STUDY

## Using the 'first-past-the-post' election: UK Parliamentary election May 2015

After the May 2015 general election, the Conservative Party had most MPs – 330. This was enough for Conservative MPs to outvote all other MPs in Parliament. The Conservatives formed a government and David Cameron became Prime Minister. They had

no need to ask any other political party to support them. The Labour Party with its 232 MPs was the second largest party in the House of Commons and so became the Official Opposition.

The table shows why the Liberal Democrats, UKIP and the Green Party feel that the first-past-the-post voting system is unfair. These political parties had far fewer MPs in 2015 than they deserved given their percentage (%) of the UK vote.

**Table 4.3** UK general election 2015 – state of the major parties+

| Party | Number of votes+ | Percentage of votes | MPs actually elected using the first past the post system | MPs that would have been elected if proportional representation had been used++ |
|---|---|---|---|---|
| Conservative | 11,334,520 | 36.9% | 330 | 240 |
| Labour | 9,347,326 | 30.4% | 232 | 198 |
| UKIP | 3,881,129 | 12.6% | 1 | 82 |
| Liberal Democrat | 2,415,436 | 7.9% | 8 | 51 |
| Green | 1,157,613 | 3.8% | 1 | 25 |
| Scottish Nationalist* | 1,454,436 | 4.7% | 56 | 31 |
| Plaid Cymru** | 181,694 | 0.6% | 3 | 4 |
| Democratic Unionists*** | 184,260 | 0.6% | 8 | 4 |
| Sinn Fein*** | 176,232 | 0.6% | 4 | 4 |
| Ulster Unionist*** | 114,935 | 0.4% | 2 | 3 |
| SDLP*** | 99,809 | 0.3% | 3 | 2 |

+Votes for minor parties have been excluded

++ This column totals 644 instead of 650 because of rounding, disregarding the votes for minor parties and the exclusion of two MPs (the Speaker and one independent MP).

*Only contests constituencies in Scotland

** Only contests constituencies in Wales

*** Only contests constituencies in Northern Ireland

### Activities

2. Analyse the UK general election result of 2015.
   a) Explain why the result would be different if a proportional representation system had been used.
   b) Describe the type of government that could have been formed if each party had the number of MPs proportionate to its vote in the 2015 election.

## Closed party list system (elections to the European Parliament in England, Wales and Scotland)

Different types of proportional representation are used for some elections in the UK.

One type of proportional representation is known as 'proportional representation – closed party list'. This was used in the elections for the European Parliament in 2014 except in Northern Ireland. In a 'closed party list' system, people vote for one political party rather than a particular candidate or candidates.

Before polling day, each political party makes an ordered list of people it would like to represent each of the UK's twelve European parliamentary constituencies. The proportion of a party's vote in a constituency then determines how many people on their list are elected as constituency MEPs.

# CASE STUDY

## Using the closed party list system: UK European election 2014, South East England constituency

In the South East constituency, 6.4 million electors were to be represented by ten MEPs. Before the election, each party drew up a list of up to ten members who it wanted to be elected as MEPs.

Thirty-six per cent of the electors voted. UKIP received most votes and so was able to have the largest share of MEPs. The top four people on UKIP's list became MEPs. Four other political parties also received enough votes for people on their lists to become MEPs.

**Table 4.4** Election result, European Parliament 2014 (South East England)

| Party | Number of votes | Share of the vote (%) | Candidates elected as MEPs from the party lists |
|---|---|---|---|
| UKIP | 751,439 | 32.14% | Nigel Farage<br>Janice Atkinson<br>Diane James<br>Ray Finch |
| Conservative | 723,571 | 30.95% | Daniel Hannan<br>Nirj Deva<br>Richard Ashworth |
| Labour | 342,775 | 14.66% | Anneliese Dodds |
| Green | 211,706 | 9.05% | Keith Taylor |
| Liberal Democrat | 187,876 | 8.04% | Catherine Bearder |
| Independence | 45,199 | 1.93% | No MEPs |
| Nine other political parties gained less than 1% of votes each and were not allocated MEPs | | | |

### Activity

3. Analyse the European Parliament election result for South East England in 2014. Write a press article or blog post describing the result and explaining how the ten MEPs were chosen.

## Additional member system (elections to the Welsh Assembly)

Elections for the Welsh Assembly use a first-past-the-post system to elect an Assembly Member for each of 40 constituencies. The total number of votes for each party within each of five Welsh regions is then used to choose twenty additional Assembly Members from party lists. The number of additional regional members a party gets is proportional to their total vote in that region.

- In the election, each voter has two votes.
- The first vote is a constituency vote for a candidate to become their local Assembly Member.
- The second vote is a regional vote for a political party.

Elections in other democracies use a similar system. New Zealand is one example.

## Single transferable vote system (elections to the Northern Ireland Assembly)

Elections in Northern Ireland for the Assembly, European Parliament and local authorities use a type of proportional representation known as the single transferable vote (STV). This is also used for local authority elections in Scotland.

# CASE STUDY
## Using the additional member system: Welsh Assembly 2011

**Figure 4.10** The constituency vote and regional vote for the Welsh Assembly elections, 2011

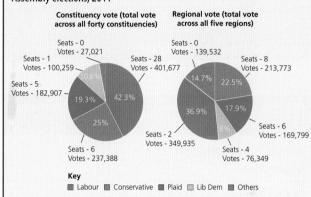

# CASE STUDY
## Using the STV system: Northern Ireland Assembly

Voters in each of the Northern Ireland Assembly's eighteen constituencies elect six representatives.

The STV system increases voter choice because they can vote for more than one candidate. Voters can choose between candidates within a party, as well as between parties. STV gives smaller parties a better chance in elections, as they may benefit from transferred votes from larger parties.

STV makes it unlikely that people will feel that their votes have been wasted. In Northern Ireland Assembly elections, around 80 per cent of all voters find that at least one of the candidates on their list of preferences is elected. This means the results represent the views of the electorate, but STV does make coalition governments more likely. This is no problem in Northern Ireland because, under the **Power Sharing Agreement** of 1998, the different political groups are required to form a coalition government anyway.

**On polling day**

Voters rank candidates in order of preference. 1 for their first choice, 2 for their second choice and so on. Voters do not have to show a preference for a candidate they do not like.

↓

**Counting the votes**

Stage 1: Candidates who get at least 14 per cent* of the total vote are elected.

↓

Stage 2: Votes for successful candidates, in excess of the 14 per cent they need for election, are redistributed among the other candidates. (The second preferences of these voters are used to do this.)

If all the vacancies are filled, the process stops.

↓

If not, it moves to stage 3.

Stage 3: The least popular candidates are eliminated in turn and the second preferences of their supporters are redistributed. The process continues until all the vacancies are filled using voters' third, fourth or other preferences as necessary.

*This is the quota for elections to the Northern Ireland Assembly. The quota is worked out depending on the number of members to be elected and the number of voters in each constituency. In Northern Ireland six members represent each constituency.

# Websites

Factsheets on the election systems used in the UK can be found on the Electoral Commission website: **http://www.electoralcommission.org.uk/**

Information on how the single transferable vote works is included on the website of the Northern Ireland Assembly: **http://education.niassembly.gov.uk**

The education section of the UK Parliament website includes a section comparing the different election systems: **http://www.parliament.uk/education/**

## Activity

4. Study the four different election systems used in the UK. Complete a grid like the one below to compare their key features and likely implications by placing a ✓ or ✗ in each cell.

**Power Sharing Agreement** This agreement helped to put an end to many years of violent conflict in Northern Ireland. Any government has to include unionists and nationalists. Elections use the STV to ensure a proportional representation of voters' intentions.

| Features and implications | First-past-the-post | Closed party list | Additional member | STV |
|---|---|---|---|---|
| Includes some proportional representation | | | | |
| Each constituency is linked to one member of the parliament or assembly | | | | |
| Electors vote for a party rather than for an individual candidate | | | | |
| Smaller parties have a good chance of getting candidates elected | | | | |
| Likely to lead to a majority government | | | | |
| Extremist parties representing minority views are unlikely to be successful | | | | |
| Easy to understand and organise | | | | |
| Most voters are likely to feel that their vote counts | | | | |

## Activity

5. Evaluate the following viewpoint.

   'We should use the closed party list system for general elections to the UK Parliament.'

   In your answer you should:
   - Describe the system used currently for elections to the UK Parliament.
   - Describe the closed party list system.
   - Compare the closed party list system with other systems.
   - Evaluate the viewpoint.
   - State which system you would prefer and explain why.

## Practice questions

In the OCR specification, this section will be assessed using objective test questions and questions needing a written response.

1. Which one of the options below best matches the term **secret ballot**?
   A Voting by the Government without the public's knowledge.
   B Voting by the Cabinet in a secret session.
   C Voting by the electorate in private.
   D Voting by Parliament with the media excluded. [1 mark]

2. Which group of people cannot vote in a **UK general election**?
   A UK citizens who have emigrated recently.
   B Citizens of other EU countries living in the UK.
   C People charged with a serious criminal offence.
   D Members of the House of Commons. [1 mark]

3. Study **Sources 1, 2** and **3**. State two reasons why the headline in **Source 2** is misleading. [2 marks]

4. Using **Sources 1, 2** and **3** and your own knowledge, evaluate the following viewpoint; 'The first-past-the-post system is unfair and should be replaced.'

   In your answer you should consider the reasons for agreeing **and** disagreeing with the viewpoint. Make your own judgement on the viewpoint and support this judgement. [12 marks]

## Source 1
### 5 May 2011 – UK votes no

*19.1 million people voted in the second UK-wide referendum in history – a higher than expected turnout of 41 per cent.*

*The final result was:*

*Yes      32.1%*

*No       67.9%.*

*UK electors were asked:*

*'At present, the UK uses the "first-past-the-post" system to elect MPs to the House of Commons. Should the "alternative vote" system be used instead?'*

## Source 2
### June 2015 – Blog post headline used by *The Daily Telegraph*

*No, Britain does not want proportional representation.*

## Source 3
### How does the Alternative Vote work?

On polling day

| Ballot Paper | |
|---|---|
| Black, Sandra | 3 |
| Brown, Yasmin | 1 |
| Green, Trevor | 2 |
| White, Winston | 4 |

*The voter ranks the candidates in order of preference.*

*They put a '1' by their first choice a '2' by their second choice, and so on, until they no longer wish to express any further preferences or run out of candidates.*

### Counting the votes

*If a candidate gains more than half of voters' first preferences, they win.*

*If not, the candidate with the least first preferences falls out of the election. Their votes are redistributed to those candidates marked as second preferences.*

*If there is still no candidate with half the total votes, the next least successful candidate has second preferences redistributed to the candidates still in the contest.*

*Eventually one candidate will have half the vote and win. (These votes will be made up of their own first preferences, as well as second and even third preferences from voters who made another candidate their first choice.)*

This chapter on *National, local, regional and devolved government* builds on learning from Chapter 4 *Democracy, elections and voting in the UK* and links with Chapter 6 on *The British constitution*.

In this chapter we explore the different forms of government in the UK and how they work.

Learning the following key concepts and terms will make it easier to organise your thinking and communicate your ideas:

- parliament
- government
- prime minister, cabinet and ministers
- monarch
- assembly
- local authority
- devolution
- centralisation.

# National governments in the UK

## Key learning

Study how elected representatives form governments and the key roles played by the Prime Minister, the Cabinet and ministers in the UK Government. Know the UK Government's key responsibilities and those of governments in Scotland, Wales and Northern Ireland.

## The United Kingdom Government

After a general election, the newly elected representatives from across the UK form a new **House of Commons**. If a political party has a majority of these Members of Parliament (MPs), it will form the Government.

If no political party has a majority of MPs, the leader of the largest party may try to go into coalition with one or more other political parties or may attempt to form a minority government (see page 87).

The **Monarch** will invite the leader of the largest political party or coalition of parties to become the **Prime Minister**.

The Prime Minister will then choose some of the most experienced, skilled and loyal MPs in his or her political party, or coalition, to help run the country. These MPs will no longer just represent their constituents. Many of them will become **government ministers** with responsibility for running one of twenty-four ministerial departments which make and implement decisions on matters such as defence, taxation and immigration.

These senior MPs will meet with the Prime Minister at least once a week to discuss the major issues facing the country and to decide what to do. This group of senior MPs is known as the **Cabinet**. (See Chapter 6 for more details of *The British Constitution*.)

**House of Commons**  Democratically elected Members of Parliament (MPs) form the House of Commons. The House of Lords is the second chamber in this Westminster Parliament.

**Monarch**  A monarch is a country's ruler. The UK has a constitutional monarch whose power is limited by the democratic system. The Monarch has important responsibilities in the British Constitution including inviting the leader of one of the political parties represented in the UK Parliament to form a government. (See Chapter 6 for more details.)

**Prime Minister**  The Prime Minister is leader of one of the political parties in Parliament – usually the party with the most MPs. He or she is asked by the Monarch to select a government to run the country. The Prime Minister is not elected directly by the UK citizens.

**Government ministers**  Senior MPs or Members of the House of Lords who have accepted the Prime Minister's invitation to be part of the Government and to lead departments responsible for matters such as defence, health or education. Together with senior civil servants, they form the executive.

**Cabinet**  The Prime Minister and the senior colleagues he or she has chosen to be part of the Government meet together at 10 Downing Street. They are known as the Cabinet.

**Figure 5.1** David Cameron, Conservative Party leader, having just been made prime minister by the Queen, outside number 10 Downing Street in London before holding his first cabinet meeting in May 2015

## The UK Government's powers

In 2016, the UK Government had the following powers over the whole of the UK. These are known as **reserved powers**.

- defence
- management of the economy
- currency
- elections
- employment
- foreign policy (international links and relationships)
- overseas development
- border control, immigration and asylum
- benefits and social security
- taxation (but with major exceptions in Scotland)
- trade and industry
- nuclear energy, oil, coal, gas and electricity
- data protection
- the constitution.

The UK Government also has responsibility for

- all laws, regulations and services that apply to England
- the legal and justice system in England and Wales
- final say on the powers for which the governments of Scotland, Wales and Northern Ireland will be responsible
- granting permission for the Scottish Parliament, and Welsh and Northern Ireland assemblies to make strategic decisions in key areas
- deciding the size of grants to Scotland, Wales and Northern Ireland from UK taxation.

## Devolved powers of national governments in Scotland, Wales and Northern Ireland

Although the governments of Scotland, Wales and Northern Ireland now have similar **devolved powers** or responsibilities, there are also some key differences.

- The Scottish Parliament has greater power over the economy, taxation and law-making than either of the Welsh or Northern Ireland assemblies.
- The Welsh and Northern Ireland governments have to ask the UK Government for permission to change policy in a greater number of key areas than the Scottish Government does.
- Although the Welsh Government does have some law-making powers, it shares England's legal and justice system.

**Figure 5.2** The UK Government controls Britain's defence and has responsibility for the armed forces

**Reserved powers** The issues on which only the UK Parliament can make laws.

**Devolved powers** The issues on which the Scottish Parliament, or the assemblies of Wales or Northern Ireland, can make their own laws.

**Figure 5.3** UK devolution of power

The Scottish Parliament

Welsh Assembly

Northern Ireland Assembly

are responsible for

- agriculture, forests and fisheries
- culture and sport
- economic development and tourism
- education and training
- environment
- health and social services
- housing
- justice and policing (not Wales)
- local government
- roads and transport
- town and country planning

The Scotland Act 2012 gave more powers to the Scottish Parliament, including the transfer of some significant financial powers. The new powers devolved to the Scottish Parliament included:

- full control of stamp duty, land tax and landfill tax from April 2015
- a new Scottish rate of income tax to be in place from April 2016
- new borrowing powers for the Scottish Government
- the power to introduce new taxes, subject to agreement of the UK Government
- giving Scottish ministers powers relating to the misuse of drugs, the drink-drive limit, the national speed limit and the administration of elections to the Scottish Parliament.

## Websites

The Government's own official website includes clear information about how government works in the UK: **https://www.gov.uk/government/how-government-works**

The websites for the Scottish Parliament, and the assemblies for Wales and Northern Ireland, provide detailed descriptions of their powers, decision-making processes and current policies:

**http://www.scottish.parliament.uk/msps.aspx**
**http://www.assembly.wales/en/Pages/Home.aspx**
**http://www.niassembly.gov.uk/**

## Activities

1. The Scottish Parliament has been described as the most devolved regional government in the world. Justify this description using evidence to support your case

2. Explain why the assemblies for Wales and Northern Ireland can be described as, 'having less power than the Scottish Parliament'.

3. Use the information from the table to decide whether these statements are true or false.
   a) Electors in Scotland are more engaged in politics than in any other part of the UK.
   b) Voters think elections for national parliaments and assemblies are more important than the UK general election.
   c) Devolved governments were felt to be less important in 2016 than in 2011.
   d) People in Wales support devolved government more than people in Scotland or Northern Ireland.

| Voter turnout in elections | | | |
|---|---|---|---|
| | 2011 | 2016 | (2015 General Election in each nation) |
| Scottish Parliament | 50% | 56% | 71% |
| Welsh Assembly | 42% | 44% | 66% |
| Northern Ireland Assembly | 55% | 54% | 58% |
| England (no national parliament or assembly) | N/A | N/A | 66% |

4. Suggest different ways to encourage more people to vote in elections for the Scottish Parliament, Welsh Assembly and Northern Ireland Assembly. Compare your ideas with those of other learners and with your teacher.

# Local and regional government

## Key learning

Study the role, structure and organisation of local and regional government in the UK.

## Local authorities

Local authorities, also known as councils, make decisions about local services. Most local authorities are controlled by representatives, known as councillors. Councillors are elected by local residents. Some local authorities are run by directly elected mayors supported by councillors.

Councillors represent a neighbourhood usually known as a ward. Larger wards may be represented by two or more councillors. Elections for English and Welsh local authorities use the first-past-the-post system. Each elector will be able to cast two votes if there are two council seats in their ward; three votes if there are three seats and so on. Most candidates in local authority elections are nominated by local political party branches, although many candidates are independents.

Some areas do not have town or parish councils so community responsibilities are taken on by the second-tier authorities.

In some parts of England, there's just one tier of local government called a unitary authority which provides all the services of a two or three tier system. Hull City Council is an example of a unitary authority.

**Table 5.2** Many parts of England have three tiers of local government

| | Local authority type | Responsibilities | Examples |
|---|---|---|---|
| First tier | county councils | <ul><li>children and families</li><li>social care</li><li>public health</li><li>libraries</li><li>strategic planning</li><li>county landscape and environment</li><li>roads, cycle routes and footpaths</li><li>fire and rescue (transferring to police and crime commissioners from 2016)</li><li>consumer protection</li><li>dealing with emergencies</li></ul> | West Sussex County Council |
| Second tier | borough or district councils | <ul><li>local planning and building control</li><li>housing</li><li>parks and leisure</li><li>refuse collection and recycling</li><li>food hygiene, public health and licensing</li><li>pest control</li><li>voting and elections</li></ul> | Arun District Council |
| Third tier | town or parish councils | <ul><li>make representations to higher tier authorities on planning applications and other matters of importance to the local community</li><li>provide local services to improve quality of life such as: floral displays; public seating; community events and allotments</li></ul> | Bognor Regis Town Council |

**Figure 5.4** Local authorities are responsible for a wide range of public services

Wales has 22 principal areas. These are unitary authorities responsible for the provision of all local government services. There are also community councils in most parts of Wales. These have similar responsibilities to England's town or parish councils. Scotland and Northern Ireland also use a system of unitary authorities but, in Northern Ireland, the national government is responsible for education, housing and roads.

## Local government in London

London is one of the world's leading cities with a population of 8.6 million (bigger than the combined populations of Wales and Scotland). It is vital to co-ordinate such things as transport, housing and policing across the whole city. This work is done by the Greater London Authority with its elected assembly and directly elected Mayor. The Mayor represents London across the world – encouraging business, investment and tourism.

Thirty-three second-tier authorities provide local services in the capital.

**Figure 5.5** London's innovative bike hire scheme – one of the Mayor's initiatives to improve transport

**Table 5.3** London's two tiers of local government

| Local Government in London | | | |
|---|---|---|---|
| | Local authority type | Responsibilities | Examples |
| First tier | Greater London Authority | • business and economy<br>• transport<br>• policing<br>• housing<br>• environment<br>• culture and sport | Greater London Authority (GLA)<br>London City Hall, GLA headquarters |
| Second tier | Borough councils | Other local authority responsibilities including:<br>• children's services<br>• social care<br>• libraries<br>• refuse collection<br>• planning | Islington Council<br>London boroughs |

# Regional government in England

The idea of devolved government for the English regions has been hotly debated over the last twenty years.

Advocates of change have argued that regional government for areas such as the North East, Yorkshire and Humberside, East Anglia and the South West would:

- give the English regions more influence
- ensure that important decisions affecting a region are made by elected representatives from that region
- enable the UK Government to devolve more power away from London
- allow the work of local authorities in each region to be coordinated more effectively.

## Regional government rejected – 2004

However, the idea of regional government was unpopular. Its opponents argued that regional government would be expensive and might simply produce more **bureaucracy** without improving people's quality of life. Most citizens identified with their county, their city, their town or their borough, and were not convinced that another tier of government was needed.

In 2004, a referendum was held in North East England on whether to introduce regional government. Voters rejected the proposal. As a result, the Government dropped plans for regional government in England.

> **Bureaucracy**   Careful, detailed and often time-consuming decision-making and implementation in which nothing is left to chance. Bureaucratic organisation is likely to be fair but it can often be slow and costly.

> ## Website
> The Local Government Association's website has information on the work of all tiers in local government and the devolution of power to local authorities: **http://www.local.gov.uk/**

> ## Activities
>
> 1. Find the local authorities that make decisions in your area. Study their websites.
>     a) List six local authority services used by you or your family.
>     b) State which political party controls local councils in your area.
>     c) Name your local councillors and explain why electors might wish to contact them.
>     d) Evaluate one local authority website for accessibility.
>         i.   How easy is it to find information about local services?
>         ii.  How easy would it be to contact your local councillor?
>         iii. Describe how the site could be improved.

## Regional government returns – 2015

In 2015, following further power devolution to Scotland, Wales and Northern Ireland, the UK Government returned to the idea of devolution within England.

This time the Government proposed to work within the existing local government structure by devolving greater power to the elected mayors of large cities such as Leeds, Manchester and Birmingham. This would place the English regions in a similar position to Wales, with its assembly, or London, with its directly elected mayor.

Devolved powers proposed for English cities:

- responsibility for local transport, housing, skills and health care
- rights to adjust taxes to match local economic plans.

These proposals were part of the Government's Cities and Local Government Devolution Bill which started its passage through Parliament in 2015.

> ## Activities
>
> 2. In 2015, the Government's Chancellor, George Osborne, proposed creating a Northern Powerhouse in partnership with local authorities.
>     a) Carry out your own research to describe:
>         - what the Northern Powerhouse is
>         - what it will do
>         - how it will operate.
>     b) Explain why the Northern Powerhouse has been proposed.
>     c) Evaluate the proposal.

# Debates about the devolution of power

## Key learning

Study the changing relationships between England, Scotland, Wales and Northern Ireland within the United Kingdom. Understand the reasons for devolution and centralisation, and evaluate arguments for further devolution.

There is general support for the idea of devolution. Devolution is seen to have the following advantages:

- Local decision-makers understand the culture and needs of their community and so will make good decisions.
- Local decision-makers live in the area, and so are able to check that money is spent well, and that services are delivered properly and on time.
- Residents can contact local decision-makers easily and so are able to hold them to account.
- Residents develop a stronger sense of identity and so increase their participation in the political process.

In 2010, the Conservative Government made a radical proposal for greater devolution of power away from national and local government to businesses, charities and community groups. Supporters of this *Big Society* idea argued that it could revitalise communities but opponents complained that the Government was just trying to save money and undermine public services. (See Chapters 7 and 11 for further details.)

### We'll pay for extra police to stop robbers, say Hampstead residents

The residents of one of Britain's wealthiest neighbourhoods have offered to help pay for extra police officers after a spate of violent robberies.

Residents plan to raise £200,000 through crowdsourcing to pay for a dedicated unit of Metropolitan Police officers – two beat officers and a sergeant for three years. The officers could not be taken for duty in other parts of London.

Some wealthier residents have already hired security firms to protect their homes, but the new proposals are being seen as a way of bringing increased peace of mind to all residents in the area. Oliver Cooper, a Hampstead councillor, said, 'Since 2010, crime has been cut by 20 per cent in Hampstead and 15 per cent across London, but with a spate of burglaries and untackled anti-social behaviour, we can't take anything for granted. This proposal would cost just £13 per person each year. As a local resident, I'd be very happy to pay that share for the peace of mind that comes from living in a more secure community.'

(Adapted from *The Daily Telegraph*, 26 September 2015)

Some government responsibilities cannot easily be devolved to a local level. Decisions about matters such as national defence, border control and overall economic policy are made by the UK Government. Such **centralisation** enables decision-makers to consider the interests of the whole country and to achieve a coordinated approach at a national level.

Centralisation   The development and management of services across a wide area from one central point.

## Activities

1. Study the advantages of devolution mentioned in this section.
   a) Rank the advantages in order of importance.
   b) Make a list of the challenges governments may face when power is devolved.
   c) Describe how governments might meet such challenges.
2. Study the scenarios below. They are based on real examples of power devolution from local authorities to community groups.
   i) A local council plans to close a local library. A community group campaigns to keep the library open and offers to run it. The council agrees. The community group arranges to pay an annual rent for the building and plans to run the library with money raised locally.
   ii) A local council plans to give parent and teacher volunteers the power to issue £70 fines to inconsiderate motorists parking outside school gates. The volunteers will be given a week's training, four week's work experience alongside a traffic warden, a uniform and ticket machine.
   iii) Individuals, businesses or charities can set up and control their own school as long as they can show that more school places are needed in a particular area. In return, the Government will provide funding linked to the number of pupils attending the new school. (Scenario based on the Government's Free School programme established in 2010.)
   a) Discuss the possible advantages and disadvantages of each scheme with other learners.
   b) Present your ideas in a slide or chart.
   c) Identify the scheme you approve of most and the one you like the least. Explain the reasons for your choices.

## Independence for Scotland, Northern Ireland and Wales?

### Scotland

In 2014, people in Scotland voted 'NO' to the proposal that their country should become independent from the rest of the UK. By autumn 2015, the Scottish National Party was calling for another referendum on independence.

### Wales

In 2011, Wales voted in favour of extending devolution by giving law-making powers to the Welsh Government. Opinion polls in 2015 indicated that Welsh people would not support independence from the UK.

**Figure 5.6** Debates about devolution usually include three questions

What rights and responsibilities should be devolved, and which should be centralised?

Should Scotland, Wales or Northern Ireland become completely independent?

Where should devolved powers go – how about devolving more power to community groups?

# SCOTTISH INDEPENDENCE

## Scotland should be independent

Independence is based on a simple truth. It is better for all of us if decisions about Scotland's future are taken by the people who care most about Scotland. It is the people who live here who will do the best job of making our nation a fairer and more successful place.

Becoming an independent country is all about making Scotland a better place to live, with greater prosperity and higher standards of living. That is the purpose and the reason why so many Scots are passionate about an independent Scotland.

People ask, can we afford to be independent? We have the people, resources and ingenuity to prosper. Instead we should be asking, why is Scotland not doing better, given all the natural and human wealth we enjoy?

As an independent country, we can speak with our own voice, choose our own direction and contribute in our own distinct way. With independence we remain part of the wider family of nations on these British Isles. And, as a member of the European Union, we will have access to the world's largest free market.

As an independent country we will have a parliament and government just as we do now. But it will take all the decisions for Scotland. It will be elected in the same way, and so the people of Scotland will be able to choose the government they want.

(Adapted from 'Choice' – a booklet produced by the Scottish National Party for the 2014 referendum.)

## Scotland should remain in the UK

A strong Scottish Parliament within the United Kingdom gives us the best of both worlds: real decision-making power here in Scotland, as well as a key role in a strong and secure UK. Now and in the future, Scotland is stronger as part of the UK and the UK is stronger with Scotland as a partner.

In the future, Scotland will be wealthier by keeping the British connection. We need more growth, more jobs, and more wealth in Scotland. We do not need uncertainty and barriers for our businesses.

The size, strength and stability of the UK economy is a huge advantage for Scotland's businesses. Scotland's largest market is the rest of the UK. The UK is better placed than a separate Scotland or England to help our businesses find and win new orders across the world.

In an uncertain world, Scotland's security will be strengthened as part of the UK. As part of the UK, we have real power and influence in the United Nations Security Council and the European Union (EU). We can afford to have British embassies around the world.

Thousands of Scots and English have made their homes in each other's nation. Half of us have English neighbours. This interdependence – the coming together of family, friends, ideas, institutions and identities – is a strength worth celebrating. The truth is we are better together.

(Adapted from information produced for the 2014 Scottish referendum campaign by Better Together – a pressure group supporting Scotland's membership of the UK)

## Northern Ireland

Northern Ireland is split between unionists who want their country to remain part of the UK, and republicans who would like there to be a single **republic** for the whole of Ireland. Unionists are currently in the majority.

**Republic**   A country with an elected head of state (usually known as a president) rather than a monarch. France and the United States of America (USA) are both republics.

### Activities

3.  Study the issue of Scottish independence.
    a)  Use the two extracts for and against independence and your own studies to help you, list the arguments for and against independence for Scotland.
    b)  Explain your reasons for either supporting or opposing Scottish independence.

### Websites

Media websites are good sources for further study of the 2014 Scottish independence campaigns. The BBC, *The Guardian* and *The Daily Telegraph* websites all carry useful archive material:
http://www.theguardian.com/
http://www.telegraph.co.uk/

Former prime minister, Gordon Brown, speaks against Scottish independence on the day before the referendum: **https://www.youtube.com/watch?v=J39bBV7CBJk**

Alex Salmond, SNP leader during the referendum campaign, outlines his party's policies for an independent Scotland: **https://www.youtube.com/watch?v=iYhPIaXyZmY**

## Practice questions

In the OCR specification, this section will be assessed using objective test questions and questions needing a written response.

1. Which **responsibility** is carried out by the UK Government?
   A defence
   B education
   C health
   D policing [1 mark]

2. Which of the following is the best definition of the term **Big Society**?
   A Greater centralisation of power.
   B One tier of local government.
   C Devolution of power to communities.
   D A United Kingdom composed of four independent nations. [1 mark]

Study **Sources 1** and **2** and answer the following questions.

3. Using the data from **Source 1**, explain why the Government decided to boost economic development in Northern England. [4 marks]

4. State two advantages of devolution that George Osborne could have added to his statement in **Source 2**. [2 marks]

5. Is devolution of power from London to English regions a good idea? Use the evidence from **Sources 1** and **2**, and your own knowledge and understanding, to answer the question above. In your answer you should consider the advantages of centralisation and of devolution. [12 marks]

# Source 1

*Gross Value Added (GVA)\* in pounds (£) per head of population 2015, comparing Inner London with ten areas of Northern England*

| Inner London | £71,162 |
|---|---|
| **Areas of northern England** | |
| Greater Manchester – South | £25,950 |
| Greater Manchester – North | £14,375 |
| Leeds (Yorkshire) | £26,741 |
| Tyneside | £20,514 |
| Sheffield (Yorkshire) | £19,995 |
| Liverpool | £22,613 |
| Bradford (Yorkshire) | £16,595 |
| Wakefield (Yorkshire) | £19,623 |
| Hull (Yorkshire) | £18,902 |
| York (Yorkshire) | £23,483 |

\*GVA measures an area's contribution to the UK economy. GVA per head is worked out by dividing an area's contribution by the number of people who live there.

# Source 2

**Viewpoints on the proposal for a *Northern Powerhouse* (a devolution of power from the UK Government to northern England)**

'… the powerhouse of London dominates more and more. And that's not healthy for our economy. It's not good for our country.

We need a Northern Powerhouse too. Not one city, but a collection of northern cities – sufficiently close to each other that combined they can take on the world.

A true powerhouse requires true power. So today I am starting the conversation about serious devolution of powers and budgets for any city that wants to move to a new model of city government – and have an elected Mayor.

A Mayor for Greater Manchester. A Mayor for Leeds. With powers similar to the Mayor of London.'

*George Osborne MP – UK Government*

'The idea of a northern powerhouse sparks alarm in other parts of the country who fear that in future they would lose out not only to London and the south-east but also to the new northern powerhouse. The north-east, for instance, fears being squeezed between this new powerhouse to the south and Scotland to the north.'

*John Humphreys, Broadcaster*

# Chapter 6:
# The British constitution

This chapter on *The British Constitution* builds on Chapter 2 *The law*, Chapter 3 *The legal system*, Chapter 4 *Democracy, elections and voting in the UK* and Chapter 5 *National, local, regional and devolved government.* This chapter links with Chapter 10 *Politics beyond the UK.*

In this chapter, we explore the distribution of power in the UK and consider law-making in more detail.

Learning the following key concepts and terms will make it easier to organise your thinking and communicate your ideas:

- executive
- legislature
- judiciary
- parliament
- government
- accountability
- oversight
- scrutiny
- parliamentary select committee
- bicameral parliament

- House of Commons
- House of Lords
- Prime Minister
- Cabinet
- ministers
- Official Opposition
- Monarch
- Commons Speaker
- party whip
- Black Rod
- uncodified constitution

- Civil Service
- department
- ministry
- agency
- bill
- act
- code of ethics
- sovereign
- parliamentary sovereignty.

## The nature of the United Kingdom's constitution

### Key learning

Study the roles of the executive, legislature, judiciary and the Monarchy in UK government. Understand the reasons why these roles are separated and why tensions can arise. Know how Parliament holds government to account through oversight and scrutiny and that Parliament is sovereign. Understand how the relationships between these institutions form an uncodified British constitution.

Many people remember the Queen's Diamond Jubilee in 2012. There was lots of flag waving, bunting and street parties as British people came together to celebrate the long reign of Elizabeth II. The Queen is the United Kingdom's Monarch and Head of State,

which means that she is the person who is in charge of the country. Her son, Charles, is next in line to become Britain's head of state.

This possibly sounds odd, because you might have thought that the Prime Minister is in charge of the UK.

You can be forgiven for any confusion because the way the UK is run is quite complicated. Yes, the Queen *is* the UK's Monarch and Head of State, but the Prime Minister is the head of **Government**.

The Queen, according to the British constitution, is the UK's sovereign. A sovereign is a ruler, so it might be expected that the Queen makes decisions and creates laws for the country. The confusion arises because while the Queen is the sovereign, it is the Prime Minister who really holds a high level of power in our political system.

Government   The Government runs the country. The Government is made up from elected members of the House of Commons and sometimes unelected members of the House of Lords. Government ministers are chosen by the Prime Minister.

Figure 6.1 The Royal Family travelling to the State Opening of Parliament

**Parliament** scrutinises the Prime Minister's decisions, votes on his or her government's proposals and makes new laws. Parliament is known as the **legislature**. So, in the UK's constitution, Parliament can be said to have the most importance. This gives us the concept of **Parliamentary sovereignty**.

This makes the UK unusual because it is the Prime Minister, along with his or her ministers in the Cabinet (together they are called the **executive**) who decides the proposals to bring to Parliament, even though it is the Monarch who, in theory, holds all the power.

This unusual arrangement has come about as a result of the UK's constitution. A constitution is a set of rules that sets out how a country is run. It regulates the relationship between a country's government and the people of that country. It also consists of rules that describe how the different parts of our political system should relate to each other and what roles each should play.

The third part of the UK's constitution is the **judiciary**. Judges apply the laws proposed by the executive and approved by the legislature. Judges are not appointed by the Government and are free to make impartial, independent decisions about how to apply the law. Tensions can arise between the executive, legislature and judiciary. There are particular problems when members of the Government or MPs attempt to influence judges' decisions. (See Chapters 2 and 3 for more details of the law and the legal system, and refer to page 113 for further information on conflicts between the executive and judiciary.)

Most countries have what is called a codified constitution. This means that all the rules about how that country is governed are set out in one document. The United States of America, for example, has a famous constitution that is codified. However, the UK has what is called an **uncodified constitution**. The rules and important guidelines about how the country should be run are not found in one single document, but are scattered across many different sources. This reflects the UK's complex union of four different nations – England, Scotland, Wales and Northern Ireland.

Figure 6.2 The Palace of Westminster – where both Houses of Parliament meet

**Parliament** The decision-making body of the UK. It has three parts: the House of Commons, the House of Lords and the Monarch. It is a law-making body and has supreme authority in the UK.

**Legislature** The name for Parliament as a whole. It means a place where laws are made. MPs and Lords work in partnership debating proposals for new laws, and making suggestions about how the laws may be made clearer and more effective.

**Parliamentary sovereignty** Parliament is the supreme authority on law-making in the UK. No other UK body or institution can make a law that is above that of one made by parliament although UK governments are bound by international law. Furthermore, no parliament can bind its successor, which means that any law that is made by one parliament can be repealed by a future parliament.

**Executive** This is the real powerhouse of government. The Prime Minister is the head of the executive and chooses people to run the big government departments. They are helped to run things by the Civil Service, which administers government decisions and provides advice to ministers.

**Judiciary** The system of courts and judges through which the law is applied.

**Uncodified constitution** A constitution in which not all parts are collected together in one document, but are found in many different sources. The UK is one of only a handful of countries that has such a constitution.

## Activities

1. The British constitution is quite complex.
   a) Design a simple survey to find out how much adults of voting age know about how the UK is run and who holds the power.
   b) Describe your findings.
   c) Share your findings with other learners.
   d) Explain the implications of these findings for citizenship education in schools and the wider community.
2. Explain why the British constitution is uncodified. Research the advantages and disadvantages of an uncodified constitution. (See page 113 for further information.)

# The structure of UK government

## Key learning

Study the separate but complementary roles of the House of Commons, House of Lords and the Monarch within the bicameral Westminster Parliament, and the differences between them. Understand the possible advantages and disadvantages of a bicameral arrangement.

**Civil Service** Makes sure that government runs properly and that decisions are carried out. Civil servants provide advice and support to ministers in their departments.

There are several branches to the UK's system of government. At the centre is the Monarchy. We have what is called a constitutional monarchy, which means that the Monarch does not get involved in the day-to-day running of the country and their power is limited. However, the Monarch still has an important role, as new laws cannot be passed without the agreement of the Queen (or a future king). The Monarch has to give what is called Royal Assent to every new law. This means that the Monarch gives their agreement that a new law can be put in place.

In the UK's uncodified constitution, the executive branch of government exercises power on behalf of the Monarch. The executive of the Prime Minister, Cabinet and senior levels of the **Civil Service** carries out the everyday business of government – making decisions and formulating policies that can be turned into laws. The executive is made up from the most senior MPs, chosen by the PM for their expertise or loyalty.

**Figure 6.3** The separation of powers in UK government

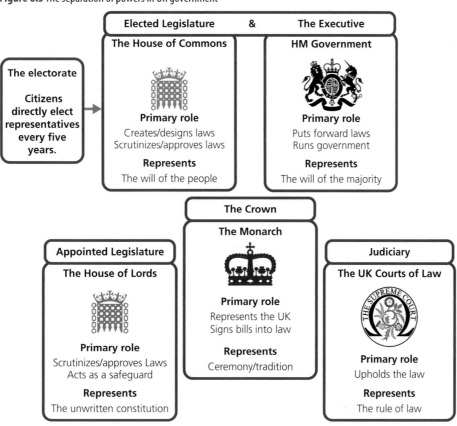

| Elected Legislature | & | The Executive |
|---|---|---|
| **The House of Commons** | | **HM Government** |

The electorate

Citizens directly elect representatives every five years.

The House of Commons
**Primary role**
Creates/designs laws
Scrutinizes/approves laws
**Represents**
The will of the people

HM Government
**Primary role**
Puts forward laws
Runs government
**Represents**
The will of the majority

The Crown
**The Monarch**
**Primary role**
Represents the UK
Signs bills into law
**Represents**
Ceremony/tradition

Appointed Legislature
**The House of Lords**
**Primary role**
Scrutinizes/approves Laws
Acts as a safeguard
**Represents**
The unwritten constitution

Judiciary
**The UK Courts of Law**
**Primary role**
Upholds the law
**Represents**
The rule of law

## The impact of bicameralism on the quality of government

### Advantages

- It improves scrutiny of legislation – a second chamber provides a way to review bills and check them. Any problems can be dealt with by suggesting changes to parts of a bill.
- As the Lords is largely an appointed chamber, it is possible to recruit expertise from the worlds of business, the arts, sport, science and industry. This helps to create better laws.
- The Lords allows groups that are under-represented in the Commons to have a voice.
- It is traditional for the UK to have a bicameral system; it reflects our history and values.

### Disadvantages

- The Commons has democratic legitimacy because its members have been elected by the British people. The Lords lacks this because it is made up of people who have inherited a seat because they were born into noble families (hereditary peers), they have been appointed (life peers) or they are high up in the Church of England (bishops and archbishops).
- The Lords can hold up the passing of new laws, which slows government down. They can do this for a year before the Government can force a bill through using the Parliament Act. (In October 2015, the Lords refused to accept proposals for welfare reform, forcing a major, last-minute change of plan by the Government. Two months later, the Government had drawn up plans to remove the Lords' power to stop bills if they had already been approved by the House of Commons.)
- It costs a lot to run the Lords as each peer can claim £300 per day in expenses to attend the chamber.

Senior MPs run the departments of government, such as the Treasury and the Home Office. There are usually about 20–25 people in the Cabinet. The Prime Minister has a lot of power in the UK's constitution because he or she exercises what is called the Royal Prerogative. This means that the PM carries out a lot of functions traditionally held by the Monarch, such as the power to declare war.

The next part of the system of government is the legislature. This is Parliament, which is made up of the Houses of Commons and Lords, plus the **Monarch**. The Commons and Lords are the two chambers of Parliament, with the Commons being the superior chamber as it is elected. This means that we have a **bicameral** legislature. Members of Parliament are elected by the voters of the UK. They take a seat in the Commons, where they represent the electors in their constituency. Members of the Lords are not elected. Some inherit their place in the Lords (hereditary peers), some are appointed (life peers) and some are bishops of the Church of England.

The existence of two Houses in Parliament helps to improve **scrutiny** of bills as the Lords can use their expertise to identify problems with potential new laws and suggest changes.

The final branch of government is the judiciary. As well as applying the law, the judiciary makes sure that the executive does not exceed its powers. If a case comes before the judiciary as a result of a judicial review, the judges have to decide whether ministers have followed the correct process when making a decision. The judges can rule that a minister has not followed the law properly and, as a consequence, their decision is illegal. Government ministers then have to go back and change their decision or make sure the correct procedure is followed.

**Monarch**    A head of state who has usually inherited their position. The power of a monarch will vary depending on how much responsibility rests with other leaders who govern on the Monarch's behalf.

**Bicameral**    The UK Parliament uses a bicameral system, with 'bi' meaning two and 'cameral' referring to chambers; the Commons and the Lords.

**Scrutiny**    Examining in detail what governments are doing, asking questions of ministers and calling witnesses to give evidence in writing or in person.

## The passage of a bill

We can see the relationship between the parts of government by following the passage of a **bill** through Parliament. Most new laws start as bills created by the Government. The bill is published as a **white paper** and is read out in Parliament (the first reading). Most bills begin in the Commons, but sometimes they can start in the Lords. There is then a debate about the bill (the second reading), where MPs can ask questions and raise any concerns they may have. At the end of this debate there is a vote. All MPs can vote on whether they support the bill.

The committee stage follows. A small group of MPs from different parties form what is called a public bill committee to go through the bill in fine detail. The committee can call on experts, including members of pressure groups, to give evidence about the issues in the bill. Eventually the committee return the bill to the Commons with any amendments, or changes, they might wish to make. This is the report stage and it includes a third reading of the bill.

If a bill has started in the Commons, it will be sent to the House of Lords for further scrutiny. The Lords will examine the bill in debate and suggest amendments. These amendments will then be sent to the Commons for consideration. This process may be repeated several times until both houses agree on the final bill. This is called the 'ping pong' stage of making a new law. Once agreement is reached, the bill is sent to the Monarch for Royal Assent. Once the bill has been signed by the Monarch, it becomes a new law or **Act** of Parliament.

## English votes for English laws

The latest development in how laws are made concerns English votes for English laws, or 'EVEL'. This is the Government's attempt to reform how MPs vote by preventing MPs from constituencies in Scotland, Wales and Northern Ireland from voting on bills that only affect England. In October 2015, the Government introduced plans to prevent non-English MPs voting on England-only matters. Committees of English MPs will consider bills after the second reading and the report stage. English MPs will have the right of **veto** over new laws that only affect England. Critics say the plans are too complicated and will not work. Others have called for an English Parliament, just for MPs representing constituencies in England.

**Bill**   A bill is a document that is published by the Government. It sets out the Government's plan to create a new law.

**White paper**   A document setting out the Government's policy on a particular issue and, at the same time, inviting opinions.

**Act**   An Act of Parliament is a new law. A bill becomes an Act once it has received Royal Assent.

**Veto**   The power to reject a proposal even though a majority of others might agree with it.

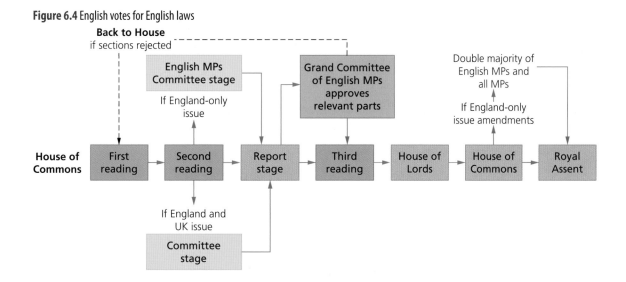

**Figure 6.4** English votes for English laws

## Website

Use Parliament's website to find out more about how a law is made and track a bill's progress through the legislative stages: **http://www.parliament.uk/**

# Why are there different branches of government?

If there were no separation of powers between the different branches of government, it would be easy for the executive to become very powerful. Imagine if the Monarch, or the Prime Minister, could just decide what laws they wanted and that was the end of the matter. Everyone would have to follow these laws and no-one would have a chance to disagree. On top of that, imagine if it was the Monarch or the Prime Minister who decided whether someone had broken the law. They would be able to find people guilty of crimes and send them to prison. This would give one person considerable power which they could abuse. It could lead to a very corrupt political system.

The executive, legislature and judiciary are separated in our constitution. This helps to spread power throughout the system so that one part of government does not become too powerful. Each part has a role in **oversight** of the others. Each part helps to hold the others to **account**.

## Activities

1. Study the key terms – monarch, executive, legislature and the judiciary.
   a) Explain the meaning of each.
   b) Explain how each branch of government is linked to the others.
   c) Explain the reasons for a separation of powers in the UK constitution.
   d) Explain why the branches of government might fail to achieve proper separation of powers. (Use information from this page to help you.)
2. Construct your own slide or diagram to show the process of making a law.
3. Research the *West Lothian Question*.
   a) Describe what it is.
   b) Explain why it was a problem.
   c) Explain how far the Government's 2015 'EVEL' plan solved the problem.

**Oversight**   The process of checking that something is being carried out properly. The legislature scrutinises the work of the executive to make sure that nothing improper is being done. MPs and Lords are involved in examining the work of the executive in order to hold it to account.

**Accountability**   The responsibility to explain how or why something is being done. Accountability can result in a government being removed from office if it does not use the correct procedure or is thought to be going beyond its powers.

## Parliamentary select committees

Parliamentary select committees hold governments to account. There are select committees in the Lords and Commons. Commons committees are groups of MPs that have oversight of the work of a government department. One example is the Home Affairs Select Committee, which subjects the Home Secretary and the Home Office to scrutiny.

**Figure 6.5** The Education Select Committee gathers evidence at a Leicestershire school

Select committees can compel ministers to appear before them to answer questions about their decisions and the workings of their departments. If something goes badly wrong, ministers are expected to resign from their job. This is called individual ministerial responsibility. Ministers can also be expected to resign if they are found to be involved in any scandal or corruption.

A prominent example of the work of select committees is the report into child and adolescent mental health published by the Health Select Committee in November 2014. The Committee found that 'there are serious and deeply ingrained problems with the commissioning and provision of the Children's and Adolescents' Mental Health Service (CAMHS)'. As a result of the committee's report, an enquiry was held into the mental health and wellbeing of looked-after children. Reports and enquiries like this help to put the spotlight on a government's effectiveness.

## Relationship between branches of government

The relationships between the branches of government are constantly evolving. This is one strength of the UK's uncodified constitution: that it is flexible. This makes it possible for Parliament to respond quickly to any crises affecting the UK. For example, new anti-terror laws were introduced soon after the London terrorist attacks in July 2005. However, this flexibility can lead to tensions between the branches of government, particularly between the executive and the judiciary.

Conflict between politicians and judges can occur over the sentencing of offenders. It is the job of judges, with help from the Sentencing Council, to decide on custodial sentences. Sometimes ministers claim to be reflecting public opinion by arguing that a particular sentence (or sentences in general) have been too lenient. Judges refer to the key constitutional principle that the judiciary should have a high degree of independence from the executive.

### Too lenient?

In September 2012, Judge Peter Bowers gave a year's suspended sentence to a burglar at Teesside Crown Court, saying:

'It takes a huge amount of courage, as far as I can see, for somebody to burgle somebody's house. I wouldn't have the nerve.'

Judge Bowers was reprimanded by the Office for Judicial Complaints – it said that his remarks had 'damaged public confidence in the judicial process'.

### Too severe?

In 2009, Sam Stanger was involved in a row over a parking fine in which he stole a traffic warden's camera. He was sentenced to two years imprisonment by Leicester Crown Court.

Two thousand supporters joined a campaign to free Stanger. The campaign was backed by his local MP. In spite of this, an appeal judge refused any right to appeal stating that: 'The starting point for sentence taken by the judge was within the bracket of appropriate sentences ... and is not manifestly excessive.'

### Websites

Use Parliament's website to find out more about the work of select committees in the House of Commons and House of Lords: **http://www.parliament.uk/**

For more about judges' approach to sentencing, go to: **https://www.judiciary.gov.uk/**

### Activities

1. Explain whether you agree with the sentences handed down in these two cases.
2. List the advantages and disadvantages of a government becoming more involved in deciding appropriate punishments for convicted offenders.

# How the constitution works: Parliament in action

### Key learning

Study the roles of different types of MPs, the Commons Speaker and the party whips. Know about the key ceremonial occasions in Parliament including the State Opening of Parliament, the budget, the Monarch's speech and the role of Black Rod. Understand the process of parliamentary debate and decision-making, including the role and importance of the Official Opposition in parliament.

## Different types of MP

We already know that some MPs have a role in the Government. Around 100 MPs from the governing party have a job as a secretary of state, a junior minister or a parliamentary private secretary.

On the other side of the House of Commons sits the **Official Opposition**. Their job is to scrutinise the Government's actions and to behave as a government-in-waiting. The Opposition leader appoints a team of MPs to 'shadow' the work of government ministers. This team is called the Shadow Cabinet. Each week the Opposition leader has the chance to hold the Prime Minister to account for his or her government in front

**Official Opposition** The Official Opposition is the non-Government party with the largest number of seats in the House of Commons.

of assembled MPs at Prime Minister's Question Time (PMQs). The Prime Minister is expected to explain the Government's actions.

If an MP is a member of the Government or Official Opposition, they are called frontbenchers because they sit on the front benches in the Commons to indicate their senior roles. Other MPs are called backbenchers as that is where they sit. Their key role is to represent their constituents by asking questions in the Commons and taking up any causes their constituents bring to their attention.

## The Commons Speaker

The **Commons Speaker** is a special and important MP. He or she sits in the Speaker's chair between the Government and Opposition benches. The Speaker is elected by the other MPs and is supposed to be politically impartial. The Speaker and his or her deputies should not take sides in a debate. If they were to try to do this, they would lose their jobs.

In debates, MPs stand up to catch the Speaker's eye. The Speaker chooses MPs to speak and makes sure that they follow the rules of the House. The Speaker can instruct MPs to withdraw comments if they use abusive language. He or she can call for quiet if the chamber is becoming rowdy, or even suspend an MP if they are deliberately disobedient.

When they are elected to the office of Speaker, an MP will step down from their party in order to remain impartial. However, they still act as a constituency MP, so people in their constituency can continue to contact them to raise issues of concern.

## Party discipline

In a large party of 200–300 plus MPs, it is important that everyone works together. This is particularly important for the party in government, as ministers need support from their party's MPs so that they can get new laws passed. It is also important for the Opposition to be united so they can present a coherent counter-argument when there are parts of bills with which they disagree. Party discipline is important. This discipline is enforced by a special group of MPs called the **party whips**. Each party has a small group of whips who make sure all its backbenchers follow the party line.

## State Opening of Parliament

It is the job of the Monarch to officially open each session of Parliament. The State Opening of Parliament

**Figure 6.6** The Speaker chairing a debate in the House of Commons with an excellent view of everyone in the chamber. (The Speaker is sitting on a large green chair in the centre towards the back of this photograph)

is an occasion of great tradition and ceremony. The Monarch travels from Buckingham Palace to the Palace of Westminster (the formal name for Parliament) and puts on the great robes of state and the Imperial State Crown. The Monarch then leads the Royal Procession to the Lords chamber and a House of Lords official, **Black Rod**, is sent along to the Commons chamber to summon the MPs to listen to the Queen.

**Figure 6.7** The Queen delivers her speech at the State Opening of Parliament in 2015

**Commons Speaker** A special MP who is the highest authority in the Commons. The role of the Speaker is to chair debates in the Commons and to keep order in the chamber.

**Party whips** MPs whose role it is to enforce party discipline and make sure all its backbench MPs follow the party line. They persuade MPs who may have doubts about a bill or policy, or threaten them with isolation if they decide to vote against their party's policy.

**Black Rod** An officer of the House of Lords who is responsible for security, and controlling access to and maintaining order within the House and its precincts. He or she plays a key role in the State Opening of Parliament.

Black Rod, upon reaching the Commons chamber, traditionally has the door shut in his or her face as a symbol of the independence of the Commons from the Monarch and Lords. After he or she knocks on the door of the Commons three times, the door is opened and the MPs follow Black Rod to the Lords' chamber and the Monarch's Speech is delivered. The speech itself outlines what the Government intends to do in the coming year. The speech is written by the Government, not the Monarch. Once the speech is over, a new Parliamentary session has begun and the Government's serious work gets under way.

## The Budget

Another important occasion in Parliament is the Budget speech delivered by the Chancellor of the Exchequer. The Budget happens every year and it sets out the Chancellor's plans for the country's finances and taxes. There has to be a Budget every year because income tax and corporation tax have to be renewed annually by law.

During the Budget speech, the Chancellor reviews the UK's finances and makes changes to levels of taxation, such as those on alcohol and tobacco. These changes usually come into effect on the day of the Budget itself. The Leader of the Opposition then responds to the Budget and several days of debate follow, where MPs discuss the Chancellor's plans, called the Budget Resolutions. Once these are agreed, a new finance bill is introduced to the Commons. It is not opposed by the Lords as, according to constitutional convention, the Lords do not examine new laws on taxes or government spending in detail. The Treasury Select Committee of MPs, however, does scrutinise the Government's proposals and produces a report, which the Government must respond to within sixty days.

### Websites

Find out who is in the Government by using the GOV.UK website: **https://www.gov.uk/government/how-government-works#who-runs-government**

Watch Parliamentary debates live on **http://www.parliamentlive.tv/Commons** or video clips of Parliament's ceremonial occasions and past debates on *YouTube*.

For more on the Speaker's role go to: **http://www.parliament.uk/**

To find out more about the role of party whips go to **https://www.gov.uk/government/ministers/parliamentary-secretary-to-the-treasury-and-chief-whip**

### Activities

1. Find out who is Chancellor of the Exchequer, Home Secretary and Foreign Secretary. Write a short biography for each person and list their main government responsibilities. Find out who shadows these government positions by using the Opposition party's website. Write a short biography for each shadow minister.

2. Describe the type of jobs the whips do during an average day in the Commons.

3. Explain why the parties appoint whips. Describe how parliamentary politics might be different without them.

4. Evaluate the viewpoint that MPs should be free to decide for themselves how to vote in the Commons.

# The Civil Service

### Key learning

Study the role of the Civil Service within the British constitution. Know that government administration is divided into departments, ministries and agencies.

The Civil Service is the administrative body that follows government instructions, implements government decisions and provides policy advice to ministers.

### What does the Civil Service do?

We are politically impartial and independent of government and work in central government departments, agencies, and non-departmental government bodies (NDPBs). The Civil Service does not include government ministers (who are politically appointed).

The Civil Service provides services directly to people all over the country, including paying benefits and pensions, running employment services, running prisons and issuing driving licences.

We also have staff working on policy development and implementation, including analysts, project managers, lawyers and economists.

We are co-ordinated and managed by the Prime Minister, in his role as Minister for the Civil Service. The most senior civil servant in a department is a permanent secretary.

(Adapted from: **https://www.gov.uk/government/organisations/civil-service/about**)

It is important that the Civil Service works effectively, otherwise government policy would not be implemented. Civil servants are supposed to be politically neutral. This means that they should not take the side of any political party or get involved in public discussion of what a government does.

## Ministries, departments and agencies

In November 2015, there were 24 government ministerial departments and 22 non-ministerial departments. As the name suggests, ministerial departments are headed by a government minister. An example of a ministerial department is the Home Office, which comes under the authority of the Home Secretary. Some government departments cover the whole of the UK, such as the Ministry of Defence. Others have more limited responsibility due to the devolution of power to Scotland, Wales and Northern Ireland.

Non-ministerial departments are headed by a senior civil servant and have a key role in delivering government policy. An important example is OFSTED, which inspects schools and colleges to make sure they are providing education that meets government standards.

There are also 360 government agencies which carry out a wide range of functions. These agencies range from the Bank of England to the Maritime and Coastguard Agency. Such agencies help to deliver government services but do not have a role in deciding policy. This is done by the government department that oversees the agency.

The most senior civil servant is the Cabinet Secretary – the Prime Minister's most senior policy adviser. Other government departments are led by a permanent secretary. These senior officials are responsible to Parliament and have to make sure that their department's budget is spent appropriately.

The Civil Service Board is responsible for the strategic leadership of the civil service. It is co-chaired by the Cabinet Secretary and the Prime Minister in his or her role as head of the Civil Service.

### Core values of the Civil Service

- Integrity – putting the obligations of public service above your own personal interests
- Honesty – being truthful and open
- Objectivity – giving advice and making decisions only after rigorous analysis of the evidence
- Impartiality – acting solely according to the merits of the case and serving equally well governments of different political persuasions

(Adapted from: **https://www.gov.uk/ government/publications/civil-service-code/ the-civil-service-code**)

### Website

For more on the Civil Service and its work try: **https://www.gov.uk/government/organisations/ civil-service**

### Activities

1. Design a chart or slide to show the key differences between civil servants and politicians.
2. Explain whether, given the choice, you would rather be a government minister or a senior civil servant.
3. Explain why the Civil Service Code is important.

## Practice questions

In the OCR specification, this section will be assessed using objective test questions and questions needing a written response.

1. What is meant by the term **Parliamentary sovereignty**?
   A Parliament is the supreme authority on law-making in the UK.
   B The Monarch can dissolve Parliament at any time of their choosing.
   C Parliament is controlled by the European Union.
   D Parliament is responsible for making money for the country. [1 mark]

2. Which statement best reflects the term **uncodified constitution**?
   A The Government has a code of ethics that guides their conduct.
   B There are guidelines from different sources that set out how government should work.
   C There is a list of the duties of the Prime Minister.
   D There is no way to hold Government to account in the UK. [1 mark]

3. What is meant by the term **Royal Assent**?
   A The last stage of making a new law when the Monarch signs off a bill.
   B When the Monarch gives her speech in Parliament.
   C It is traditional that the Monarch cannot enter the Commons chamber.
   D When the Monarch tells the Prime Minister that Parliament is dissolved. [1 mark]

4. State two ways in which a government is **accountable** to Parliament. [2 marks]

5. Explain why it is important for the **judiciary** to be independent of any government. [4 marks]

# Chapter 7:
# The economy, finance and money

This chapter on *The economy, finance and money* builds on Chapter 5 *National, local, regional and devolved government* and Chapter 6 on *The British constitution*.

In this chapter, we explore some of the links between politics and the economy by studying issues linked to taxation, welfare, the health service and education.

Learning the following key concepts and terms will make it easier to organise your thinking and communicate your ideas:
- taxation (direct and indirect)
- public expenditure
- economic growth
- administrative efficiency
- benefits
- welfare.

**Figure 7.1** Governments can spend more on roads in a growing economy

In a growing economy, it is easy to borrow money as banks and other lenders are confident that people will be able to pay back their loans. Businesses are likely to borrow money so they can expand and, in doing so, will create more jobs. Consumers tend to borrow more money too – spending it on higher value items such as houses and cars. This leads to higher levels of business activity and the creation of further jobs.

The Government also benefits from economic growth. Higher earnings and spending mean that more tax is collected. The Government has more money available and so will be able to expand public services by, for example, building more schools, improving transport, training more doctors or increasing pensions. Governments can also pay back money they may have borrowed in the past.

## How does the Government help to manage the economy?

### Key learning
Study the relationships between taxation, administrative efficiency, economic growth and public spending. Know how public taxes are raised by local and national government, and how this money is spent. Apply this knowledge to understand how governments manage risk and make complex decisions about public spending.

## What is the economy?
The term 'economy' is used to describe all the business activity and wealth creation that takes place in a country.

### A growing economy
In growing economies levels of business activity are high; people have jobs and money to spend.

### An economy in recession
Where business activity declines, people often lose their jobs. They may be unable to pay back their loans and even banks may go out of business. People have less money to spend and start saving more in case they become unemployed. As people spend less, demand for products falls, some businesses fail and people lose their jobs. The Government receives less money from taxation and may have to make cuts, borrow or print extra money to keep public services going. The economy is in 'recession'.

**Figure 7.2** People need extra help to get jobs when the economy is in recession

**Figure 7.3** Ways in which action by the Government and Bank of England can affect the economy

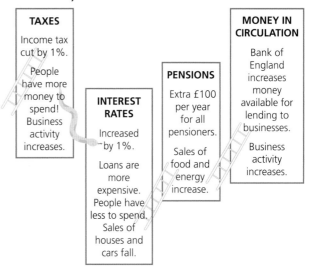

## Managing the economy

One of the main ways any government manages the economy is to encourage business activity.

When the economy is in recession or growing very slowly, a government might support businesses by:

- encouraging investment in new products and equipment
- creating work by funding major public projects such as housebuilding, and rail and road improvement
- encouraging consumer spending by cutting taxes – so giving businesses a welcome sales boost and encouraging them to employ more workers.

The Bank of England may assist the Government by cutting interest rates. This encourages business investment and consumer spending. The Bank can also encourage more lending by increasing the quantity of money in circulation.

However, the Government will need to make sure that the economy does not grow too rapidly. Rapid economic growth can result in: large increases in borrowing, steep price rises and high wage growth. This can damage economic activity in the long term.

## A global economy

A government does not manage an economy in isolation. Natural disasters and wars anywhere in the world can have a negative effect on business activity everywhere. Economic problems in one country can have knock on effects far beyond its borders.

### Financial crisis

In the early part of the twenty-first century, during a time of economic growth, banks in the USA and Europe had lent money to people who were unable to pay it back when the economy became less strong. By 2009, many banks were in debt. Investors panicked and withdrew their savings. Governments lent money to the banks to save them from collapse. American consumers spent less money on goods made in the USA and on **imports** from around the world. World trade declined and everyone lost out. Governments stepped in to encourage more business activity and consumer spending but, by 2016, Chinese economic growth began to slow and many economists predicted a further global recession.

**Imports** Goods and services brought from overseas.

### Activity

1. List the different types of action the Government and the Bank of England can take when the economy is in recession. Explain which of these types of action is likely to be:
   a) most effective
   b) most controversial
   c) most difficult to organise.

# Tax and government spending

## Where does the money come from?

The data used in the chart in Figure 7.4 is from the Office for Budget Responsibility's estimates for 2013–14. It shows total money received by central and local government in 2013.

**Figure 7.4** Central and local government receipts (£ billions)

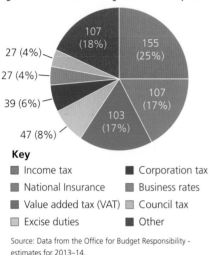

**Key**

- ■ Income tax
- ■ National Insurance
- ■ Value added tax (VAT)
- ■ Excise duties
- ■ Corporation tax
- ■ Business rates
- ■ Council tax
- ■ Other

Source: Data from the Office for Budget Responsibility - estimates for 2013–14.

## What does the Government spend our money on?

The data used in the chart below shows the cost to central and local government of providing public services.

**Figure 7.5** Government spending: the cost of public services in 2013 (£ billions)

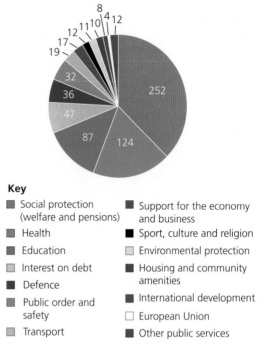

**Key**

- ■ Social protection (welfare and pensions)
- ■ Health
- ■ Education
- ■ Interest on debt
- ■ Defence
- ■ Public order and safety
- ■ Transport
- ■ Support for the economy and business
- ■ Sport, culture and religion
- ■ Environmental protection
- ■ Housing and community amenities
- ■ International development
- ☐ European Union
- ■ Other public services

Source: Data from HM Treasury.

## Government receipts explained

| | |
|---|---|
| **Income tax** | A **direct tax** tax people pay on their earnings. This is usually taken directly from people's pay by their employers. |
| **National Insurance** | A charge paid by people who have jobs, National Insurance is used to help fund pensions as well as benefits for workers who become ill, need parental leave or lose their job. |
| **Value Added Tax (VAT)** | An **indirect tax** paid by consumers on what they spend. Some items have a zero or low VAT rate. These items include: food, books, children's clothing, electricity and gas. |
| **Excise duty** | A tax paid when buying fuel, alcohol and tobacco. |
| **Corporation Tax** | Businesses pay this tax on their profits. |
| **Business rates** | Businesses pay this tax on the value of their premises. |
| **Council tax** | Residents pay this tax on the value of their homes. |
| **Other government income** | This includes: vehicle excise duty; taxes on house purchases; inheritance tax; and income from government activities, loans and investments. |

**Direct tax**   A tax on the income or profits of individuals and businesses.

**Indirect tax**   A tax, such as VAT, which is charged on the goods and services bought by individuals and businesses.

## What makes the money go further?

All governments try to make public money go further.

From 2010 to 2016, the Government took action to cut spending but this was opposed strongly by the Labour Party and the trade union movement.

**Table 7.1** Examples of Government actions to reduce spending

| Government action from 2010 | Examples |
|---|---|
| Reducing 'unnecessary' spending | Cutting child benefit for higher earners |
| Increasing **administrative efficiency** to give better value for money | Ensuring that the Government acts as a single customer when purchasing goods and services |
| Making savings on the delivery of existing services | Health and social care services began to work more closely together to avoid people needing expensive hospital care |
| Controlling wage costs | Limiting annual pay increases to 1% for most public sector employees |

## Complex decisions

### Making difficult choices

In a democracy, governments must remain popular with voters if they are to stay in power. This is never easy, especially when hard choices need to be made about taxes, welfare benefits and public services. Nobody likes seeing their taxes increase or having their welfare benefits or services cut.

The years from 2010 became known as a period of **austerity**. Governments felt a need to cut public spending so that taxes could be reduced and the national debt repaid. Many people experienced falls in their **standard of living** as a result. The Conservative/Liberal Democrat Coalition Government (2010–15) claimed that it was acting fairly as its policies required everyone to make sacrifices. In spite of criticism from rival political parties that the poorest were suffering most from austerity, the Conservatives won the 2015 general election. (See pages 86 to 89 for the economic policies of different political parties.)

**Administrative efficiency**   Managing a government's work well so as to avoid delay, duplication and confusion, and to achieve the best value for money.

**Austerity**   Reductions in people's wealth resulting from government measures to reduce public expenditure.

### Websites

The Government's own website describes the measures being taken to manage the economy: **https://www.gov.uk/government/topics/uk-economy**

The Local Government Association's website describes local authority action to boost the economy: **http://www.local.gov.uk/economy**

The National Audit Office tries to make sure that governments spend public money wisely. Its website includes advice on risk management and a report, *Over-optimism in government projects*: **http://www.nao.org.uk**

The Bank of England website has details of its role in helping to manage the economy: **http://www.bankofengland.co.uk**

### Managing risk

**Risk management** is a key government responsibility but one that is sometimes difficult to carry out effectively, as the following two examples show.

### Overreaction – the Millennium Bug 2000

In the final months of 1999, concern grew into panic that the Millennium Bug was going to cause computers to malfunction and endanger everything from televisions to power stations. It was expected that many computer clocks would see 00 on 1st January 2000 and understand that to mean 1900. Tony Blair, Prime Minister at the time, claimed that the Millennium Bug was, 'one of the most serious problems facing not only British business but the global economy today'.

The UK Government, in common with other governments around the world, launched a huge and expensive advertising campaign to show businesses and individuals how to adjust their clocks. In the end, the anticipated disaster did not happen. The Government had overreacted.

### Lack of preparation – Somerset floods 2014

In January 2014, very serious flooding occurred in Somerset. Over 600 houses were flooded and 16,000 acres of farmland were under water for more than a month. Rivers that usually drained the area had not been dredged and, when the rains came, water was not able to get away quickly enough. The Government had seemed ill-prepared for flooding in such low-lying areas even though winters were clearly becoming much wetter. A government minister made a public apology. Flood prevention schemes were given a higher priority in response to the increased risks caused by climate change.

**Figure 7.6** A local resident is rescued from rising flood water by a police boat team

**Standard of living**   A measure of the wealth and material support available to individuals and communities.

**Risk management**   A process for identifying, assessing, and prioritising risks of different kinds. Once the risks are identified, a plan will be created to minimise the impact of negative events.

## Planning for the future

Governments need to plan up to fifty years ahead to meet the country's future needs. This is a complex process in which politicians and civil servants have to anticipate such things as:

- changes in the UK population
- global warming and its effect on climate, sea levels and farming
- changes in the availability of natural resources such as coal, oil and gas
- technological change.

Sometimes governments are forced to change long-term plans if the short-term effects of these plans prove to be unpopular. For example, fuel duties were increased in the early years of this century to encourage people to use public transport instead of cars. Public protest and concerns about the impact of higher fuel costs on standards of living, forced the Government to change its policy.

# CASE STUDY
## Bikers stop motorways in fuel protest – June 2008

Bikers formed a slow-moving convoy to cause traffic chaos as part of a protest against the increasing cost of fuel. Up to 500 protesters gathered near Manchester after two bikers had organised the demonstration via social media.

The bikers eye-catching gesture followed a rally held by angry lorry drivers in London in May. Many onlookers backed the protest and were critical of the Government's policy of increasing fuel duty as part of a move to reduce carbon emissions.

**Figure 7.7** Bikers hold up M62 motorway traffic in a protest about high taxes on fuel

# Deciding priorities for tax and public spending

## Key learning

Study different viewpoints on taxation and spending. Apply this knowledge and understanding to evaluate different approaches to the provision of services for welfare, health, education and the needs of the elderly.

## Different views on tax and public spending

Opinions differ about whether the State or individuals and private businesses should have most responsibility for welfare, health, education and the care of the elderly.

Businesses increasingly work in partnership with central government and local authorities to provide public services such as transport, refuse collection and housing.

Successful partnerships provide good services at a competitive price as well as making a profit for the business involved. This is possible because the businesses are specialists in their field and can make savings by providing a similar service in several local authority areas. Trade unions have not always been happy with such partnerships. Working conditions and pay rates have often been less favourable than when workers were employed directly by a government or local authority.

UK political parties hold different views about the involvement of businesses in public services such as health and education. They also disagree about how far the State should be expected to support people who are elderly, sick, unemployed or vulnerable. (See Chapter 4 for more details on party policies.)

# CASE STUDY

## Refuse collection – a partnership between local authorities and private businesses

In the case of refuse collection, local authorities invite businesses to compete for a waste disposal contract. The local authority chooses the proposal representing the best value for money and pays the contactor to deliver the service. The local authority has the power to fine a contractor if their service is not up to standard.

**Figure 7.8** Kier, a private sector business, has a contract to collect household waste with four neighbouring local authorities in South East England

**Advantages of direct government (state) provision**

- Everyone receives a similar standard of service.
- People receive a service based on their needs rather than their ability to pay.
- As everyone is receiving a similar service, everyone has a stake in its success.
- Elected politicians can maintain close supervision and control of the service.
- Workers' pay and conditions are the same across the whole country.

**Advantages of private provision**

- People can choose the service they want and pay for it accordingly.
- People are encouraged to look ahead and anticipate their needs. This will make them more likely to take responsibility for meeting those needs.
- Business involvement brings in new ideas and drives standards up as companies compete with one another for contracts.
- Companies lose business if their service is poor so they have the incentive to provide a good service.
- Elected politicians can concentrate on checking service standards and getting good value for the taxpayer.

# Different approaches to welfare, health, education and the needs of the elderly

There are differences of opinion about how far governments should be responsible for providing services and support for citizens. Political parties are divided. The Conservatives, UKIP and the Liberal Democrats believe that people should take as much responsibility as possible for their own lives. On the other hand, Labour, the Green Party and the Scottish and Welsh Nationalists think that governments should provide services and support for everyone according to personal need.

## Viewpoints on welfare

> The Government spends too much on welfare, it should encourage people to work.

> The Government should spend more to help people out of poverty.

**Strategy**

1. Make work pay:
   - Pass laws to make businesses pay a 'living wage'.
   - Cut taxation so that people keep more of their earnings.
   - Increase training so that people can develop new work skills.
   - Cut welfare benefits.

2. Deal with the individual behaviour that causes poverty:
   - Encourage families to stick together by rewarding married people with special tax incentives.
   - Train adults to be better parents so that their children become confident and ready for school.
   - Intervene directly with 'problem' families to break the cycle of poverty.

**Strategy**

1. Make sure everyone has a decent standard of living:
   - Pass laws to make businesses pay a 'living wage'.
   - Set minimum family incomes to prevent poorer people from falling behind.
   - Increase taxes paid by the wealthy and use this money to support the poor.
   - Increase benefits in line with the cost of living.

2. Deal with the structural factors that cause poverty:
   - Improve medical and educational services in poorer areas of the country.
   - Improve housing conditions and community facilities.
   - Improve child care so that more single parents feel able to work.

## Viewpoints on health

We can't afford the keep paying more and more for a National Health Service. People must be ready to pay for their own health care.

Everyone has a right to free health care. We must increase taxes as necessary to fund the NHS properly.

**Strategy**
- Change the law so that everyone pays something for the health services they use – the wealthy will pay most; the poorest the least.
- Encourage personal and preventive care linked to community health centres; scale down large general hospitals.
- Support privately provided 'end of life' care at home or in a hospice.

**Strategy**
- Pay for health from taxation – so that those who can afford it pay the most but everyone benefits according to their health needs.
- Make health services efficient through large general hospitals and specialist units in which staff are asked to meet clear targets.
- Encourage health professionals to work cooperatively within one nationalised health service.

## Viewpoints on education

Schools must meet the needs of the local community and businesses. Parents who can afford to, should be prepared to pay.

Democratically elected local authorities should control schools in there area. It's unfair for parents to buy a better education just for their own children.

**Strategy**
- Turn all schools into academies so that head teachers and governors can make decisions that fit local community needs.
- Encourage competition, innovation and choice by enabling groups of parents, charities and businesses to run schools.
- Require people to pay towards the cost of their education as long as they can afford to.

**Strategy**
- Achieve consistent educational standards by placing all schools in local authority control.
- Make sure all children have access to a common curriculum, at least in their early years, so that all have an equal chance of success.
- Restrict private education so that wealthy people cannot buy their children advantages that others cannot afford.

## Viewpoints on care for elderly people

Older people can no longer expect the State to provide. They must take responsibility and save for their own retirement.

We all have a responsibility to look after older people. Taxes from those in work should be used to pay pensions for the retired.

### Strategy

- Pay people a bonus from government funds to encourage them to save for their retirement.
- Increase personal responsibility and choice by requiring people to take out personal insurance to cover their care home fees.

### Strategy

- Collect sufficient funds from taxation to meet the income and care needs of all elderly people.
- Reorganise community care for elderly people – local authorities and the National Health Service should be working together.

## Websites

Websites of the Trade Union Congress and the major trade unions describe their viewpoints on taxation and public spending: **https://www.tuc.org.uk/**

The Institute for Economic Affairs promotes low taxation and low public spending: **http://www.iea.org.uk/**

Websites of the political parties provide their viewpoints and current policies (See Chapter 4 for more details.)

## Activities

1. Design an opinion poll to find your friends' or family's views on welfare, health, education, and care for the elderly.

2. Find out where you and other learners stand on public service provision.

   a) Prepare a case for or against the viewpoint that 'the Government should provide services and support for everyone according to their needs'.
      - Include information from this book, and policy statements, election manifestos, speeches or media releases from the main political parties and elsewhere.
      - Use examples from welfare, health, education and care for elderly people.

   b) Ask your teacher to help organise a class debate on this issue.

3. Organise a 'Question Time' with invited guests representing different viewpoints on these issues. Prepare questions carefully in advance.

## Practice questions

In the OCR specification, this section will be assessed using objective test questions and questions needing a written response.

1. A government is more likely to **cut** public expenditure if:
   A  Immigration is rising.
   B  Taxes are being increased.
   C  The economy is in recession.
   D  Risk management has been completed. [1 mark]

2. Which of the following does the Government **spend** most money on?
   A  membership of the European Union
   B  education
   C  defence
   D  public order and safety. [1 mark]

Study **Sources 1** and **2** and answer the questions that follow.

## Source 1
### Viewpoint of the teaching trade unions

*We are against making all schools become academies.*

*Independent academies have no real link with the local authority (council) and so are not democratically accountable to their local communities. Schools used to cooperate with each other as part of the local authority. Academies no longer have to do this.*

## Source 2
### Extract from Bedford Free School's website

*We are a state-funded independent secondary school serving the communities of Bedford and Kempston. We teach students from Year 7 to Year 11. Working with you, the local community, our aim is to improve the prospects of local students through a supportive learning environment, expanded curriculum, and top class teaching.*

3. State **two** UK political parties that would be likely to **support** the NUT's statement in **Source 1**. [2 marks]

4. Use your own knowledge and understanding to help you describe the different forms of **community involvement** mentioned in **Sources 1** and **2**. [4 marks]

5. Support the following viewpoint:
   'Businesses should be allowed to run schools and hospitals at a profit.'
   In your answer you should consider the **advantages** of privatising public services. [8 marks]

This chapter on *The role of the media and free press* builds on Chapter 1 *Rights and responsibilities* and links with Chapter 9 *Citizen participation in the UK and taking citizenship action*.

In this chapter we explore the role of the media in a democracy by discussing freedom of expression and how far this should be limited by governments.

Learning the following key concepts and terms will make it easier to organise your thinking and communicate your ideas:
- free press/media freedom
- public interest
- media regulation
- censorship
- social media
- privacy
- libel.

# The media's rights and responsibilities

## Key learning
Study the legal rights and responsibilities of a 'free press'. Understand the media's moral responsibility to report accurately and to respect people's dignity.

## Legal rights

The media is allowed to exercise the same legal rights to free speech as those enjoyed by ordinary citizens. Journalists and other people working in the media have **freedom of expression**, which gives them the right to criticise governments without fear of prosecution – this is an important feature of a democratic society and, in the UK, is a right protected by the Human Rights Act of 1998.

> **Freedom of expression**   The right to hold opinions and to express them freely without government interference. This includes the right to express views aloud or through: published articles; books or leaflets; television or radio broadcasting; works of art and communication on the internet.

The media also shares another important right with ordinary citizens: right of access to information held by public authorities including government departments, local authorities and state schools. This legal right, under the Freedom of Information Act 2000, gives the media access to any recorded information held on computers, in emails and in printed or handwritten documents as well as images, video and audio recordings. Information of a personal nature is protected. For example, a person's medical record would be 'protected information'.

> **Example: Freedom of Information request and response**
>
> ## Information requested from Kent Police
> The number of child on child assaults in schools and educational settings that were reported to Kent Police in 2013, with outcomes (resulting in a charge, etc.)
>
> ## Information provided
> A search of Kent Police's crime database was conducted on 17 April 2014 for crimes reported between 1 January 2013 and 31 December 2013 where the scene was recorded as either 'educational' or 'school'; both the victim and the offender/suspect was aged seventeen or under; and the offence category description was 'violence against the person'. There were 69 results whose outcomes were as follows:
>
> active investigation 1; caution 17; charge 10; community resolution 20; undetected 21.

The media also has rights to prevent others copying reports and articles without permission.

## Legal responsibilities

The media is protected by law but also has a responsibility to obey the law.

Just as the Human Rights Act protects freedom of expression, it also requires the media to conform to the restrictions specified in Article 10 shown on page 129.

# Extract adapted from Article 10 of the Human Rights Act 1998

*Everyone has the right to freedom of expression. This right shall include freedom to hold opinions and to receive and impart information and ideas without interference by public authority and regardless of frontiers.*

*The exercise of these freedoms may be subject to restrictions that are necessary in a democratic society – in the interests of national security, territorial disorder or crime, for the protection of health or morals, for the protection of the reputation or rights of others, for preventing the disclosure of information received in confidence, or for maintaining the authority and impartiality of the judiciary.*

## Activities

1. Study the Freedom of Information request made to Kent Police on page 128.
   a) Suggest why such a request might be made and who might make it.
   b) Explain why it is important that UK law enables such requests to be made.
2. Study Article 10 of the Human Rights Act. Rewrite the Article so that it could be understood by some of the youngest learners in your school.

## Balancing rights and responsibilities

The dividing line between media 'investigation' and 'intrusion' is not always clear. Judges can find it difficult to settle legal disputes over media reporting.

The media has a right to hold people to account in the **public interest**, so that all citizens are aware of what is being done on their behalf and know about the behaviour of public officials. However, sometimes reporters have justified unreasonable invasions of people's privacy by claiming to be acting in the public interest (see pages 133 to 134 for more details).

Nevertheless, most journalists accept a moral responsibility to report accurately and to treat people with dignity. These standards are reflected in media organisations' codes of practice.

**Public interest**   Information that the public have the right to know, such as a plan to close a local hospital. This is different from information that might interest some members of the public, such as a celebrity's private life.

# Extract adapted from *The Guardian*'s editorial code – August 2015

*Five questions we should ask ourselves about a situation before intruding on privacy:*

1. *There must be sufficient cause – the intrusion needs to be justified by the scale of potential harm that might result from it.*
2. *There must be integrity of motive – the intrusion must be justified in terms of the public good that would follow from publication.*
3. *The methods used must be in proportion to the seriousness of the story and its public interest, using the minimum possible intrusion.*
4. *There must be proper authority – any intrusion must be authorised at a sufficiently senior level (from within the organisation) and with appropriate oversight.*
5. *There must be a reasonable prospect of success; fishing expeditions are not justified.*

## Websites

Full details of the Human Rights Act and all other legislation can be found at: **http://www.legislation.gov.uk/**

The Office of the Information Commissioner (ICO) website includes guidance on how to request information under the Freedom of Information Act: **https://ico.org.uk/**

## Activities

3. Design a simple slide or chart to describe the media's legal rights and responsibilities.
4. Do you think reporting these stories would be in the public interest or just of interest to the public?
   a) A royal princess has complications with a pregnancy.
   b) A hospital surgeon belongs to a racist organisation.
   c) A TV news broadcaster is splitting from her partner.
   d) A secondary school teacher has a social media profile containing sexual images.
5. Describe how *The Guardian's* editorial code seeks to safeguard privacy and explain what a 'fishing expedition' means in this context.
6. Debate these viewpoints:
   a) The balance between the right to a private life and the right to freedom of expression should come down on the side of free expression.
   b) The media has too many rights but not enough responsibilities.

# The media's role and importance in a democracy

## Key learning

Study the role of the media in: informing and influencing public opinion; providing a forum for communication; and exchanging ideas and opinions. Understand the importance of the media holding those in power to account by investigating and reporting on matters of public interest. Evaluate the effectiveness of the media in carrying out these roles.

## Informing and influencing public opinion

Democracies rely on the media to:

- reveal information that enables the public to make decisions
- expose wrongdoing and injustice

**Figure 8.1** Front pages like this alert readers to politicians' plans for their community

- protect the public from danger
- prevent the public from being misled.

UK citizens get much of their information from social, digital, broadcast and print media. This helps citizens to know what is going on. Keeping up to date with news, and other people's reactions to that news, helps citizens to form opinions on issues such as whether students should pay tuition fees or whether the Government should provide more resources for the National Health Service.

**Figure 8.2** Newspapers are becoming a less popular news medium as people rely on their phone to keep up with events

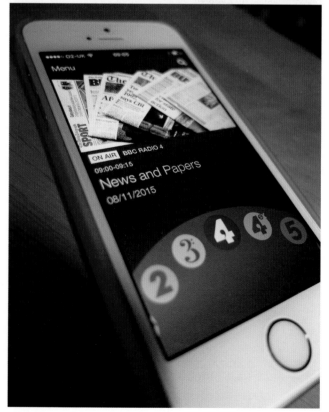

## The British Broadcasting Corporation (BBC)

The UK is unusual because one of the most influential media organisations, the **BBC**, is regulated by the Government and currently funded largely from money paid by the public through an annual **licence fee**. As a result, the BBC has to be impartial – it is not allowed to promote a particular viewpoint or support a particular political party. An advantage of this lack of bias is that people tend to trust the BBC for news. The BBC also has a World Service that broadcasts news internationally in 31 different languages. This helps to promote the UK and British culture around the world. The World Service is paid for by the UK Government.

**Figure 8.3** BBC news is trusted throughout the world

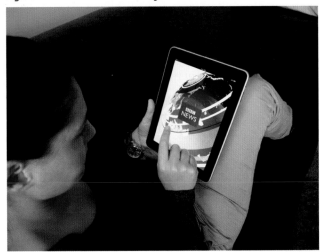

**BBC**   The UK's publicly owned media organisation. It is regulated by Royal Charter. This sets out the BBC's responsibilities to be impartial, and to inform, educate and entertain the public. The BBC also has a responsibility to represent all that is good about Britain.

**Licence fee**   The BBC is currently funded directly through a fee paid by each household owning any electronic device used for receiving TV programmes. This reliable source of income allows the BBC to run a wide range of popular output without the need for revenue from advertising. The licence fee arrangement protects the BBC from those who might wish to influence programme schedules and content.

### Extract from the BBC Royal Charter

The public purposes of the BBC are as follows:

- sustaining citizenship and civil society
- promoting education and learning
- stimulating creativity and cultural excellence
- representing the UK, its nations, regions and communities
- bringing the UK to the world and the world to the UK.

### Website

The BBC's website includes details of its mission, charter and privacy policy: **http://www.bbc.co.uk/**

## Privately owned media organisations

Other news organisations are owned privately and are more likely to try to influence public opinion than the BBC. For example, *The Sun* and *The Times* newspapers, Sky TV and Fox News are largely owned by the Murdoch family. The Murdochs like to have some control over the viewpoints expressed by the media they own. For example, in the 2015 UK general election, *The Sun* supported the Conservative Party and ran a special feature on its front page advising its 1.8 million readers to vote Conservative. The decision to do this was supported by Rupert Murdoch.

### English news media support for the political parties – general election, May 2015

| Conservative | Daily Mail |
| --- | --- |
| | The Sun |
| | The Daily Telegraph |
| | Financial Times |
| | The Times |
| Labour | The Guardian |
| | Daily Mirror |
| | Morning Star |
| UK Independence Party | Daily Express |
| No party supported | The Independent |

## Websites

Most of the private media companies' websites have details of their values, mission and policies as well as advice on how to complain. Try *The Guardian* website: **https://www.theguardian.com/**

Social media sites also include pages about: mission, values and aims (often headed 'about us' or 'about'); privacy; and advice on comments or complaints. Try Instagram's site: **https://instagram.com/**

## Media campaigns

Privately owned media also run campaigns to influence their readers and to put pressure on the Government. In 2015, the *Daily Mail* newspaper and website (owned by Viscount Rothermere) celebrated the success of its campaign to release UK citizen, Shaker Aamer, from fourteen years' detention without trial.

### Justice at last!

#### Shaker Aamer's story

Shaker Aamer is a British citizen born in Saudi Arabia. In December 2001 United States forces arrested Shaker Aamer in Afghanistan and took him to their detention camp at Guantánamo Bay, Cuba.

He was imprisoned as a suspected terrorist but was never charged and didn't face trial.

Fourteen years later he was still there – the only British citizen still held at Guantánamo by the Americans. After a high profile campaign supported by the *Daily Mail* newspaper, the United States Government responded to mounting demands for justice and the 48-year-old was released.

On 30th October 2015, Shaker Aamer flew home to Britain to meet the son he had never seen.

## Exchanging ideas and opinions

Most news organisations encourage discussion and debate. Some shows on broadcast media use a debate format. This gives viewers and listeners access to a wide range of ideas and opinions. Any Questions on BBC radio and Question Time on BBC TV were amongst the first shows to ask politicians and other important opinion-formers to face questions from a studio audience. Talk radio thrives on contributions from the public.

The internet has given everyone a platform from which to talk to millions. This has huge benefits but has also led to concerns about bullying as well as anxiety over the sharing of ideas and opinions damaging to vulnerable people. While internet service providers have attempted to remove the most offensive or dangerous material, there have been calls for further action. Others, though, object to any control of digital media and worry about the increasing number of 'takedown' requests from government officials. (For more details on censorship, see page 135.)

## Holding those in power to account

One of the media's main responsibilities in a democracy is to help scrutinise the actions of:

- the royal family
- MPs and members of the House of Lords
- civil servants
- judges and lawyers
- the clergy
- military leaders
- business and trade union leaders
- political parties
- pressure groups
- charities
- heads of schools, hospitals, police forces, prisons and other organisations.

The media's role is to expose any wrong doing, mistakes or broken promises. They also sometimes offer praise and encouragement.

## A small selection of media headlines holding powerful people to account

**Corbyn dodged kissing the Queen's hand in Privy Council ceremony by going HIKING in the Scottish Highlands**

*MailOnline* 11 October 2015

**MPs' expenses: The Maltesers are on the taxpayer**

*Daily Telegraph* 8 May 2009

**David Cameron grins as he plunges 600,000 more people into poverty**

*Daily Mirror* website 8 October 2015

**Scandal and incompetence stalk the SNP**

*The Guardian* 11 October 2015

**Facebook paid only £4,327 in UK tax last year – less than the average worker**

*The Independent* 11 October 2015

## Activities

1. Explain why it is important for the media to inform and educate the electorate.

2. Compare coverage of the day's news from organisations working in digital media, broadcast media and print media.
   a) Describe their coverage – which headline stories were chosen?
   b) Explain whether you felt coverage was sufficiently informative.
   c) Explain how far you felt coverage was impartial.
   d) Evaluate each organisation's news coverage – which news service would you recommend?

3. Research and describe a campaign run by a media organisation.
   a) What is or was the campaign about?
   b) What methods are or were being used to inform and persuade?
   c) How far do you think the campaign has been or will be successful?

4. Evaluate the viewpoint that the power of news media owners should be controlled by the Government.

# Media regulation and censorship

## Key learning

Study how media regulation operates in the UK. Understand the reasons for media regulation and censorship. Evaluate the effectiveness of media regulation.

## Media power and the Leveson Enquiry

Most people agree that the media should have the right to publish any story involving ordinary people, organisations, businesses, politicians or celebrities as long as it is accurate and in the public interest. People's privacy should only be infringed if the 'public interest' requires such intrusion. For example, a reporter wanting to expose a people-trafficking gang would be justified in infringing the gang's privacy. However, reporters should not obtain information by using unreasonable methods such as 'hacking' into people's mobile phones.

### Missing Milly Dowler's voicemail was hacked by *News of the World*

Milly Dowler disappeared at the age of thirteen on her way home in Walton-on-Thames, Surrey, on 21 March 2002.

The *News of the World* illegally targeted the missing schoolgirl and her family, interfering with police inquiries into her disappearance, an investigation by *The Guardian* has found.

*News of the World* journalists intercepted – and deleted – Milly Dowler's voicemail messages to free up space for more messages. As her friends and parents called and left messages imploring Milly to get in touch with them, the *News of the World* was listening and recording their every private word.

Thirsty for more information from more voicemails, the paper continued to delete older messages – and as a result Milly's friends and relatives concluded wrongly that she might still be alive. Police feared evidence may have been destroyed.

The Dowler family's lawyer issued a statement describing the *News of the World*'s activities as 'heinous' and 'despicable'.

(Adapted from an article in *The Guardian*, July 2011)

In 2011, the Government set up the Leveson Enquiry, a **judicial public enquiry** into the culture, ethics and practice of the press. This followed revelations of widespread phone hacking by newspaper reporters. One of the Leveson Enquiry's main aims was to investigate the balance between privacy and media freedom.

**Judicial public enquiry**   An independent investigation by an experienced judge into a matter of concern. Most meetings are open to the public and can be reported by the media. Pressure groups and members of the public may present evidence to the enquiry. Public enquiries are initiated and funded by the Government.

### Activity

1. Explain why the Milly Dowler case helped to change media regulation in the UK.

## Leveson's findings and media regulation

The Leveson Enquiry found that the media's own system of **self-regulation** through the Press Complaints Commission had failed to prevent abuses of power by reporters and newspaper editors. Lord Leveson's report recommended that the people should be more easily able to make a claim against the media if their right to privacy was being ignored or if stories were untrue. The outcome of the Leveson Report was that the Government set up a system for approving new proposals for media self-regulation. (The Government felt that it would be a dangerous infringement of press freedom to control the media itself.)

In response, some media businesses set up their own **regulatory body**, the Independent Press Standards Organisation (IPSO). This angered many of the victims of media reporting who had already formed a pressure group, Hacked Off, to represent their interests. Hacked Off felt that IPSO would not go far enough in controlling the press.

**Self-regulation**   Some activities are regulated by independent organisations funded by the Government. For example, the Office for Standards in Education (OFSTED) is the independent inspector and regulator for schools and other educational establishments. Self-regulation occurs when a group of businesses or organisations engaged in a common activity such as providing news, set up their own regulator. This can lead to suspicions about the extent of its independence.

**Regulatory body**   An organisation responsible for the oversight of an activity or service. Members of the public can complain to the regulatory body if they are unhappy about the quality of the activity or service. A regulatory body often publishes reports on the effectiveness of the service-providers. These reports are made available to the media and general public.

### Hacked Off unhappy with IPSO

IPSO is the 'Independent Press Standards Organisation' – the press regulator backed by the Murdoch papers, the *Daily Mail*, the *Daily Mirror*, *The Telegraph* and *Daily Express*.

- They claim it's new.
- They claim it's far better than the discredited Press Complaints Commission (PCC).
- They claim it delivers what the Leveson Enquiry recommended.
- They claim that it's 'the toughest press regulator in the world'.

### IPSO is none of these things

IPSO is biased and unfair, just like the PCC. And just like the PCC it will allow the big newspapers to bully, lie and intrude with impunity, so ordinary people will suffer.

Don't get fooled again. Learn the truth about IPSO, and its former incarnation, the PCC – and how it is the same organisation, pulling the wool over everyone's eyes again.

(Adapted from the Hacked Off website: **hackinginquiry.org**)

### Website

The BBC website has a clear and concise summary of the Leveson Report's recommendations and includes a useful link to a question and answer page on press regulation: **http://www.bbc.co.uk/news/uk-20543133**

### Activities

2. Explain why the Government does not take the simple step of regulating the press through an official regulator in the same way that OFSTED regulates education.

3. Explain why Hacked Off is unhappy with IPSO (the regulator set up by some media businesses).

4. Identify the human right that the pressure group Hacked Off thinks is still under threat.

# Media censorship

The UK Human Rights Act safeguards freedom of expression in line with Article 10 of the European Convention on Human Rights. However, there are still some restrictions about what can be written or broadcast as follows:

- threatening, abusive or insulting words intending or likely to cause harassment, alarm or distress or cause a breach of the peace
- incitement of racial or religious hatred
- incitement of terrorism including encouragement or glorifying terrorism and dissemination of terrorist publications
- gross indecency
- court reporting that includes the names of victims or young offenders
- interviews with jurors
- endangering national security or military operations.

Films and videos are classified according to the ages of people allowed to see them. This form of age-related censorship is designed to protect young people from bad language, sex and violence.

OFCOM regulates the broadcasting media under the Communications Act 2003. OFCOM has to make sure television programmes reflect 'generally accepted standards' and prevent harm. OFCOM's Broadcasting Code governs what can be broadcast on TV and radio. The Code exists to protect viewers and listeners from harmful and offensive content but also ensures that broadcasters have the freedom to make challenging programmes.

> **Website**
> The IPSO and OFCOM websites include a description of the regulator's role, their codes of behaviour and guidance on how to complain: **https://www.ipso.co.uk/IPSO/index.html** and **http://www.ofcom.org.uk/**

Social and digital media are more difficult to regulate. Governments do intervene with internet service providers to control potentially harmful content, but many people are worried about how easy it still is to find content that is sexually explicit, violent or promotes potentially dangerous behaviour. There have been campaigns for internet bullies to face more severe punishments and for young people to be banned from using devices that allow free access to the internet.

On the other hand, some people are worried about the growing tendency to report content deemed 'offensive' and demand its removal. This is seen as a threat to free speech.

> **Sarah Wollaston, MP, – 'Sexting' bullies should have their phones confiscated**
>
> Sarah Wollaston, a Conservative MP, has asked the Government to stop young people from owning smartphones if they bully others online. In her statement to the House of Commons at Home Office questions, Ms Wollaston explained that many young people were being bullied into sending intimate photographs of themselves over the internet. She went on to describe how the images are then often posted or shared without permission causing massive distress to the victims.

**Figure 8.4** Should internet access be restricted?

> **Guru, Steve Hilton, calls for teen smart phone ban**
>
> *'As society adapts to the digital age, we need to push back a bit and make the digital age adapt to us. On the one hand, technology – especially in the form of mobile devices – has built a whole new world of progress. On the other hand, devices have unintended and serious negative side effects that we need to recognise and address if we are to maintain a healthy relationship with technology and retain our humanity. Ending children's unsupervised access to the internet is a step in the right – and more human – direction.'*
>
> Steve Hilton, *More Human*, 2015

## Libel

Under English and Welsh law, citizens are protected from libel – publishing a false statement that is damaging to a person's reputation. Libel is a civil matter and respondents are expected to prove their innocence. A person accused of libel has the responsibility of proving that their published comments were either true or, if they were false, did no damage to the person's reputation.

# CASE STUDY

## Comedian wins over £54,000 in libel damages against newspaper

Comedian Frankie Boyle won £54,650 in damages in 2011 after a High Court jury concluded that the *Daily Mirror* had libelled him by describing him as 'racist'. *Daily Mirror* publisher Mirror Group Newspapers (MGN) defended the piece 'on the basis of truth and fair comment', but jurors ruled in favour of Boyle.

Boyle claimed to have been 'pretending' to be someone with racist views during a television show. In doing so he was making fun of racists and drawing attention to their despicable attitudes.

**Websites**

The Index on Censorship website includes news on media censorship around the world: **https://www.indexoncensorship.org/**

Reporters Without Borders produces the World Press Freedom Index: **http://rsf.org/**

**Activities**

5. Assess how far you would censor the internet by deciding whether you would:
   - Ban sites that promote activities such as: blood sports; assisted suicide and drug use?
   - Ban sites that promote negative attitudes to such groups as: girls and young women; ethnic minority groups; gay people and religious groups?
   - Restrict internet access for young people?
   - Introduce harsher punishments for trolling (making abusive personal comments) or sexting?
6. Debate the viewpoint that censorship is a threat to democracy.

# Using the media

**Key learning**

Study how the media is used by those in power and by groups wishing to influence public opinion.

Citizens often get information from the media when carrying out research or planning a campaign. For example, the BBC website is a favourite for citizenship students as it shows both sides of an argument and has links to other relevant sources of information.

An individual with their own well-designed website or blog can have considerable influence. Social media messages can spread quickly – sometimes with huge impact – and it takes moments to post on other people's sites.

Videos posted on an influential website can easily go viral. YouTube **https://www.youtube.com/** and The Huffington Post UK **http://www.huffingtonpost.co.uk/** are two of the most influential sites on which to find videos with a citizenship focus.

Citizens running a campaign use **digital media**, print media (newspapers and magazines), radio and TV to gain publicity and to encourage support from others. Citizens can also use websites such as change.org **https://www.change.org/** to start an online petition. (See also Chapter 9.)

**Digital media** Digital media is created and shared using computers. Examples of digital media include: blogs and websites; social media; and digital video and audio.

Most pressure groups have a media or press officer. Their job is to send out regular messages through social media, email and texts; update their social media sites and websites; and write and send press releases to newspapers, radio and TV. This has to be done frequently to keep the pressure group in the public eye, and to give an impression that the group's ideas are important and should be taken seriously by politicians.

**Figure 8.5** Most political parties and pressure groups use social media to project a positive image

Citizens' opinions about politicians and their policies are strongly influenced by media coverage. As a result, politicians are keen to have good relations with reporters and media owners. Politicians strive to project a positive image and sometimes hire media consultants to help them achieve this. Media consultants can help politicians adjust their hairstyles, style of dress or even the way they speak. Most politicians use social media, hiring professional assistants to update their blogs and websites. Government ministers have their own blogs and social media profiles to publicise their activities and promote their policies.

### Website
The Government's own websites include ministerial blogs. The Secretary of State for Energy and Climate Change's blog is at: **https://decc.blog.gov.uk/**

## CASE STUDY
### Extract from the Secretary of State for Energy and Climate Change's blog, August 2015

*We said in our Manifesto that we would support the safe development of shale gas and as a One Nation Government that's what we will do, because it's good for jobs, it is part of our plan to ensure the potential of all parts of the UK is realised and it's good for our energy security.*

*We're dealing with the problems left by an energy system which for too many years saw a lack of investment and where vital decisions were put off because they were seen as too difficult. But a responsible, long-term energy policy demands a willingness to take decisions today for the good of tomorrow.*

Two months later, there had been just nine posts in response. All were opposed to the Government's policy. They included comments similar to the ones below:

*Mike: Fracking is stupid and short-term. Fracked oil and gas will increase carbon emissions. Big oil companies will make money but future generations will pay a heavy price for years to come.*

*What happened to the Government's green agenda?*

*Stuart: Fracking makes no sense! We should invest in solar energy – it's sustainable and safe. If everyone had solar panels on their home, we could all generate energy. People will be part of the solution instead of part of the problem.*

### Activities

1. Evaluate a digital campaign about a citizenship issue.
   a) Find some suitable digital campaigns and choose one that appeals to you.
   b) Describe what the campaign is about.
   c) Describe the methods used by the campaign to encourage support.
   d) Evaluate the campaign's effectiveness and suggest ways it could be improved.

2. Evaluate the effectiveness of a government minister's blog and an MP's website.
   How far are they successful at:
   a) getting the politician's message across
   b) engaging the public?

3. Design a short guide for MPs on how best to use digital media.

# Practice questions

In the OCR specification, this section will be assessed using objective test questions and questions needing a written response.

1. According to its Charter, which one of the following is a purpose of the BBC?
   A  Provide good value for money for licence fee payers.
   B  Compete with independents such as ITV and Sky.
   C  Represent the United Kingdom, it's regions and communities.
   D  Support the Government of the day. [1 mark]

2. What is the main reason politicians try to achieve a good relationship with the media?
   A  Many want to work in the media once they leave politics.
   B  So that they can support media campaigns.
   C  It is a requirement of being a politician.
   D  So that the public hear about their policies. [1 mark]

3. Study the two statements.  Choose option **A**, **B**, **C** or **D** to describe their accuracy.
   **First Statement**  An independent organisation regulates the media in the UK
   **Second statement**  Government regulation could endanger press freedom
   A  Both statements are true ...... **and** the second statement is a correct explanation of the first.
   B  Both statements are true ...... **but** the second statement **is not** a correct explanation of the first.
   C  The first statement is false but the second statement is true.
   D  Both statements are false. [1 mark]

4. State **two** reasons why the media may be censored in the United Kingdom. [2 marks]

5. Use your knowledge and understanding from across the whole Citizenship course to evaluate the following viewpoint:
   *A free media is more important than anything else in a successful democracy.*
   You should consider
   • the media's role in supporting a democratic society
   • other things that contribute to democracy being successful. [12 marks]

# Chapter 9:
# Citizen participation in the UK and taking citizenship action

This chapter on *Citizen participation in the UK and taking citizenship action* builds on Chapter 1, *Rights and responsibilities* and Chapter 4, *Democracy, elections and voting in the UK*.

In this chapter, we explore the different ways citizens can participate in UK democracy, including by organising campaigns to bring benefit or change to their community or wider society.

Learning the following key concepts and terms will make it easier to organise your thinking and communicate your ideas:

- advocacy
- petition and e-petition
- lobbying
- volunteering
- interest groups, pressure groups and voluntary groups
- National Citizen Service
- digital democracy
- public life.

## Getting involved and having a voice

### Key learning

Study the opportunities for citizen participation in UK democracy and consider barriers to participation. Research the roles played by public institutions, public services, interest and pressure groups, trade unions, charities and voluntary groups in providing a voice for and support to different groups of citizens. Understand the importance of participation for democracy.

Active citizenship is about taking an active role in community life and making a positive contribution to society. Ways in which active citizenship can be achieved include: taking part in voluntary work;

involvement in community organisations; and participation in local and national politics. People can join political parties (see Chapter 4) or join trade unions (see Chapter 1). Citizens can also become directly involved in their communities as special constables, magistrates and a range of other roles in the legal and justice system (see Chapter 3).

People can also dedicate their time to their wider community and country by working for a **public institution** or in the public services. People working in the armed services, judges, doctors, nurses, teachers, care assistants, school employees and many more public sector employees serve the community. The same is true of elected politicians who choose to provide **public service** when they could often earn much more than their parliamentary salary in an alternative career.

> **Public institution**   A school, college, library, hospital or other place that is run for public benefit.
>
> **Public service**   Using knowledge, understanding, skills and experience for community and / or national benefit.

This section considers further opportunities for community involvement.

### Opportunities for young people

*As young people we are the next generation of voters, business leaders, charity leaders, bankers, artists, actors, celebrities, politicians and lawyers. Politics affects everything – and you have to take an interest, you have to let your voice be heard. No matter what your political opinion is: do your research, take a stance, join a party, write to your MP, start a revolution, do something!*

Oli Coulson, National Citizen Service graduate and aspiring Member of Parliament

Government policy aims to achieve five overarching aims for young people – one of which is 'making a positive contribution'.

# Making a positive contribution – a government aim for young people

*'Young people engage in decision-making, support their community and environment, engage in law-abiding and positive behaviour in and out of school, develop positive relationships, choose not to bully and discriminate, develop self-confidence, successfully deal with significant life changes and challenges and develop enterprising behaviour.'*

## The National Citizen Service

National Citizen Service (NCS) is open to all sixteen and seventeen-year-olds in England. It brings together young people from different backgrounds to develop skills for work and life, through team-based challenges to sharpen leadership, teamwork and communication.

The three NCS phases take place outside school term times in spring, summer and autumn.

- **Phase 1 Adventure** A week is spent away from home at an outdoor activity centre learning new skills such as canoeing, archery and rock climbing.
- **Phase 2 Future** Participants learn to live independently, cook for themselves, budget and think about a career. They meet decision-makers from their local community and prepare to help make a difference.
- **Phase 3 Making a difference** All participants work in teams on a social action project to bring a change or benefit to their community.

A large majority (90 per cent) of young people enjoyed National Citizen Service and thought it was worthwhile, because it had:

- given them the chance to meet people they would not normally mix with
- given them the chance to develop skills for the future
- made them proud of what they had achieved.

(NatCen Independent review of the National Citizen Service, 2011.)

## Website
National Citizen Service: **http://ncsyes.co.uk/**

## The UK Youth Parliament (UKYP)

UKYP aims to give a voice to young people aged eleven to eighteen. The Youth Parliament gives young people a chance to influence local, regional and national government, providers of young people's services and other agencies with an interest in the views and needs of young people.

UKYP is independent of government and has a programme of activities including a debate in the House of Commons, regional meetings, dialogue with government ministers and inputs to policy development.

There are 369 UKYP representatives elected each year from special constituencies across the UK.

In 2016, members of the UK Youth Parliament voted for the top five issues that they wanted to campaign on as follows:

- Combat racism and discrimination to give particular support to people of Jewish or Muslim faith.
- Improve public transport by making it less expensive and more accessible.
- Improve mental health services and help young people understand more about mental health.
- Develop the curriculum in schools and colleges so that all young people can learn more about politics, finance and relationships.
- Modify the living wage to make it applicable at a full hourly rate of £7.85 to everyone aged 16 and over (£9.15 in London).

## Website
The UK National Youth Parliament's website includes a record of the Parliament's activities and links to all the MYPs across the country: **http://www.ukyouthparliament.org.uk/**

## Activities

1. Find out more about how to become involved in the National Citizen Service or the UK Youth Parliament. Does your school or college have a link to either scheme?
2. Study the UK Youth Parliament's top five campaigning issues. Add issues of your own to the list and then rank all the campaign issues in order of importance as you see it. Compare your ideas with other learners in your group.

# Interest groups and pressure groups

People enjoy meeting those who share their interests. Such interest groups might follow a football team, walk their dogs together or play computer games. **Pressure groups** go further. In a pressure group, people have similar views on a single issue. They work together to promote those views and **advocate** change.

A pressure group is different from a political party because it does not aim to form a government. Instead, a pressure group seeks to influence decision-making by persuading politicians and civil servants to take action on a particular issue.

Pressure groups use the following tactics to influence decision-makers:

- give evidence to Parliamentary committees
- **lobby** decision-makers
- present a petition or e-petition supported by as many people as possible
- persuade people to contact decision-makers individually
- run media campaigns
- organise protests
- organise **direct action**.

> **Pressure group** A group of people with similar views on a single issue who lobby elected representatives.
>
> **Advocate** *(verb)* Make a case for a particular viewpoint, cause or policy. 'Advocate' is also used as a noun to describe someone whose job it is to provide advocacy (speak on behalf of a viewpoint or person).
>
> **Lobbying** The process of trying to influence the opinions of decision-makers. Methods of lobbying vary and include sending messages, making presentations, providing briefing material and organising rallies.
>
> **Direct action** To seek an immediate result by doing things to disrupt the work or life of the Government or the people thought to be responsible for a problem. Examples include strikes, boycotts and road blocks.

**Figure 9.1** People have the legal right to protest peacefully in the UK

## Pressure groups – in their own words

Information in the following boxes is taken from each group's own website. Claims made by the groups should be checked carefully.

---

**Amnesty International**

**www.amnesty.org.uk**

We protect people, defending their right to freedom, truth, and dignity. We do this by:

- investigating and exposing abuses where they happen
- encouraging our global movement of seven million people to intervene where individuals are at risk
- educating future generations so that one day the dream of human rights for all becomes a reality.

---

**Migration Watch**

**www.migrationwatchuk.org**

We believe that sustainable levels of properly managed immigration are of distinct benefit to our society. Many migrants make a valuable contribution to our society in terms of both their skills and experience. At present immigration is neither sustainable nor well-managed. Our purpose is to monitor developments, conduct research, and provide the public with full and accurate facts placed in their proper context. We also make recommendations for policy.

**Animal Aid**

**www.animalaid.org.uk**

We campaign peacefully against all forms of animal abuse and promote cruelty-free living. We investigate and expose animal cruelty. Our undercover investigations and other evidence are often used by the media, to bring these issues to public attention.

**Website**

Parliament's website offers advice about effective lobbying: **http://www.parliament.uk/**

## Charities and voluntary groups

Many people make a contribution to their community by supporting the work of a charity. According to the Institute for Volunteering Research, 42 per cent of adults volunteer at least once each year and 27 per cent do so at least once each month.

Organisations such as Oxfam, the Samaritans and Citizens Advice rely on people giving up their time to raise money or to work free of charge. Volunteering is particularly popular with: retired people who have valuable skills to offer, young people building their CVs or people seeking to make a bigger contribution to their community.

People who volunteer all get something different from their work. Some of the most common benefits are:

- making a difference to people's lives
- changing the way things work for the better
- gaining valuable work experience
- putting existing skills to good use
- developing new skills
- getting involved with the community
- making new friends.

**Charity** An organisation set up to provide help and raise money for those in need.

**Volunteer** *(verb)* To work without pay to support a good cause. (Also used as a noun to describe someone who does this.)

# CASE STUDY
## Citizens Advice

**www.citizensadvice.org.uk**

**Figure 9.2** Advice centres like this one can be found across the UK

Citizens Advice is a charity that provides free, independent, confidential and impartial advice to everyone on their rights and responsibilities. Citizens Advice is also a pressure group. It campaigns to improve government support for poorer people and those with money problems.

Citizens Advice has centres in most towns for face-to-face advice. People can also get help from the charity's website, by web chat or by phone. Without volunteers, Citizens Advice would not be able to provide these services.

Over 20,000 Citizens Advice volunteers work as:

- advisors
- receptionists
- information assistants
- advice line staff
- administrators
- trustees
- financial education volunteers
- campaigners
- fundraisers
- IT support staff
- marketing and media officers
- witness service volunteers.

When asked 'why they do it', Citizens Advice volunteers often mention:

- Making a difference to individual lives.
- Helping people to stand up for their rights.
- Giving people the skills and confidence they need to manage their own finances.

## The importance of community participation for democracy

Citizen participation is vital for a healthy democracy. People develop greater feelings of well-being and self-worth by engaging with others, sharing their skills and ideas, and by making their voices heard.

Decisions are likely to be better if everyone is involved and, if people have had their say, they are more likely to support those decisions.

Community participation also brings people together: breaking down barriers to encourage mutual respect and tolerance – important values that underpin UK democracy.

Finally, think of what would happen if people didn't question decisions or campaign for change. Decision-makers would be much less accountable to public opinion and the UK would cease to be a fully democratic country.

### Examples of community participation in action

What have these examples got in common?

### Neighbourhood and Home Watch, nationwide

**www.ourwatch.org.uk**

Neighbourhood & Home Watch is a voluntary network of schemes where neighbours come together, along with the police and other local partners, to build safe and friendly, active communities where crime and anti-social behaviour are less likely to happen.

### Website

The Neighbourhood and Home Watch website explains how the scheme works and provides advice about how to set one up: **http://www.ourwatch. org.uk/**

### St Paul's Community Development Trust, Birmingham

The Trust has its origins in local people from Balsall Heath, an inner-city area of Birmingham, working together to start a nursery, adventure playground and small school, and to reduce crime. The Trust continues to promote education, recreation and life-long learning. Many users of the Trust's facilities have gone on to become volunteers, committee members or Trust employees.

### Bexhill Town Forum, East Sussex

**bexhilltownforum.co.uk**

The Forum was launched in 1996 and is run by a committee of volunteers. The Forum was set up to improve the town and make it easier for Bexhill residents to get their voice heard by local decision-makers. Public Forum meetings are held throughout the year to address issues of concern and discuss any residents' suggestions.

### Barracks Lane Community Garden, Oxford

The Garden Project has charitable status and is run by members of the local community who volunteer their time and expertise. Anyone can use the garden and eco building by visiting, booking for a private function or by joining one of the various events and activities held throughout the year.

## Overcoming barriers to community participation

Sometimes people feel unable to participate actively in their community. Reasons for this might include:

- not having enough time
- not knowing where to begin
- being generally de-motivated
- feeling they have nothing to offer
- thinking that their contribution will not make any difference.

Such barriers can be overcome by:

- successful citizenship action in school
- experience of the Duke of Edinburgh Award or National Citizen Service
- confidence-building
- working with activist mentors.

Many businesses encourage their employees to take on a community commitment alongside their normal work. This is good for the business as it often helps to improve employees' skills and motivation as well as giving the business a more positive image in the community. Employees often extend their commitment by building on their positive first experience of community action.

At Barclays, 65,000 employees worldwide (around half) have volunteered in their communities.

Employees are encouraged to share their skills with young people through:

● mentoring

● running CV and mock interview workshops

● advising young entrepreneurs

● teaching money management.

## Website

Volunteering England is an independent charity committed to supporting, enabling and celebrating volunteering: **www.volunteering.org.uk**

The Do-it website helps organisations to recruit suitable volunteers and advises potential volunteers about how to get started: **https://do-it.org/**

## Activities

3. Interview school / college governors, directors or trustees, or other non-executive post holders in charities or public organisations to find out:
   a) what skills they bring to the role
   b) how they became involved
   c) why they do it
   d) what they get out of it.

4. Research and classify a range of volunteering opportunities available to people of different ages and with different skills. Design a slide or poster to display the information. Choose a volunteering opportunity that you think might suit you or someone you know well.

5. Choose an example of a pressure group and describe at least three ways in which it tries to influence decision-makers. To what extent has it been successful?

# Increasing participation in politics

## Key learning

Study different measures to increase participation rates and voter engagement in UK democracy, and explore the potential impact of social media and digital democracy.

There has been a worrying decline in the number of UK electors turning out to vote (Figure 9.3). However, since 2001, numbers have started to rise. In the Scottish independence referendum of 2014, voter turnout was very high at 84.5 per cent. On the other hand, UK voter turnout for the European Parliament election in 2014 was only 35.6 per cent.

Electors are far more likely to vote when they feel something important is at stake, understand the issues and feel their vote matters.

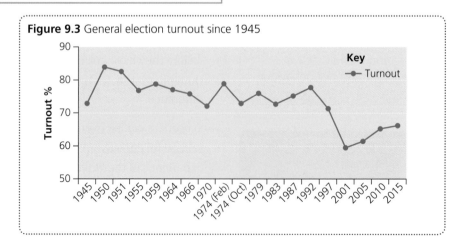

**Figure 9.3** General election turnout since 1945

## Making politics interesting and relevant

Governments have used a variety of approaches to make parliamentary politics more interesting and relevant.

- 1989 – Parliamentary debates televised.
- 2002 – Citizenship becomes part of the National Curriculum.
- 2011 – Parliament's online petition relaunched.

Political parties have also done their best to attract new members. Until recently though, political party membership has been in decline, matching the fall in election turnout.

More people have bypassed 'traditional politics' to campaign directly on issues they care about. Some people are less committed to the main political parties not because of lack of interest in politics but because they no longer feel represented by these parties.

The *British Social Attitudes Survey* of 1987 found that 46 per cent of people identified very or fairly strongly with a political party. This had fallen to 37 per cent by 2014. Identification with a political party was particularly low among the young.

Since 2010, there has been a surge of support for 'new' political parties such as the Green Party and the United Kingdom Independence Party (UKIP). Both these parties started life campaigning on single issues, gained support and now have a range of policies on a variety of issues. (See Chapter 4 for more details of political parties.)

There was increased interest in party politics at the 2015 general election. The rise of the Scottish National Party, and the increased popularity of UKIP and the Greens, coincided with much more obvious policy differences between Conservatives and Labour. Party politics had become more interesting and significant. Turnout in the election increased. This trend has continued. Policy differences between the main parties are becoming even clearer and all the main political parties are attracting more members. (See Chapter 4 for more details.)

### Activity

1. Design a poll to find out older students' views on party politics. Do they see party politics as 'interesting and relevant'? What might encourage them to become active in party politics or campaigning in general?

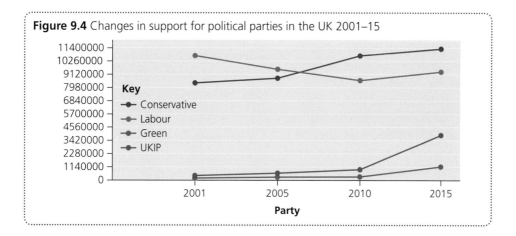

**Figure 9.4** Changes in support for political parties in the UK 2001–15

# GREEN PARTY MEMBERSHIP IS BOOMING

## LibDem membership up 10,000 since general election

# UKIP membership has almost tripled in two years
## Labour Party sees record surge in membership
## Conservative Party membership is up 11.7%

## Changing the way we vote

The way people vote in the UK has changed very little since Victorian times. Everyone votes on the same day (almost always a Thursday) and those who turn up in person must make a special journey to a designated polling station between 7 a.m. and 10 p.m. It is easier to qualify for a postal vote than in the past, but only motivated electors take the time and trouble to apply.

Could changing the way we vote encourage more people to become involved in elections?

## Electoral registration

In order to vote, people must first make sure they register as an elector. In the recent past, each head of household had responsibility for registering all people over eighteen living in their property. This system was misused by some heads of household. Now people must register individually and, although they can do so electronically, the number registering to vote has fallen. This has caused concern. People who change their addresses most often, such as students and welfare claimants, are less likely to register to vote.

## Casting a vote

In 2000, the UK Government recommended that local authorities try out alternatives to the paper ballot. In May 2007, five UK local authorities tried out electronic voting, accepting votes over the internet registered from anywhere. However, the Electoral Commission found 'issues with security' in these pilot schemes. They recommended that local authorities should carry on using their polling stations and ballot boxes. Concerns about fraud continue to be a concern especially because hundreds of different local authorities organise UK elections. One national system might be needed to deal with the challenges of electronic voting. (See Chapter 4 for more on voting and elections.)

*'There have been few substantial changes (to the election system): we still use mediaeval statutes. But we will have to change – what we have is not suitable for lifestyles of the 21st century. More than half, sometimes two-thirds of people are not voting. We have a problem. There are other ways than going to a draughty church hall and marking an X in a box with a stubby pencil – which of course was traditionally the sign of the illiterate. Why not try text or online voting?'*

*David Monks – former Chief Executive,*
*Huntingdonshire District Council*

**Figure 9.5** Phone polls may increase voter turnout if concerns about fraud can be overcome

## Using digital media

Worldwide use of the internet and social media has made it much easier to become directly involved in campaigning and decision-making.

### Digital campaigning – starting and signing petitions

Change.org, Avaaz and Digital Democracy are examples of petitioning websites where people can sign existing petitions or start their own. By 2016 nearly 125 million people worldwide had signed petitions on the Change.org site, while Avaaz claimed 42 million members campaigning in fifteen different languages internationally. The Digital Democracy site is largely UK-based and a favourite with local councillors and MPs, many of whom get involved directly.

---

**Activity**

2. Evaluate methods to increase participation in UK democracy including:
   - citizenship education in schools
   - changes in elections and voting
   - e-petitions.

   List your priorities for increasing participation and debate your choices with other learners.

---

# CASE STUDY
## A digital campaign success

Emily Clarke from Wiltshire started a petition to the Government of Sudan demanding that they should respect freedom of religion and free a young mother, Meriam Yehya Ibrahim, from prison. 1,029,283 people signed Emily's petition and, in June 2014, Meriam was released following an international campaign that included Emily's petition.

*'Over a million people from around the world signed my petition on change.org and joined the chorus of international voices demanding freedom and justice for Meriam.*

*Over the past few months world leaders like UK Prime Minister, David Cameron, and US Secretary of State, John Kerry, have spoken out against Meriam's imprisonment, and media coverage of her story has raised an important conversation about religious freedom and women's rights around the world.*

*Now, thanks to our voices, a young mother and her children have been freed from prison and we have stood together to protect the right to religious freedom.*

*This campaign sends an important message that we will not stand by and let injustice happen. We've proven that coming together online can make a real difference toward the goal of human rights for everyone.'*

Emily Clarke

The UK Government has an on-line petitioning system that enables people to raise issues and enlist support. Petitions remain live for six months. Any petition with at least 100,000 signatures will be considered for a debate in Parliament. If a petition gets at least 10,000 signatures, the Government will make a public response. Videos of debates and government responses are posted on Parliament's website at **https://petition.parliament.uk**

### Examples of petitions on the Parliament website
- End cuts to Merseyside police.
- Accept more asylum seekers and increase support for refugee migrants in the UK.
- Stop allowing immigrants into the UK.
- Introduce a tax on sugary drinks in the UK to improve our children's health.
- Make the production, sale and use of cannabis legal.
- Reconsider the new Dividend Tax for small businesses.
- Make an allowance for up to two week's term time leave from school for holidays.
- Don't kill our bees! Immediately halt the use of Neonicotinoids on crops.

Unfortunately e-petitions have their disadvantages. As it is so easy to set up a campaign electronically, sometimes petitions are frivolous or of little value. Others contain misinformation or remain in circulation long after they become outdated. Fraud is also a problem as e-signatures are difficult to verify.

## Digital campaigning – group action for change

**Figure 9.6** There's never been a greater need for people power

38DEGREES is a campaigning website committed to democracy, human rights, peace and sustainability. Its website features campaigns that anyone can join. 38DEGREES also supports people who want to start a campaign of their own. During the 2015 election, 38DEGREES members organised a campaign to protect the National Health Service. The campaign was directed at all political parties. So far, 38DEGREES has supported over 5,500 different campaigns.

It is easy to start a campaign blog. A simple social media page can be an important information point for project team members and campaign supporters. Campaigners often build their own websites using one of the many guides freely available online.

### Websites
View petitions and reports of campaigners' progress at **https://www.change.org/** and **http://avaaz.org/en/**

View petitions and government responses on the Parliament website at: **https://petition.parliament.uk**

View examples of campaigns at: **https://home.38degrees.org.uk/**

*Wordpress* is one of the most well-established and reliable sites for people building their own website: **https://wordpress.com/**

## Activities

3. 'Avaaz' means 'voice' in several European, Middle Eastern and Asian languages, while 38 degrees is the angle at which snowflakes come together to form an avalanche.
Visit the Avaaz and 38DEGREES websites and explain why they chose these names.

4. The *Democracy Index* gives the UK a rating of 96 per cent for 'organising elections and pluralism', but only 67 per cent for 'political participation'. Using information from this chapter and Chapter 4:

    a) Give two reasons why the UK has a high score for organising elections and pluralism.

    b) Give two reasons why the UK's score for political participation is much lower.

    c) Describe two ways in which organising elections and pluralism could be increased in the UK.

    d) Describe two ways in which political participation could be increased in the UK.

    e) Discuss your proposals with other learners in your group.

# Making a difference

## Key learning

Study two different examples of how young citizens work together to change or improve their communities.

## Citizenship GCSE campaign, underpass safety in Didcot

# CASE STUDY

## Didcot girls on subway mission

Teenagers have launched a campaign to improve safety at a notorious Didcot underpass.

Pupils at Didcot Girls School said they are scared to walk through the Cow Lane underpass alone following a series of violent attacks.

The Year 10 pupils are calling for CCTV and better lighting to boost safety in the dingy subway.

Since July, the underpass has been the scene of fifteen crimes, including knifepoint robberies and an attack in which a man's jaw was shattered.

As part of their GCSE in citizenship, the students have launched a poster campaign, collected a 120-signature petition, met police officers and conducted a survey of 100 underpass users.

Eighty-one of the people questioned said they would feel safer if the underpass were monitored by CCTV.

The town council's deputy leader, Tony Harbour, said: 'The council fully supports what the girls are trying to do. With the CCTV, although we're concerned about the level of violent acts there has been, there is a financial implication.'

(Adapted from *The Oxford Times*, 19 March 2010)

## Outcome

In autumn 2011, South Oxfordshire District Council arranged for the underpass walls to be painted. Once the work had been carried out, people reported feeling safer.

Subsequent major works to transport systems in the area have led to further improvements to the underpass.

## National Citizen Service, Team Keyn, defibrillator training in Milton Keynes

**Figure 9.7** Team Keyn, a group of 16 to 17-year-olds making a difference in their community by promoting the use of defibrillators in local schools

### Plan

- Support the charity SAD UK (Sudden Arrhythmic Death) in their campaign for every UK school to have at least one defibrillator by law.
- Raise £300 to train eight staff to use defibrillators in Milton Keynes schools.

### Action

- Set up a social media page with a donation link.
- Arranged an on-line survey to check public awareness of the issue.
- Produced an awareness-raising video and posted it on their page and on YouTube.
- Ordered SAD leaflets and stickers to give out at fundraising events.
- Made special T-shirts and cupcakes for fundraising.
- Advertised T-shirts for sale.
- Ran a stall at the NCS 'culture fest'.
- Inspired by their success, organised a tea and cake afternoon in a community centre.
- Made a 'last push' to promote their social media page's donation link.

### Outcome

- Target exceeded. Eight people can now be trained.

### Activities

1. Evaluate each of the two citizenship action projects in this section.
   a) List their achievements.
   b) Explain what impresses you about each project.
   c) Describe how the projects could have been developed or extended.

## Planning your own action

Citizenship action project teams can make a difference by:

- contributing to campaigns on local, national or international issues
- raising awareness of local, national or international issues or debates
- lobbying decision-makers in the school or college, local authority, pressure group or national government to protect or extend citizens' rights or opportunities
- organising or contributing to an event, project or programme to address a school, college or community need.

Go to page 150 to find out how to make a success of your own citizenship action.

### Websites

Step Up to Serve is a national campaign that aims to make social action part of life for as many 10 to 20-year-olds as possible by the year 2020. Their website signposts a range of volunteering opportunities: **http://www.stepuptoserve.org.uk/**

Further examples of successful citizenship action projects can be found at the Future Creative website: **http://www.future-creative.org/what-we-do/community-engagement/community-engagement-projects/**, and at 38DEGREES. Their site also includes campaigning tips: **https://home.38degrees.org.uk/**

For further advice on planning your citizenship action, download the Association for Citizenship Teaching's Make it Happen Social Action Toolkit: **http://www.teachingcitizenship.org.uk/resource/social-action-toolkit**

### Activities

2. Research further examples of citizenship action that have taken place in your school, college or community, or through the National Citizen Service. Ask people who have completed such projects to reflect on their experiences and achievements.
   a) Describe how far these projects followed the eight stages of successful action outlined on page 150.
   b) Describe what could have been done differently to achieve further success.
   c) Make your own list of project 'dos and don'ts'.

## Eight stages for successful action

**Stage 1** Choose an issue that you and your team care about and that will bring a change or benefit to your school, community or wider society.

↓

**Stage 2** Seek help and information, especially from decision-makers who can advise you.

↓

**Stage 3** Seek support from those who might benefit from or care about your project.

↓

**Stage 4** Find out more about your issue and research people's opinions.

↓

**Stage 5** Decide exactly what you hope to achieve from your project with the resources and time you have available.

↓

**What you hope to achieve – questions to ask yourself**

- What will a successful outcome look like?
- How will you get feedback from your group, your supporters and the wider community?
- How will you celebrate and publicise project outcomes?

↓

**Stage 6** Decide the form your action will take. At this stage think carefully about:

- targeting a decision-maker – choose an individual or organisation with the power and influence to help you achieve your goal
- keeping all team members and supporters safe
- staying within the law
- asking for necessary permissions
- safeguarding personal information and respecting privacy
- using democratic processes to contact, inform and lobby decision-makers
- protecting and promoting people's freedoms and equalities
- communicating within the project team
- communicating with supporters, decision-makers and the general public.

↓

**Thinking about freedoms and equalities – questions to ask yourself**

- How inclusive is your project; is everyone able to play a part?
- If you are holding an event, will everyone be able to get to the venue and use it safely?
- If you are providing refreshments, will people with special dietary needs be catered for?
- When you are communicating information, what types of media will you use to enable everyone access to information about your project?

↓

**Stage 7** Agree an action plan.

- Break your project down into tasks.
- Sequence the tasks.
- Allocate responsibility and deadlines for each task.
- Build in regular team meetings to review progress and adjust your plans.

↓

**Stage 8** Evaluate your action in relation to the objective you agreed at Stage 5. Consider how you or others could extend or enlarge your project.

## Practice questions

A key task in the OCR exam is to evaluate an aspect of your own project by drawing on your knowledge and understanding of other projects. You may also be asked how far your project was inclusive, reflected democratic values, or took account of rights, freedoms and equalities.

## Example

Using your experience of taking Citizenship Action, explain how you attempted to **involve and include others** and describe other methods you could have taken to achieve this.

Your response should include the following:

- a description of what your aims were and how your project set out to deliver a benefit or change for a particular community or wider society
- what you did to involve and include others
- suggest other methods that could be used to involve and include others.

You should draw upon your studies of citizenship action from across your whole Citizenship course **and** from examples in your own school or college.  [12 marks]

# Chapter 10:
# Politics beyond the UK

This chapter on *Politics beyond the UK* builds on Chapter 1, *Rights and responsibilities*, Chapter 4, *Democracy, elections and voting in the UK*, Chapter 6, *The British constitution* and Chapter 9, *Citizen participation in the UK and taking citizenship action*.

In this chapter, we compare government and politics in the UK with another democratic country, Switzerland, and a non-democratic country, the People's Republic of China.

Learning the following key concepts and terms will make it easier to organise your thinking and communicate your ideas:
- democracy
- pluralism
- authoritarian regime
- political participation
- political culture
- civil liberties.

# Comparing systems of government

## Key learning
Understand the concept of democracy and the key features of democratic societies. Know how different countries can be ranked and compared.

There are three main democracy ranking systems. Each aims to measure the extent to which each country in the world is democratic:

- Democracy Ranking from the Alpen-Adria University in Austria
- Democracy Index from The Economist Intelligence Unit, based in the UK
- Democracy Barometer from the Swiss National Science Foundation.

Although each ranking system uses slightly different ways of measuring democracy, they tend to agree about which countries are most and least democratic. We will use Democracy Ranking here because it

includes the 'quality of society' (as an outcome of good government) as well as the 'quality of politics'. In this way, Democracy Ranking can tell us about people's quality of life as well as about how far they are able to engage in decisions about their lives.

## Website
Find Democracy Ranking at:
**http://democracyranking.org/**

Find the Democracy Index at the Economist Intelligence Unit website: **http://www.eiu.com/**

Find the Democracy Barometer at:
**http://www.democracybarometer.org/**

In Chapter 4, democracy was defined as 'rule of the people'. Each person with voting rights has a say in decision-making. We also learned that pluralism is a feature of democracies – all groups are included in decision-making.

Democracy in the UK and most other democratic countries is underpinned by interconnected values:

- personal freedom
- tolerance and respect for diversity
- equal opportunity
- the rule of law.

(See Chapter 4 for more details.)

## Democracy Ranking – making comparisons between countries
Democracy Ranking measures the quality of politics and the quality of society to decide how far a country is democratic. According to Democracy Ranking the two are linked. If people are fully involved in decision-making, then their society should become a satisfying place to live.

In the table on the opposite page, each of the criteria or measures is given a weighting which shows how much it contributes to the quality of democracy. For example, political rights contribute 12.5 per cent of the total democracy measure.

**Table 10.1** Measuring the quality of democracy

| Quality of politics –<br>including freedom and civil liberties 50% | | Quality of society –<br>the effects of government 50% | |
|---|---|---|---|
| Criteria | % weighting | Criteria | % weighting |
| **Political rights**<br>Is everyone able to vote regularly and in secret, stand as a candidate and join a political party? | 12.5 | **Economy**<br>Wealth, inflation, government debt and employment | 10 |
| **Civil liberties**<br>Legal rights connected with<br>• personal freedom<br>• tolerance and respect for diversity<br>• equal opportunity<br>• the rule of law | 12.5 | **Environment**<br>Carbon dioxide emissions<br>Sustainable use of energy | 10 |
| **Gender equality**<br>This includes political empowerment. Are women fairly represented in the executive, the legislature and the judiciary? | 12.5 | **Gender equality**<br>Do males and females have similar levels of life expectancy, education and employment? | 10 |
| **Press freedom**<br>Can the media express itself freely without censorship or restriction? | 5 | **Health**<br>Infant mortality, percentage of country's wealth spent on health care. | 10 |
| **Lack of corruption**<br>Are there laws against unfair political and business deals? Are the laws enforced in all cases? | 5 | **Knowledge**<br>School and college enrolment, internet access, personal communication | 10 |
| **Peaceful changes of government**<br>Do political parties and heads of state respect election results? | 2.5 | | |

**Figure 10.1** World democracy ranking, 2014

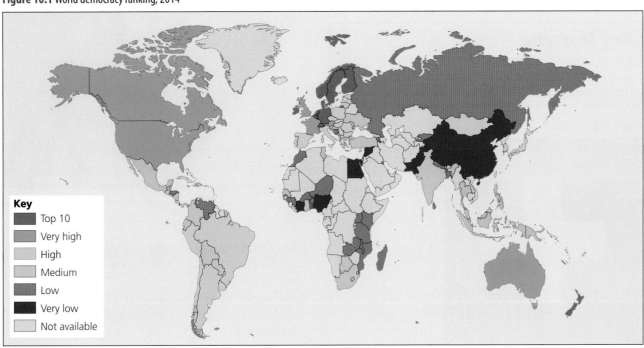

## Activities

1. Study the criteria used in the Democracy Ranking table on the previous page.
   a) Explain why the quality of society is included in the ranking.
   b) Identify any criteria that you think should be added to the ranking.
   c) To what extent does the Democracy Ranking enable a fair comparison between countries?

The chart below compares the UK, China and Switzerland using the Democracy Ranking criteria. Each score is out of 100.

**Table 10.2** Comparing the UK, China and Switzerland using the Democracy Ranking criteria

| | | UK | Switzerland | China |
|---|---|---|---|---|
| | Quality of politics | 86.3 | 91.1 | 25.0 |
| Quality of society | Economy | 55.7 | 76.1 | 44.9 |
| | Environment | 66.1 | 79.5 | 49.1 |
| | Gender equality | 82.2 | 81.8 | 69.1 |
| | Health | 81.1 | 87.2 | 65.1 |
| | Knowledge | 67.2 | 79.1 | 39.2 |
| | Overall score | 78.4 | 85.9 | 39.2 |
| | Rank | 13th | 2nd | 106th |

# Switzerland – a direct democracy

## Key learning

Know the key differences between the nature and extent of citizens' political participation in the UK and one other democratic system.

**Figure 10.2** The Swiss flag

Switzerland is a relatively small but influential and wealthy country. Switzerland is not a member of the European Union, but enjoys strong trading relationships with the rest of Europe. Switzerland is known as a **direct democracy** – citizens elect representatives to their parliament and assemblies, but they also have the right to vote in referendums on a range of issues affecting their country, region or community.

Switzerland is a **federation** of cantons (regions). Cantons have considerable independence from the federal (national) government. There are four languages spoken in Switzerland – German, French, Italian and Romansh. Most Swiss people also speak English.

**Figure 10.3** Switzerland – famous for chocolate, watches, cheese, army knives and democracy

**Direct democracy**   A type of democracy where citizens are dominant and have a key role in making decisions.

**Federation**   A union of partially self-governing states or regions under a central (federal) government.

Switzerland has no defence agreements with any other country and has not fought a war for over 200 years.

Switzerland was one of the last countries in the world to allow women to vote. Women have only been able to take part in elections at federal level since 1971. One canton, Appenzell Innerrhoden, only allowed women the right to vote in cantonal matters when forced to do so in 1990 by a Federal Supreme Court decision.

# Quality of politics

## System of government – a federal republic

Switzerland is a federation – a system of government in which power is shared between the central state and the regions. The laws of the central authority apply to the whole country, whereas those of the federal states apply only to their regions.

Other countries with a federal system include Germany, the USA, India, Australia and Brazil.

Switzerland is also a **republic**: it has no monarch. Instead, the seven members of the Swiss Federal Council (Switzerland's executive) share the Head of State role. A president is elected to chair meetings of the Federal Council for a one-year term.

**Figure 10.4** The Swiss cantons

Authority in Switzerland is shared between the Confederation (central state), the 26 cantons ( federal states) and the 2,929 municipalities (town or village councils). Each of these three levels of government has legislative powers (to draw up laws and regulations) and executive powers (to implement them). The Confederation and the cantons also have judicial powers – through their courts – to ensure that the laws are enforced.

Swiss cantons have considerable devolved power, being responsible for education, hospitals and policing in their region.

## Forming governments

Every four years, citizens elect the 200 members of the National Council and the 46 members of the Council of States (representing each of the cantons) using a system of proportional representation (see page 90 in Chapter 4). These two chambers form a United Federal Assembly which jointly elects the President and federal judges.

After the 2015 federal election, eleven different political parties had representatives in the National Council. The largest party, the Swiss People's Party, won 53 seats – far too few to form a government on its own.

Switzerland is used to coalition government and has developed a **political culture** based on **consensus** rather than on conflict between a government and an opposition as in the UK. In Switzerland, Federal Council posts are divided between the biggest parties according to a formula agreed in 1959.

**Figure 10.5** Swiss government

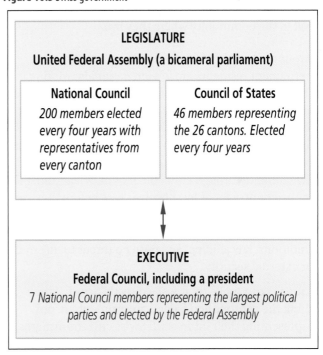

**Republic**   A country in which power is held only by elected representatives. There is no monarch.

**Political culture**   The attitudes and beliefs that underpin practices and behaviour in the political system.

**Consensus**   General agreement.

**Figure 10.6** Power in Switzerland

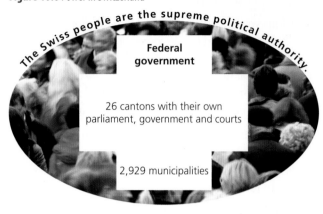

## Political rights and political participation

All Swiss citizens over eighteen can vote, unless they lack the mental capacity to make decisions. The different cantons can allow sixteen-year-olds voting rights in regional elections. Only one canton has done this so far. As soon as Swiss citizens become entitled to vote, they are automatically registered on the electoral roll in the community where they live.

Around a quarter of Switzerland's eight million permanent residents are foreign nationals working in the country with permission. As most foreign nationals are not Swiss citizens, they are not allowed to vote at federal level. Around one-third of Swiss cantons allow foreign nationals to vote in cantonal and/or municipal ballots. Foreigners with no direct blood ties to Switzerland, through either birth or marriage, must live in the country for at least twelve years before they can apply for citizenship. Applicants for citizenship must be well integrated, familiar with Swiss customs and traditions, law abiding, and pose no threat to internal or external security.

Citizens can make their voice directly heard, if they think the cantons and federal government are not representing their interests. If Swiss citizens disagree with an act of parliament, they can oppose it by launching a referendum. As long as 50,000 signatures are collected in support, the contested law is put to the vote. Only hand-written signatures are accepted and all are checked using official electoral registers.

**Political participation**   Involvement in decision-making.

Any member of the Swiss electorate, including leaders of political parties, can also demand an amendment to the Federal Constitution. 100,000 signatures are needed for a referendum to be held on their proposal. Any change to the law requires both a majority of the valid votes cast and the majority of the cantons (double majority).

**Figure 10.7** A poster supporting a YES vote in the 2014 referendum to stop mass immigration to Switzerland. 56% of the electorate turned out to vote. 50.4% of those voted YES. Swiss laws were changed to curb immigration.

'In many countries, parliamentary elections present the only opportunity for the citizens to have a say in politics. Things are very different here. Switzerland is the world champion in holding referendums. Over 30 per cent of all referendums held globally since the 18th century have been held in Switzerland.

In no other country in the world is politics so intensively debated as it is here. Three to four times a year we vote on issues that have a direct impact on our lives; issues such as health policy, education, Switzerland's relations with other countries or the future of energy. Nothing is taboo. We have even voted on abolishing the armed forces and whether or not Switzerland needs new fighter jets.'

Corina Casanova, Swiss Federal Chancellor, 2015

A referendum can also be requested by a minimum of eight out of the twenty-six cantons. Citizens also have the right to launch a referendum at cantonal and municipal level.

Some acts passed by parliament, including all changes to the constitution, must automatically be voted on by the Swiss electorate. A double majority is needed for the constitutional change to be accepted.

Swiss citizens are generally called on four times a year to vote in referendums on federal proposals. There are additional referendums on proposals from citizens. Average turnout in Swiss federal elections and referendums is 48 per cent.

Citizens have the right to petition any authority. There is no time limit for petitions and no minimum number of signatures. Authorities have to acknowledge petitions but they do not necessarily have to respond.

## Criticisms of direct democracy

One of the criticisms of democracy is that it can be a **'tyranny of the majority'**. In Switzerland, for example, a referendum vote can pass a law discriminating against a minority group. In 2009, Swiss citizens voted to ban minarets. The country's constitution was changed and the ban came into force. This was in spite of many Swiss politicians believing that the ban was unfair to the country's 400,000 Muslims, infringed international human rights law and contradicted one of the core values of the Swiss constitution – respect for minorities.

Direct democracy can also limit the actions of elected representatives. Governments may be reluctant to make a necessary but unpopular decision because a referendum might reverse it. This threat encourages Swiss governments to consult fully on their plans before trying to pass new laws.

### Websites

The Swiss Government's own website provides a clear and useful guide to Switzerland's political system: **https://www.ch.ch/en/swiss-political-system/**

Find a brief guide to Swiss politics and government at: **https://www.bk.admin.ch/dokumentation/02070/index.html?lang=en**

### Activities

1. List the advantages and disadvantages of direct democracy.
2. Switzerland is often described as a 'model on which all other democracies should be based'. Evaluate this viewpoint.

**Tyranny of the majority**  A majority of people making decisions that discriminate against a minority.

**Politburo**  The main policy-making committee of a communist party.

# The People's Republic of China (PRC) – a non-democratic political system

### Key learning
Know the key differences between the nature and extent of citizens' political participation in the UK and one non-democratic system.

**Figure 10.8** The flag of the PRC

The People's Republic of China was founded in 1949 by the victorious Community Party following a civil war lasting twenty years.

In 1949, China was an underdeveloped, largely agricultural society with low life expectancy and limited education. Now China is the world's second-largest economic power, one of five permanent members of the United Nations Security Council, and the only **communist** state in the G-20 grouping of major world economies.

In 2015, the UK and China became close trading partners, even though the two countries have very different approaches to politics and human rights.

## Quality of politics

### System of government – a state with a single political party in power

China has a complex political system that is very different from those in democratic countries. The Chinese Communist Party is the prime authority. It is led by its 370-person Central Committee and a **Politburo** of 25 people. Within the Politburo is the seven-person Standing Committee. The Standing Committee includes the Communist Party's top leadership including the General Secretary/President.

The Standing Committee sets policy for the State Council – China's executive and cabinet – and is accountable to the Politburo and to the Central Committee.

The National People's Congress (NPC) is a **unicameral** parliament and China's legislature. It is dominated by the Communist Party, but around a third of the seats are taken by members of the eight smaller parties allied to the Communist Party. This helps to provide a greater diversity of views but not a political opposition.

**Figure 10.9** Shanghai is one of China's most lively and prosperous cities

**Figure 10.10** NPC meeting in the Great Hall of the People, Beijing

The NPC meets once each year – for a period of two weeks. A Standing Committee of the NPC meets more regularly. NPC members discuss recommendations from the State Council and usually approve these

new laws. In recent years, the NPC has become more willing to challenge the State Council on issues in the public spotlight, such as environmental protection and public finance. The NPC appoints the judiciary and elects the Chinese President. The Chinese leadership is accountable to the NPC. Leaders present annual 'work reports' to the NPC and are keen to receive the parliament's full approval.

People's congresses make decisions in China's provinces and towns. These congresses interpret Communist Party policy to fit local circumstances. Chinese local government is much more heavily influenced by national government than in either the UK or Switzerland.

## Forming governments

Delegates to the National People's Congress are elected for five-year terms by an **indirect election system**. Delegates to the NPC are chosen by members of provincial congresses. Delegates to the provincial congresses are chosen by members of several smaller congresses within each province. Locally based people's congresses in towns, large workplaces or villages are the first stage of this whole process. Local people's congresses are chosen directly by the electorate.

Communist Party members elect the top party officials to govern China's provinces. The influential Central Committee of the Communist Party is composed largely of these officials. The Central Committee chooses members to serve on the Politburo.

## Political rights and political participation

All citizens over eighteen have the right to vote by secret ballot in direct 'general elections' for local people's congresses. Political parties, organisations and groups of ten electors can nominate candidates but, in practice, people opposed to the Communist Party's policies are unlikely to stand for election.

Citizens have their political voting rights removed if they are in custody, being investigated, charged or tried because of 'endangering national security or other serious criminal activities'.

---

**Communist** A system of government in which the community rather than the individual, is seen to be more important. In theory each person is supposed to contribute to the community according to their ability and, in return, the community should be prepared to meet their needs.

**Unicameral** A parliament with a single chamber, in contrast to the bicameral parliaments in the UK and Switzerland.

**Indirect election system** Citizens elect representatives who then take responsibility for electing delegates to a higher layer of government.

Citizens over eighteen can also apply to become one of the Chinese Communist Party's 60 million members. The application process is rigorous – two existing party members must act as sponsors – and all applicants must serve a period of probation to prove themselves suitable for membership. Communist Party members vote in elections to choose party officials and can stand for office themselves. All members must swear an oath of loyalty to their party.

*'It is my will to join the Communist Party of China, uphold the Party's programme, observe the provisions of the Party constitution, fulfill a Party member's duties, carry out the Party's decisions, strictly observe Party discipline, guard Party secrets, be loyal to the Party, work hard, fight for communism throughout my life, be ready at all times to sacrifice my all for the Party and the people, and never betray the Party.'*

Communist Party admission oath

All Communist Party members are free to discuss policy but, once the decision of the party is made by majority vote, all members are expected to uphold and enforce that decision. This is known as the principle of 'democratic centralism'.

## Criticisms of the Chinese approach

The Chinese Government has been described as an **authoritarian regime** – a government that enforces strict obedience at the expense of personal freedom.

The main criticisms of the Chinese approach are that human rights are not fully respected and that people do not have enough say about how their country is run.

- Those who campaign for democracy are not tolerated (see case study on page 160).
- News media is controlled by the Chinese state.
- Minority groups are repressed if they are seen as a threat to China's stability.
- People have limited political influence especially if they are not Communist Party members.

Chinese leaders fear chaos if opposition groups are allowed to speak out against the Government and if the Communist Party begins to lose control. This helps to explain the robust system of monitoring and control designed to restrict the growing pressure for political change in China.

**Authoritarian regime** A government that uses its power to enforce strict obedience to its policies and practices. As a result, personal freedom is restricted.

**Figure 10.11** People's Republic of China government

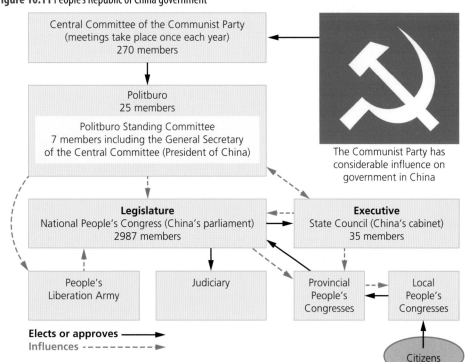

The Communist Party has considerable influence on government in China

# CASE STUDY

## Amnesty International case – Liu Ping, China

*'My mother, Liu Ping, is in prison for standing up for human rights in China.'*

Liu Ping was an ordinary factory worker who became a passionate anti-corruption activist in China. Her daughter, 22-year-old Liao Minyue, tells their story.

*'My mom started giving speeches on the streets and giving out leaflets. She also tried to run for the local People's Congress as an independent candidate so she could help workers who had been forced to retire. She was away from home for days at a stretch.*

*I was completely against what she was doing and tried everything to stop her. The police and local party officials would also approach me to get her to stop.*

*I had no idea what she was involved in. There was talk that she was up to no good, and I started believing what I heard. Our relationship became badly strained as a result.'*

## Arrested for denouncing corruption

*'My mom and two other anti-corruption activists were arrested for holding a small private gathering and displaying a banner demanding that government officials make their assets – like property and investments – public. After that, I lost faith in the Chinese Communist Party, and I posted an open letter online announcing my withdrawal from it. I was prepared to face the consequences.*

*My mother and the other two activists are said to be linked to the New Citizens' Movement, a loose network of human rights activists. When she was sentenced to six and a half years in prison in June, I was outraged. I posted another letter online, expressing my deep disappointment.'*

(Extract adapted from Amnesty International, USA)

## Website

The Global Times, China's official English language newspaper, is a good source of political news stories from the official Chinese Government's point of view: **http://globaltimes.cn/**

The Chinese Government's website provides further details of the country's political system and human rights: **http://www.china.org.cn/english/Political/25060.htm**

Several websites take a critical view of human rights in China. Try Human Rights Watch and search for China: **http://www.hrw.org/**

## Activities

1. Describe three ways in which the Communist Party keeps a grip on power in China.

2. Describe two ways in which democracy and human rights are restricted in China.

3. Design and complete a chart or table to compare politics in the UK, Switzerland and China. (See Chapters 1, 4, 8 and 9 to remind you about the UK.) Include the following:
   a) political rights
   b) elections
   c) devolution
   d) forming a government
   e) political participation.

4. Evaluate the political systems of Switzerland and China. Describe what features of each, if any, you might like to bring to the UK. Explain your choices.

# Practice questions

In the OCR specification, this section will be assessed using objective test questions and questions needing a written response.

1. What is likely to cause most concern to a **supporter** of democracy?
   A Low turnouts in elections.
   B Hostile coverage of the Government from some media websites.
   C Campaigns to give people under eighteen the right to vote.
   D An independent judiciary criticising a government policy. [1 mark]

2. Which of the following is the strongest argument against the use of referendums in a democracy?
   A The electorate expect their representatives to make decisions.
   B The rights of minority groups can be threatened.
   C The result isn't always clear.
   D The Government usually takes no notice. [1 mark]

3. Which country (A, B, C or D) is likely to gain the **highest** score on a democracy ranking?

4. State **two** ways in which civil liberties are restricted by an authoritarian regime. [2 marks]

5. Evaluate the following viewpoint: 'Citizens' political participation in the UK is very high in comparison with other democracies and non-democratic countries.' In your answer, you should:
   - Describe the opportunities for citizen participation in UK politics.
   - Describe how far citizens do participate.
   - Describe citizens' participation in **either** another democracy **or** a non-democratic country you have studied.
   - Evaluate the viewpoint by comparing the UK with the other country selected. [12 marks]

| Country | Devolution | Separation of powers | Media |
|---------|-----------|---------------------|-------|
| A | Most decisions are made centrally for the good of the whole country | The judiciary are chosen by the elected government | Censorship is used only to protect vulnerable people from harm |
| B | Power is devolved to communities resulting in different policies in different areas | The judiciary is appointed by an independent organisation | Censorship is used only to protect vulnerable people from harm |
| C | Power is devolved to communities resulting in different policies in different areas | The judiciary are chosen by the elected government | Censorship is used to protect national security and keep people safe |
| D | Most decisions are made centrally for the good of the whole country | The judiciary is appointed by an independent organisation | Censorship is used to protect national security and keep people safe |

[1 mark]

This chapter on *Identities and diversity in UK society* builds on Chapter 1, *Rights and responsibilities* and Chapter 9, *Citizen participation in the UK and taking citizenship action*.

In this chapter, we explore UK citizens' sense of identity and consider the importance of tolerance and respect for diversity, and ways to promote greater community cohesion. After studying the main reasons for migration to and from the UK, we will assess the benefits and challenges of immigration and evaluate different viewpoints on this controversial issue.

Learning the following key concepts and terms will make it easier to organise your thinking and communicate your ideas:

- sense of identity
- multiple identities
- migration
- immigration
- emigration
- economic reasons for migration
- political reasons for migration
- asylum
- British citizenship
- community cohesion.

# Our sense of identity

## Key learning

Study the main factors that affect people's **sense of identity**. Understand that, in UK society, people have a range of identities which are often diverse, complex and relate to their heritage connections with the nations of the UK, Commonwealth or the wider world.

**Sense of identity**   Feelings of belonging and loyalty. People may identify with their religion, culture, place of birth, family or community.

## A sense of Britishness

The UK is a multi-cultural society. Groups of people from all over the world have come to settle in the UK, bringing their cultural traditions with them.

Some of these traditions have been widely adopted across the country. Here are two examples.

- Settlers from the Caribbean brought their tradition of street carnivals to London. The Notting Hill Carnival is now one of the biggest carnivals in the world and is enjoyed in late August each year by tens of thousands of people from different backgrounds.

**Figure 11.1** Street carnival, brought to the UK from the Caribbean, is becoming a cultural tradition in the UK

- Immigrants from India and Pakistan brought their tradition for hot, spicy food that had already been popular with the British in India for 200 years. Now there are Asian restaurants in every town and many villages across the UK.

**Figure 11.2** Indian restaurants are now part of the British landscape

There are many other British cultural traditions that people take for granted when they live in the UK but miss if they go to live in another country. Examples include school uniform, Remembrance Sunday, Bonfire Night, Mothering Sunday and the English pub. Such traditions are often linked to the UK's official protestant religion or to British history.

**Figure 11.3** Britain's history has given rise to several important annual events that bring people together

People across the UK are passionate about certain sports. Rugby and football are two examples. For the English, cricket is a traditional summer sport enjoyed by many. Horse racing, show jumping, motor racing, boxing, rowing and sailing are also sports that are seen as British specialities. The UK is also well known for the quality of its education, music, theatre, film and television.

Many people are intensely proud of their home nation or region within the UK. These differences in heritage are celebrated through dress, music, literature, food, drink, and support for particular football, rugby or cricket teams.

As the home of the English language, the UK remains a place that interests and attracts people from across the world. Our culture is seen as rich and varied. The cultural traditions brought with them by immigrants to the UK has added to this cultural richness and variety.

## British values

Values are the moral principles or accepted standards held by an individual or group of people. To find out what official British values are, we should study the rules that govern public bodies connected with the law, justice, communication and education. These rules are usually based on the following core values – all four of which also underpin our democracy:

- the rule of law
- personal freedom
- tolerance and respect for diversity
- equal opportunity.

(See Chapter 4 for more details.)

Other people can sometimes judge our values and behaviour more accurately than we do. The British Council's survey, *As Others See Us*, asked 5,000 foreigners what they thought of the UK and the British. This is what they said.

- Culture and history are the UK's most attractive features; weather and food its least.
- Shakespeare, the Queen and David Beckham are our biggest cultural icons.

**Table 11.1** Characteristics of British people – what foreigners think of us

| Worst | Percentage (%) support | Best | Percentage (%) support |
|---|---|---|---|
| Drink too much | 27 | Polite and well mannered | 46 |
| Have poor eating habits | 23 | Educated and skilled | 37 |
| Ignorant of other cultures | 22 | Friendly | 31 |
| Too nationalistic | 22 | Respect the rule of law | 27 |
| Intolerant towards people from other countries | 20 | Have a sense of humour | 25 |

**Figure 11.4** Artist Grayson Perry created *Comfort Blanket* in 2014 to illustrate British values and the characteristics of British people. This provides an insight into how we see ourselves.

## Website

The British Council's report *As Others See Us* is available on their website at: **http://www. britishcouncil.org/organisation/press/best-and-worst-british-eyes-world**

## Activities

1. Study the British Council's report *As Others See Us* and Grayson Perry's *Comfort Blanket*.
   a) Which of them, in your opinion, gives the more accurate view of British values and characteristics? Explain your views.
   b) Explain why foreigners may have developed the positive and negative impressions shown in the British Council's report.
   c) Describe how you would like foreigners to regard British people.
   d) Describe what can be done to create this more positive image.
2. Describe the main influences on your own sense of identity and describe how British you feel. Compare your descriptions with those of other learners in your group. Identify and explain any similarities and differences that you find.
3. Ask one of your parents or carers about the main influences on their personal identity and their sense of Britishness. Describe the differences and similarities between their response and your own.

## Complex identities

We develop our sense of who we are (our identity) from different sources. When we are very young, we spend most time with our parents and learn from them. Parents shape our values, habits and behaviour. We follow their cultural traditions without question.

As we get older, we mix with a wider variety of people. This first happens at school, and then at college or university and at work. Our friends' values, habits and behaviour may contrast with those of our parents, relatives and members of our community. Reading, using electronic media, listening to music, travelling or just shopping intoduces us to new ideas and ways of behaving. The UK is a diverse society with many different options to help us shape our sense of identity. In doing so, we may begin to question our parents' values and traditions, and move away from the cultural ties that were so important when we were young. We may have **multiple identities**, switching from one to another depending on circumstances.

**Multiple identities** People have a multiple identity when they identify with more than one source of belonging or loyalty. For example, a person may describe themselves as a 'British Muslim, originally from Sudan'.

**Figure 11.5** What contributes to our sense of identity?

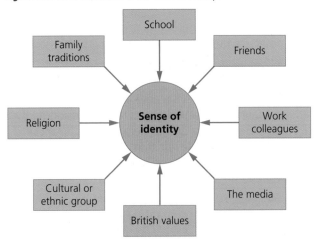

Young people who belong to a black or minority ethnic (BME) group have to balance the values, culture and traditions of that ethnic group against mainstream British traditions, culture and values. This is usually not a problem. People who are part of a BME group can still celebrate their Britishness. However, there can be difficulties if ethnic group traditions are seen to be out of step with mainstream UK culture. For example, some Muslim girls have serious disputes with their parents about appropriate behaviour with boyfriends.

All this can result in people developing a complex sense of identity. This can be a particular issue for the 1.3 million people in the UK with a mixed ethnic background.

---

**Institute for Social and Economic Research finds that ethnic minorities feel most British**

As part of the Institute for Social and Economic Research (ISER) long term study, Understanding Society, people living in 40,000 UK households were asked about their feelings of 'Britishness'. The 2012 report's rather surprising findings contradict the common view that ethnic minority groups prefer to identify with their family's country of origin, and are unwilling or unable to fit in with British culture, values or traditions.

When asked to indicate how important being British was to them on a scale of 1 to 10, people of Pakistani origin scored highest with an average of 7.76, closely followed by respondents with Bangladeshi and Indian heritage. It was the white population who scored lowest with a 6.58 average.

Chief researcher, Dr Alita Nandi, also found that identification with Britain increased from generation to generation with younger people from black and mixed ethnic (BME) backgrounds feeling more British than their parents or grandparents. Many of the respondents seemed to have little trouble managing 'dual identities' – respecting their cultural heritage while also embracing British culture, values and traditions.

White people had low scores on British identity because many of them preferred to see themselves as English, Scottish, Welsh or Irish first and British second.

---

## Website

The Understanding Society research studies can be found at: **https://www.understandingsociety.ac.uk/**

## Activities

4. Study the Understanding Society research.
   a) Did you expect the study to come to these conclusions? Explain your answer.
   b) Describe the implications of this study for the future of British society.

## Contribution of black and minority ethnic (BME) groups to the UK

People from a wide range of ethnic and religious backgrounds contribute very substantially to the national economy and to the success of the UK as a nation.

In the 1950s, 1960s, 1970s and 1980s, many immigrants from the Caribbean, Africa and Asia came to the UK to work in low-skilled and poorly paid jobs. They faced widespread racism and discrimination.

Even though racial discrimination became illegal in 1976, people from BME groups still found it difficult to break out of poverty. However, as the UK has become a much more diverse society and racism has become less acceptable, it has been easier for people from BME groups to achieve success. While many BME children still have problems to overcome, especially at school, others have now achieved very prominent positions in business, politics, the media, sport and entertainment. Four examples of the many success stories are given below.

### Assem Allam – entrepreneur and philanthropist

Assem Allam came to the UK in 1968 as a refugee from Egypt. He studied economics at Hull University and then worked as an accountant. In 1992 he founded Allam Marine, leading the company to international success. He was named the UK Entrepreneur of the Year in 2006.

Assem has been grateful to the area that gave him refuge. He has supported sport and the arts in East Yorkshire as well as becoming a trustee of the Daisy Appeal, a local medical research fund. He has provided financial support to the Labour Party and, in 2010, took over Hull City, rescuing the football club from likely bankruptcy.

### Baroness Scotland of Asthal – lawyer

Patricia Scotland was born in the Caribbean. Her family moved to London when she was two years old. Patricia gained a law degree at London University in 1976 and in 1991 became the first black woman to be appointed a Queen's Counsel. She received a life peerage in 1997 to represent the Labour Party in the House of Lords. She became the chief legal advisor to the Queen, Parliament and the Government by being appointed Attorney General in 2007. She held this post until 2010, when there was a change of government. During her time in Parliament, Patricia has been voted Peer of the Year and Parliamentarian of the Year.

Patricia continues to sit in the House of Lords and is Chancellor of Greenwich University.

### Sajid Javid MP – politician

Sajid was born in London and is one of five sons; his father is a bus driver. Sajid went to state schools before studying Economics and Politics at Exeter University.

At the age of 24, Sajid became a Vice President of Chase Manhattan Bank. He was later headhunted by Deutsche Bank in London to help build its business in poorer countries. He left that role in 2009 to enter politics and was elected as Conservative MP for Bromsgrove the following year.

In 2014, Sajid became the first British Asian MP to lead a government department when he was appointed Secretary of State for Culture, Media and Sport and Minister for Equalities. Following two further political promotions, including to the Cabinet, the Prime Minister appointed Sajid as Secretary of State for Business, Innovation and Skills in 2015.

Sajid has been involved in community work all his life, raising money for the Disaster's Emergency Committee and hiking to the summit of Mount Kilimanjaro.

### Shazia Mirza – comedian and writer

A trained biochemist, Shazia was born and educated in Birmingham – the daughter of first-generation Pakistani immigrants. Raised in a strict Muslim family, Shazia first became a science teacher whilst secretly developing her writing, acting and comedy skills part-time at drama school and through late-night gigs across the country.

Shazia writes extensively and her articles have appeared regularly in the *New Statesman*, *The Guardian*, *Observer* and Virgin's *Hotline* magazine.

In March 2009, Shazia was listed as one of the twenty most successful Muslim women in the UK and, by 2015, had built her reputation as one of the UK's leading comedians and writers.

### Activity

5.  Carry out further research on the contributions made by people from different ethnic origins to business, the public services, science and technology, national defence, the media, entertainment, politics or sport. Work with other learners to design a presentation celebrating the range of achievement revealed by your research.

# Migration and asylum

## Key learning

Study the reasons for migration, and the broad patterns of migration into and out of the UK in the last 60 years. Understand why people seek asylum. Study the main benefits and challenges of immigration to the UK and its impact on communities. Evaluate different viewpoints on the control of immigration to the UK.

## Why do people migrate from one place to another?

The movement of people (**migration**) from one place to another is normal. Try some research on your own family or one that you know. Where do grandparents, aunts, uncles and cousins live? Have they always lived in the same place? What were their reasons for moving? The family tree below helps to tell one family's story.

**Migration**   Moving from one place to another.

**Figure 11.6** Migration – one family's story over three generations

**Grandparents**

**Archie**
Born in Aberdeen, Scotland. Met Susan on holiday in Wales. Moved to Birmingham to be close to Susan's family. Now retired to Scarborough in Yorkshire.

**Susan**
Born in Birmingham. Lived there all her life but now retired to Scarborough with Archie.

**Marlon**
Born in Jamaica but moved to Florida to get a better job. Met Kate in Florida, moved to London with her and became a British citizen.

**Kate**
Born in Germany where parents were based (father in the army). Moved back to London but spent time working in the USA where she met Marlon.

**Parents**

**Tom**
Born in Birmingham but moved to London to go to college. Now a self-employed plumber in Brighton where the family moved because housing was cheaper than London.

**Rose**
Met Tom in Spain where she was working for a travel company. Now works in a bank in Brighton. She has a sister who emigrated to Canada with her family.

**Children**

**Archie**
Went to university in Edinburgh. Now works in China teaching English.

**Alicia**
At college in Scarborough where she lives with her grandparents to keep costs down.

**Beatrice**
On a gap year in Australia. Now has a boyfriend over there and may decide to stay.

## Activity

1. Find out about the migration experiences of your family or friends. Show their journeys on a map and explain their reasons for moving.

**Figure 11.7** Migration explained

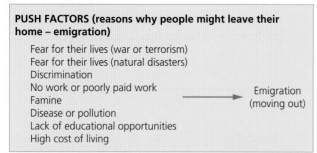

**PUSH FACTORS (reasons why people might leave their home – emigration)**

Fear for their lives (war or terrorism)
Fear for their lives (natural disasters)
Discrimination
No work or poorly paid work
Famine
Disease or pollution
Lack of educational opportunities
High cost of living

→ Emigration (moving out)

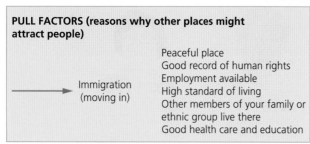

**PULL FACTORS (reasons why other places might attract people)**

Immigration (moving in) →

Peaceful place
Good record of human rights
Employment available
High standard of living
Other members of your family or ethnic group live there
Good health care and education

## Patterns of UK migration

The UK's history helps explain the country's cultural diversity. The UK has been a great trading nation for many hundreds of years. During the eighteenth and early nineteenth centuries, much of this trade involved the buying and selling of slaves. Ships from Bristol and Liverpool carried cargoes of people from Africa to the Caribbean and USA. One result of this trade was the growth of small black communities in Bristol, Cardiff and Liverpool over 200 years ago. At the same time, refugees from Europe had come to the UK to settle in cities such as London, Hull and Norwich.

Throughout this period, the UK was **colonising** land all across the world. This brought great wealth and influence to the UK. The Indian subcontinent, large parts of Africa, most of the Caribbean and even parts of Asia were under British control by the end of the nineteenth century. People across this **British Empire** were encouraged to think of Queen Victoria as their monarch, to learn English and to see the world from a British point of view. Many residents of the British Empire were given rights to a British passport and to live in the UK if they wanted to.

**Colony**   Land overseas governed and controlled by another country.

**British Empire**   Countries governed and controlled by the UK.

One of the largest nineteenth and early twentieth century migrations to the UK was from Ireland as people escaped from widespread famine and unemployment. Irish immigrants helped to build the

# CASE STUDY

## Migration from Syria – one of the largest movements of people in history

A violent civil war in Syria started in 2011. By 2016, nearly five million Syrians had been forced to leave their country for safety in neighbouring Turkey, Jordan, Lebanon or Iraq. Most sheltered in camps where conditions were poor. For many it seemed unlikely that they would ever be able to return to their homes.

The United Nations, the British Government and aid agencies such as Oxfam and Save the Children had supported refugees in the camps by providing food, shelter, health care and education. But Syrians were desperate for a new life and many hundreds of thousands began to make the long journey to Europe in order to find work, housing and a brighter future.

European countries found it almost impossible to cope with the overwhelming number of desperate migrants.

**Figure 11.8** Migrants, trying to reach EU countries, walk near the Greek border at the city of Gevgelija

UK's canals, railways, docks and roads, as well as the homes needed for an expanding population.

**Figure 11.9** Map showing the main areas of the UK where immigrants settled 1950–90

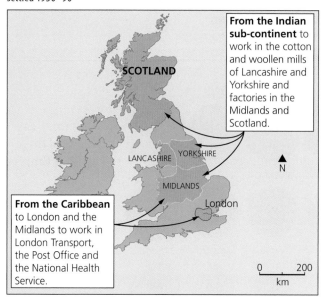

Persecution of minority groups throughout Europe at this time resulted in refugees seeking a new home in the UK. Jewish people, in particular, made their homes here after seeking refuge from discrimination, violence and death in Russia, Eastern Europe, Germany and France.

During the twentieth century, most British colonies gained their independence and joined the British Commonwealth (see Chapter 12 for more details). When additional workers were needed in the UK after the Second World War in 1945, it made sense to recruit labour from these former British territories. People were keen to start a new life in what many regarded as their 'mother country'. Large numbers of immigrants arrived from British Commonwealth countries from 1950 through to 1990.

Free movement of workers within the European Union (see Chapter 12 for more details) has resulted in many thousands of young people coming to the UK for work, particularly from Eastern Europe and France. London and the south-east of England have also been popular destinations for **immigrants** from Australia and the USA, most of whom have helped to fill vacancies for skilled workers. Recently there has been an increase in **asylum** applications

by refugees – adding further to the numbers of people coming to live here (see page 173).

The number of immigrants to the UK for the year ending November 2015 was a record 636,000. The Government was committed to reducing these numbers.

**Figure 11.10** In 1949, the *SS Empire Windrush* brought one of the first groups of immigrants from the Caribbean to the UK. They filled job vacancies in London after the Second World War

**Figure 11.11** Most towns have several shops serving the needs of recent immigrants to the UK

**Immigration**   Arriving in a country.

**Asylum**   Refuge and protection from discrimination or violence.

169

**Figure 11.12** Top ten countries of birth for people living in the UK but born overseas
(Adapted from Office for National Statistics data (2014))

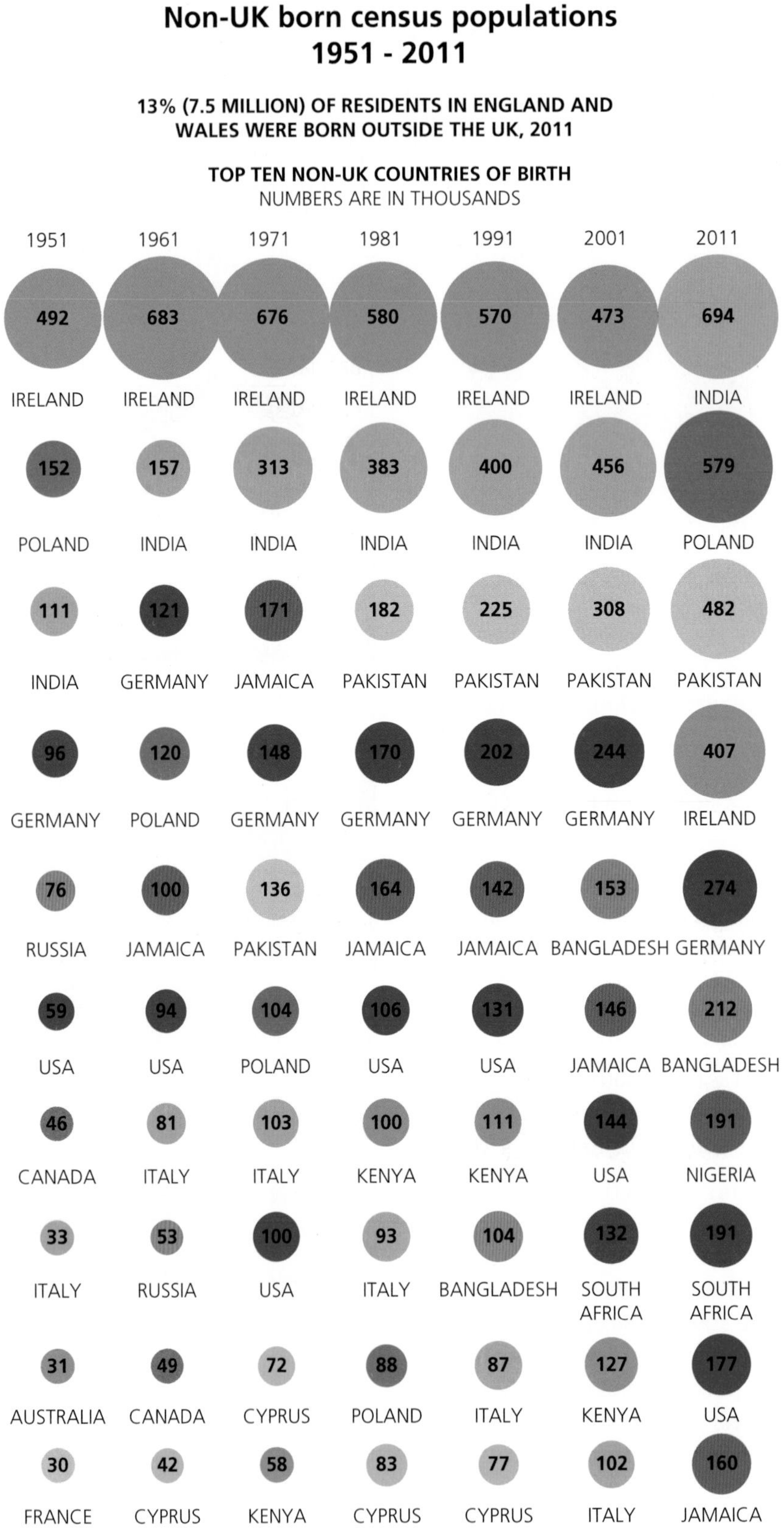

# Non-UK born census populations
# 1951 - 2011

**13% (7.5 MILLION) OF RESIDENTS IN ENGLAND AND
WALES WERE BORN OUTSIDE THE UK, 2011**

**TOP TEN NON-UK COUNTRIES OF BIRTH**
NUMBERS ARE IN THOUSANDS

| 1951 | 1961 | 1971 | 1981 | 1991 | 2001 | 2011 |
|---|---|---|---|---|---|---|
| 492 | 683 | 676 | 580 | 570 | 473 | 694 |
| IRELAND | IRELAND | IRELAND | IRELAND | IRELAND | IRELAND | INDIA |
| 152 | 157 | 313 | 383 | 400 | 456 | 579 |
| POLAND | INDIA | INDIA | INDIA | INDIA | INDIA | POLAND |
| 111 | 121 | 171 | 182 | 225 | 308 | 482 |
| INDIA | GERMANY | JAMAICA | PAKISTAN | PAKISTAN | PAKISTAN | PAKISTAN |
| 96 | 120 | 148 | 170 | 202 | 244 | 407 |
| GERMANY | POLAND | GERMANY | GERMANY | GERMANY | GERMANY | IRELAND |
| 76 | 100 | 136 | 164 | 142 | 153 | 274 |
| RUSSIA | JAMAICA | PAKISTAN | JAMAICA | JAMAICA | BANGLADESH | GERMANY |
| 59 | 94 | 104 | 106 | 131 | 146 | 212 |
| USA | USA | POLAND | USA | USA | JAMAICA | BANGLADESH |
| 46 | 81 | 103 | 100 | 111 | 144 | 191 |
| CANADA | ITALY | ITALY | KENYA | KENYA | USA | NIGERIA |
| 33 | 53 | 100 | 93 | 104 | 132 | 191 |
| ITALY | RUSSIA | USA | ITALY | BANGLADESH | SOUTH AFRICA | SOUTH AFRICA |
| 31 | 49 | 72 | 88 | 87 | 127 | 177 |
| AUSTRALIA | CANADA | CYPRUS | POLAND | ITALY | KENYA | USA |
| 30 | 42 | 58 | 83 | 77 | 102 | 160 |
| FRANCE | CYPRUS | KENYA | CYPRUS | CYPRUS | ITALY | JAMAICA |

**Figure 11.13** Reasons for migration to the UK 2014 (migrants born overseas) (Adapted from Office for National Statistics data)

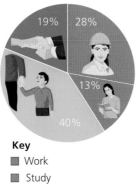

**Key**

- ■ Work
- ■ Study
- ■ Accompanying or joining a partner or parent
- ■ Visiting, marriage or civil partnership

**Activity**

2. Design a chart or slide to show which groups of people have come to the UK, when they came and their reasons for coming.

## Emigration from the UK

Migration has not been 'one way traffic', particularly during the last 70 years. Tens of thousands of UK citizens have **emigrated** to the USA, Canada, South Africa, Australia and New Zealand in search of more skilled work and a higher standard of living.

Thousands of Britain's students and workers have taken advantage of their right as EU citizens to study or work anywhere in the EU.

**Emigration**   Leaving a country.

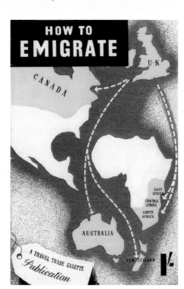

**Figure 11.14** Many UK citizens have emigrated to find a better life overseas. This guide was published to help them

UK senior citizens have emigrated to southern Europe in search of warmer weather and a less expensive way of life. This form of emigration has become more attractive since the UK joined the EU, especially as UK citizens can receive their pensions and some free health care while living overseas.

**Table 11.2** Most popular destinations for emigrants from the UK (2013)

| European Union | 114,000 |
|---|---|
| Australia | 44,000 |
| USA | 24,000 |
| India, Pakistan and Bangladesh | 24,000 |
| Middle East | 14,000 |
| Europe (non-EU countries) | 12,000 |
| Canada | 11,000 |
| New Zealand | 10,000 |

(Adapted from Office for National Statistics data)

300,000 people emigrated in the year ending November 2015, some of whom were returning home after working or studying in the UK.

## Net migration

Net migration is the difference between numbers of people arriving in the UK (immigration) and people leaving (emigration). In the twelve months to November 2015, net migration was 336,000. Net migration figures help us to track the effect of migration on population growth.

**UK migration, November 2014 – November 2015**

| Immigration | – | Emigration | = | Net migration |
|---|---|---|---|---|
| 636,000 | – | 300,000 | = | 336,000 |

## Impact of migration on UK population

In 2015, the Office for National Statistics (ONS) made some predictions about the possible effects of migration on the UK population. This is shown in the graph in Figure 11.16 on page 172.

The ONS has made population projections based on different levels of net migration. If net migration was reduced to zero, the population would rise gradually from 65 million in 2016 to 67 million by 2031.

**Figure 11.15** Net migration (UK) 1975 to 2015

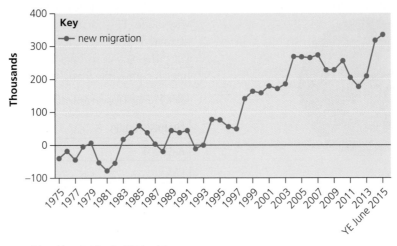

Adapted from the Migration Watch website

**Figure 11.16** UK-population projections based on different levels of net migration

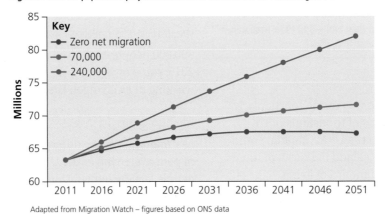

Adapted from Migration Watch – figures based on ONS data

On the other hand, if net migration continues at 240,000 (the average of the last ten years), then the population is expected to rise by 2.5 million over the next five years and to reach 73 million by 2031; an increase of 8 million people in fifteen years. This would have a considerable impact on the Government's plans for future public services.

### Activity

3. Explain why net migration has increased in the UK over the last twenty years.

## Seeking asylum

When people seek asylum, they are asking for refuge or protection. A person needing refuge is known as a refugee. Refugees feel unable to return to their country. They have a realistic fear that they or members of their family may be killed, injured, tortured, imprisoned or subjected to unreasonable discrimination. There are nearly twenty million people worldwide who are now receiving protection in this way.

People often migrate for **economic** and family reasons. Refugees do not have this choice. Refugees are forced to leave and need help. This type of migration is often known as **political migration**. One hundred and forty seven countries across the world have signed the 1951 United Nations Convention Relating to the Status of Refugees giving refugees the right to protection in their territories.

The United Kingdom has a long record of providing refuge for people who have had to leave their own country because of discrimination or threats to their lives. The first refugees were from Europe but, more recently, people from the Middle East, Asia and Africa have asked for asylum in the UK.

**Economic migration**   Moving from one place to another to improve standards of living.

**Political migration**   Moving from one country to another to improve human rights.

However, the UK government refuses protection to those who are thought not to need it and removes asylum seekers who are found to have made false claims.

## People seek refuge in the UK because:

- The UK has a good record on human rights. (See Chapter 1 for more details.)
- English is spoken across the world and is a familiar language to many people.
- People belonging to the asylum seeker's ethnic group may already live somewhere in the UK.
- The UK is a wealthy country that can afford to support asylum seekers.
- Jobs are available in the UK. Many of these jobs are unskilled and it is not always necessary for applicants to speak good English.
- People who live in the UK have a right to housing, education and health care.

In 2014, 38 out of every 100 people who applied for asylum were recognised as refugees and given asylum. Another four out of every 100 who applied for asylum,

but did not qualify for refugee status, were given permission to stay for humanitarian or other reasons.

In 2015 there were almost 30,000 applications for asylum in the UK. In the same year, the UK Government arranged to take a further 5,000 refugees each year up to 2020 as part of an international effort to help people escaping civil war in Syria.

**Does the UK have more asylum seekers than most countries?**

With an estimated 173,100 asylum applications, Germany was the largest recipient of new asylum claims in 2014. The USA was second with 121,200 asylum applications, followed by Turkey (87,800), Sweden (75,100), and Italy (63,700).

(Source: United Nations High Commission on Refugees [UNHCR] 2014 Asylum Trends Report)

**Where do asylum seekers in the UK come from?**

The top three countries of origin are: Eritrea (3,568), Pakistan (2,302), and Syria (2,204). The vast majority of refugees stay in their region of displacement. This means that 86 per cent of the world's refugees are hosted by poorer countries. Turkey now hosts the highest number of refugees at 1.6 million, followed by Pakistan at 1.5 million.

(Source: Office for National Statistics Migration Statistics Quarterly Report, August 2015, and UNHCR 2014 Global Trends Report)

## Asylum seekers' rights and responsibilities

The UK Border Agency, the public body responsible for dealing with asylum and immigration, sets out rights and responsibilities for people claiming asylum in the UK, as shown in the two boxes on page 174.

**Figure 11.17** Asylum applications to the UK 2004–15 (Adapted from ONS data)

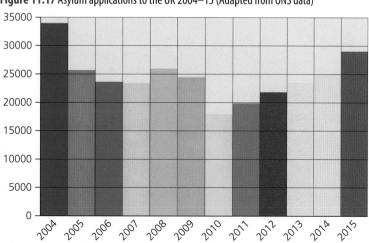

**Asylum seekers' rights in the United Kingdom**

- Fair and lawful treatment regardless of race, gender, age, religion, sexual orientation or any disability.
- Freedom of religion and the responsibility to show respect to people of other faiths.
- Fair and accurate consideration of asylum claims.
- Support and accommodation.
- Free health care from the National Health Service (NHS).
- Legal representation and financial support to pay for legal help if necessary.

Deportation   Being returned to a country of origin.

**Asylum seekers' responsibilities in the United Kingdom**

- Co-operating with the UK Border Agency and telling the truth. (It is a crime to make a false asylum application. A false claim could lead to imprisonment and **deportation**).
- Making regular contact with the Border Agency.
- Obeying the law.
- Caring for children (an adult must always supervise children under the age of sixteen, and if they are aged between five and sixteen they must have full-time education, usually at school).
- Leaving the UK if an asylum application is refused.

# CASE STUDY

## United Nations High Commission for Refugees (UNHCR)

UNCHR's mission is to make sure that everybody has the right to seek asylum and find safe refuge, if they have had to escape from violence, persecution, war or disaster at home.

Since 1950, UNHCR has faced multiple crises across continents and provides vital assistance to refugees, asylum-seekers, internally displaced and stateless people, many of whom have nobody left to turn to. UNHCR, with support from governments and citizens across the world, helps to save lives and build better futures for millions forced from home.

## Website

UNHCR is the United Nations Refugee Agency. On their website you will find the real stories of refugees and their life-threatening sea journeys: **http://stories.unhcr.org/**

## Activity

4. Browse the UNHCR's collection of refugee stories at **http://stories.unhcr.org/**. Choose one of your favourite stories and summarise it for presentation to your class. Include the following in your presentation:
   - an explanation of why the refugee left home
   - a description of where they travelled and what happened to them
   - a description of where they settled and what they did there
   - an evaluation of their whole experience.

**Figure 11.18** Lesbos, Greece, 25 August 2015. An inflatable boat carrying some fifty refugees approaches the shore on the northeastern part of Lesbos. More than 30,000 refugees reached the Greek island during August 2015, according to Amnesty International

## British citizenship

People can apply for British citizenship as long as they:

- are 18 or older
- do not have a serious or recent criminal record and have not broken any immigration laws
- intend to continue to live in the UK
- have passed the English-language and citizenship tests
- have lived in the UK for at least five years and have been granted the right to stay.

British Citizenship gives people important rights including:

- living permanently in the UK
- leaving and re-entering the UK at any time, without any restriction
- protection and assistance while overseas
- all the legal rights granted by the UK to its citizens including the right to vote.

### Activity

5. Research two further case studies of asylum-seekers' own experiences and use these to help you explain why people seek asylum.

## The migration debate

### Supporting migration

### An economic view

According to John Cridland, former Director-General of the Confederation for British Industry (CBI), migration brings major benefits to the UK particularly at a time of economic growth.

- 63 per cent of CBI members say that free movement of labour within the EU has been beneficial for their business.
- Many migrants are well-educated and solve labour shortages in sectors such as IT and engineering.
- UK hospitals and care homes could not function without overseas workers. Housebuilding and big infrastructure projects, such as the roll-out of broadband, would also stall.
- It is a myth that migrants come to the UK for our benefits system rather than to work. Data from the ONS shows two-thirds of EU citizens in the year to 2013 migrated for work, and a fifth for study. Research from University College London shows that an average EU migrant pays over £2,700 more in taxes annually than they receive in benefits.

### A political view

The Green Party is more supportive of immigration than any other political party. It argues that it is inevitable that people want to escape the effects of global warming, environmental degradation and shortages of resources. The Green Party believes that international action and a willingness to share resources are needed to meet migrants' needs. The Greens argue that richer countries have no right to protect their privileges from others by using migration controls.

Green Party policy is to:

- support development in poorer countries to reduce the need for migration
- reduce UK immigration controls.

*We value the cultural diversity and intercultural awareness resulting from both temporary residence and migration.*

Green Party policy statement, 2015

## Restricting migration

### An economic view

Migration Watch is an independent policy institute and pressure group. Migration Watch believes that, 'At present immigration is neither sustainable nor well managed'.

Migration Watch points out that England is already one of the most overcrowded countries in the world, with a population density of 410 people per square kilometre. Among its economic concerns are:

- Rapid population growth has made it difficult to provide public services such as education.
- Migrant women have a higher fertility rate than women born in the UK and so place an extra burden on maternity healthcare – more than one in four babies born in England and Wales in 2014 was to a migrant mother.
- Strains are being placed on public transport and roads.
- Adequate housing will have to be built to accommodate all the extra people, either by making our urban areas more overcrowded or by building on green field sites.

### A political view

Both UKIP and the Conservative Party have responded to public concerns by promising to reduce immigration. Both parties would continue to grant asylum to those refugees protected by international law. UKIP would go furthest to control the numbers of migrants coming to work and study in the UK. At the general election of 2015, UKIP's policy was to return immigration to what it described as 'normal levels' by:

- leaving the EU so that EU citizens would no longer have a right to work and study in the UK
- allowing only workers with essential skills to move to the UK with permission to stay for five years.

In February 2016, the Prime Minister negotiated with the leaders of other European member states to reduce immigration from the EU to the UK. He hoped to do this by cutting the welfare benefits to EU immigrants working in the UK.

*'The fact is that in scores of our cities and market towns, this country in a short space of time has frankly become unrecognisable. Whether it is the impact on local schools and hospitals, whether it is the fact in many parts of England you don't hear English spoken any more, this is not the kind of community we want to leave to our children and grandchildren.'*

Nigel Farage, Leader of UKIP, 2014

## Public opinion

Opinion polls show consistently high levels of public concern about immigration. However, the public also has positive things to say about multi-cultural Britain.

- 65 per cent were worried about the level of immigration to the UK, while 31 per cent were not worried and 4 per cent did not know (YouGov poll for Channel 5, 2014).
- 31 per cent thought immigration had had a good or very good impact on the economy, 20 per cent thought its impact was neither good nor bad and 47 per cent thought that immigration had had a bad or very bad impact (British Social Attitudes Survey, 2014).
- The British Attitudes Survey of 2013 found that 40 per cent of respondents thought that immigrants had improved British society by bringing new ideas and cultures, compared to 33 per cent in 2003.
- 53 per cent of respondents thought that a variety of cultures and backgrounds had strengthened the UK (YouGov poll, 2013).

**Table 11.3** Positive views on immigration and its effects according to an IPSOS/MORI poll in 2011

| Immigration's effect on: | Positive responses (%) | Negative responses (%) |
|---|---|---|
| Food and restaurants | 68 | 8 |
| Business start ups | 47 | 11 |
| Premier League football | 38 | 13 |
| Films and music | 36 | 7 |
| Art and literature | 32 | 6 |
| Media | 25 | 14 |

## Websites

The Office for National Statistics (ONS) provides a series of charts and interactive graphs to show UK migration patterns from 1975 onwards:
**http://www.neighbourhood.statistics.gov.uk/HTMLDocs/dvc215/index.html**

For a history of immigration, some of the latest statistics and arguments for reducing immigration, try the Migration Watch website:
**http://www.migrationwatchuk.org/**

UNHCR is the United Nations Refugee Agency. It helps to coordinate international action to support refugees and gathers worldwide information about people seeking protection:
**http://www.unhcr.org/pages/49c3646c125.html**

Refugee Action is a pressure group that supports asylum seekers. Its website contains information about refugees, their rights and their personal stories:
**http://www.refugee-action.org.uk/**

### Activities

6.  Research the benefits and challenges of migration in your community.
    a)  Describe the main migrations into and out of your community.
    b)  Explain these patterns.
    c)  Describe the benefits and challenges of migration for your community.
7.  Evaluate the viewpoint that further immigration to the UK should be stopped.

# Building cohesive communities

### Key learning

Study the importance of cohesive communities in a democratic society and understand how to promote community cohesion. Analyse and evaluate citizen actions that improve community cohesion. (See also Chapter 9.)

## The importance of community cohesion

**Community cohesion** means people sharing values and goals and living together well. Community cohesion is at its strongest when people have the opportunity and the capacity to participate in their community as much as they want and on an equal footing with others.

In a neighbourhood with high levels of community cohesion, you might find:

*   People of all ages out on the streets without fear.
*   Tidy streets, gardens, parks and public areas.
*   Houses and flats lived in and cared for.
*   People mixing in shops, cafes and parks.
*   Successful schools, libraries and community centres with lots of services for the whole community.
*   Low levels of discrimination and racism.

**Figure 11.19** This street of well-kept, brightly-painted houses shows that people have a pride in their community

In a neighbourhood with low levels of community cohesion, you might find:

*   People afraid to leave their homes, especially at night.
*   Vandalism, graffiti and litter.
*   Houses and flats empty.
*   People going to particular shops and cafes to avoid other groups.
*   Failing schools with little provision for the community.
*   High levels of discrimination and racism.

**Community cohesion** Neighbours living together with respect and cooperation.

**Figure 11.20** Litter, garden rubbish and houses needing repair are often indicators of low community cohesion

**Figure 11.21** Most football clubs in the UK run community programmes

## Promoting community cohesion

UK governments have been keen to promote community cohesion. It is widely accepted that a more equal society is more cohesive and at ease with itself. The Equality Act of 2010 gave all public authorities a legal responsibility to promote equality of opportunity and foster good relations between different groups of people. The Act also made it necessary for all public authorities to publish equalities data on their workforce and services. (See Chapter 2 for more details.)

National initiatives to devolve more power and influence to a local level can also help to empower individuals and communities, encouraging social responsibility and influencing change at a local level. (See Chapter 5 for more details.)

In addition, government, local authorities, businesses and charities all support projects and programmes to improve community cohesion.

The National Citizen Service (NCS) is one example of a government programme to promote community cohesion. (See Chapter 9 for more details.)

**Figure 11.22** Local authorities often promote community cohesion by encouraging people to have a say in the decisions that affect their communities

## Local authorities promote community cohesion

Many local authorities help to co-ordinate or facilitate a community cohesion strategy in their communities.

This usually starts with the formation of a working group or committee bringing together faith groups, the police, sports clubs and other community groups. Their mission is to promote equalities and fairness, and help the whole community to gain the confidence to change things for the better. Only with local residents' personal involvement can communities become more cohesive. Clear goals and effective communication are essential for overall success.

**Table 11.4** Typical local authority community cohesions goals and strategies

| Goals | Local authority actions | What local people can do |
|---|---|---|
| Increase people's pride in their community | Involve local people in decision-making | Make the most of opportunities to make your voice heard and get others to do the same |
| Give people access to a wider range of life chances | Provide English language classes and citizenship classes for immigrants | Encourage your children to be positive about school and join local clubs |
| Encourage people to value diversity and get on with their neighbours | Help organise community events to celebrate diversity and bring people together | Welcome and respect your neighbours. Report anti-social behaviour |
| Make sure people are active in helping to make their community more cohesive | Take appropriate legal action against anti-social residents | Oppose discrimination and racism whenever you see it |

### Website

Find out more about Slough's community cohesion strategy at: **http://www.slough.gov.uk/council/strategies-plans-and-policies/community-cohesion.aspx**

### Activities

1. Study Table 11.4. List five additional actions residents could take to help improve community cohesion in their area. Compare your lists with other learners and devise five recommendations for possible action in your own community. Ask your teacher for support in organising a meeting with your local councillor. Discuss your recommendations.
2. Community cohesion strategies focus on what could be achieved by the local authority or police and what could be achieved by residents themselves. Explain why both are important.

# CASE STUDY

## The Prince's Trust – a national charity promoting community cohesion by supporting young people

## Prince's Trust

According to the Prince's Trust, 'around one in eight young people in the UK are not in work, education or training. Youth unemployment costs the UK economy £10 million a day in lost productivity, while youth crime costs £1 billion every year.'

That's why the Prince's Trust supports thirteen to thirty-year-olds who are unemployed, and those struggling at school and at risk of exclusion. Many of the young people helped by the Prince's Trust are in or are just leaving care, facing issues such as homelessness or mental health problems, or have been in trouble with the law.

Prince's Trust programmes give young people the confidence, skills, and practical and financial support they need to move successfully into work, education or training.

## Example of Prince's Trust project from north-west England – *Donna's Dream House*

Young people with lives blighted by unemployment and underachievement found themselves united by a Prince's Trust project to help terminally ill children and their families. Spurred on by a shared goal, they changed their own lives while helping others.

Fifteen young people aged 17–25 came together on a twelve-week personal development course which helps unemployed young people to turn their lives around and find work, training or education.

Benefitting the local community is a key part of the Team programme, and the young people quickly decided to help a Blackpool charity, *Donna's Dream House*. The charity provides free holidays for terminally ill children and their families, but had been hit by a recent arson attack. The Team members decided to help rebuild the Dream House by designing and constructing a new relaxation area with a beautiful pagoda.

Stepping outside their comfort zones, the group sought expertise and funding from local businesses, and put in hard physical work day after day. The media coverage they attracted proved crucial in raising the necessary funding and support to rebuild this desperately needed facility for local people.

Everyone was bursting with pride the day *Donna's Dream House* finally reopened bigger and better than before, giving families and their terminally ill children a place they can escape to and create happy memories they will always cherish.

'The project at *Donna's Dream House* got me motivated to get up in the morning and get my life back on track', says Michael Naylor, a Team member. Since the project, every Team member has pursued training, further education or volunteering opportunities – including Michael, who returned to *Donna's Dream House* as a volunteer.

(Adapted from the Prince's Trust website)

## Website

Find out more about the Prince's Trust and its work at: **http://princes-trust.org.uk/**

## Activities

3. Describe successful actions taken in your school or college to improve community cohesion.
4. Describe projects or programmes run by the Prince's Trust in your area. (Check the map on their website for the nearest activities.)
5. Describe and evaluate the work of your local authority, the police or a local community organisation to promote community cohesion in your area. Describe what else could be done by residents themselves and how they could be encouraged to take these actions.

## Practice questions

In the OCR specification, this section will be assessed using objective test questions and questions needing a written response. The following are examples of questions that require a short written answer and a question needing an extended response. All four questions are based on Sources 1 and 2 on page 182.

Study **Sources 1** and **2** on page 182. Answer the questions below.

1. State two pieces of evidence in **Source 1** that could be used **against** the following viewpoint: 'UK has more than its fair share of immigrants.' [2 marks]

2. State one additional piece of information that would need to be **added** to the diagram in **Source 2** to **bring it up to date**. [1 mark]

3. Describe one additional piece of information that could be **added** to the diagram in **Source 2** for it to show **net migration**. [1 mark]

4. Use information from both sources to help you make a case **against** the following viewpoint: 'Most migrants to the UK have come for a better quality of life. For example, this explains the massive wave of immigration from Ireland – a country that accepts very few immigrants today.' [8 marks]

# Source 1

## Immigrants in European countries for every 1000 inhabitants

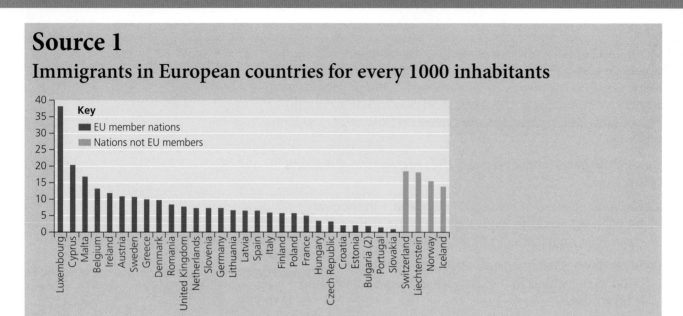

# Source 2

## Key waves of UK immigration

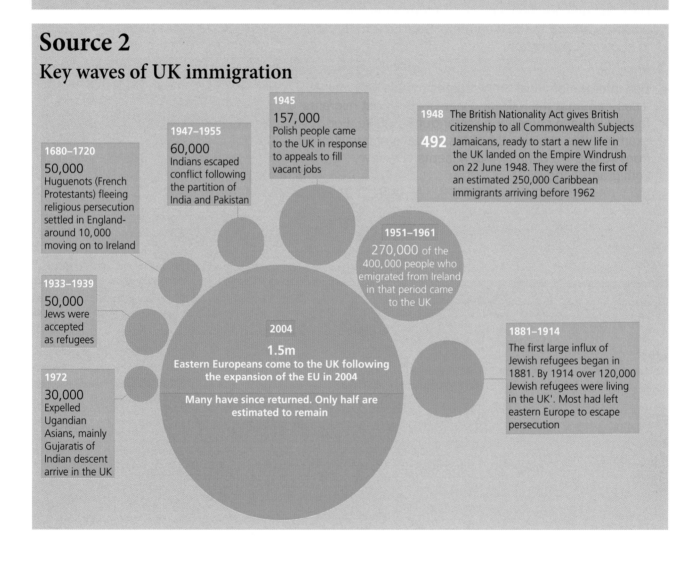

**1680–1720**

**50,000** Huguenots (French Protestants) fleeing religious persecution settled in England- around 10,000 moving on to Ireland

**1933–1939**

**50,000** Jews were accepted as refugees

**1972**

**30,000** Expelled Ugandian Asians, mainly Gujaratis of Indian descent arrive in the UK

**1947–1955**

**60,000** Indians escaped conflict following the partition of India and Pakistan

**1945**

**157,000** Polish people came to the UK in response to appeals to fill vacant jobs

**2004**

**1.5m**

Eastern Europeans come to the UK following the expansion of the EU in 2004

Many have since returned. Only half are estimated to remain

**1951–1961**

**270,000** of the 400,000 people who emigrated from Ireland in that period came to the UK

**1948** The British Nationality Act gives British citizenship to all Commonwealth Subjects

**492** Jamaicans, ready to start a new life in the UK landed on the Empire Windrush on 22 June 1948. They were the first of an estimated 250,000 Caribbean immigrants arriving before 1962

**1881–1914**

The first large influx of Jewish refugees began in 1881. By 1914 over 120,000 Jewish refugees were living in the UK'. Most had left eastern Europe to escape persecution

# Chapter 12:
# The UK and its relations with the wider world

This chapter on *The UK and its relations with the wider world* builds on Chapter 1, *Rights and responsibilities* and Chapter 9, *Citizen participation in the UK and taking citizenship action*.

In this chapter, we consider the UK's international role and evaluate our changing partnerships and alliances with other countries. We will also take a more detailed look at two international organisations – the European Union (EU) and the United Nations (UN).

Learning the following key concepts and terms will make it easier to organise your thinking and communicate your ideas:
- international organisation
- Commonwealth
- Council of Europe (COE)
- European Union (EU)
- North Atlantic Treaty Organization (NATO)
- United Nations (UN)
- World Trade Organization (WTO)
- mediation
- sanction
- intervention
- non-governmental organisation
- International Humanitarian Law.

# International partnerships

## Key learning
Study the purpose of those international organisations that include the UK as a member. Understand why the organisations were established and the role played by the UK in each of them.

International partnerships are important for peace and prosperity. Governments work together for economic, political, social and environmental reasons. Cooperation reduces the risk of conflict. It also enables individuals, organisations and businesses to share expertise and work on joint development projects.

**Figure 12.1** Without international cooperation over trade, there would be far less choice for UK consumers

The United Nations (UN) is the largest, most important and most widely known **international organisation** in the world. Through the UN, countries cooperate to promote peace and prosperity. Almost all nations are members of the UN, but most also have membership of a range of other political and economic international organisations.

> **International organisation** A group of countries that agree political and economic priorities, and set up structures (organisations) that enable them to work together on joint projects.

### Activity
1. List the advantages for the UK of belonging to international organisations.

**Organisation: Commonwealth**

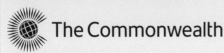 The Commonwealth

**Foundation year**: 1931. Established to maintain relationships between the UK and its former colonies as they became independent nations.

**Purpose**: Encourages and safeguards:

- cultural understanding
- links between people and communities
- democracy
- human rights
- economic development
- sport (through events such as the Commonwealth Games)
- improve the quality of teaching and school leadership in all member nations.

**Membership**: 53 developed or developing countries with historic ties to the UK – most are former British colonies. The Commonwealth is often described as a 'family of nations'.

**UK contribution**: The UK was a founding member. Each member country has an equal say in decision-making. All member nations make a financial contribution towards the Commonwealth's costs. As a wealthy member country, the UK pays a larger membership contribution than the less prosperous members. The British Monarch is Head of the Commonwealth and also Head of State for many of the Commonwealth nations.

**Government policy** (2016): Strengthen the Commonwealth to promote democracy in its 53 member states. Encourage the Commonwealth Secretariat to strengthen its institutions, so it can do more to promote human rights, democratic values and the rule of law. Support sustainable development across the Commonwealth.

**Organisation: European Union (EU)**

**Foundation year**: 1957. The EU's predecessor organisation was founded in 1951 with six member countries. Its aim was to prevent another European war by encouraging greater cooperation and union. The UK joined in 1973.

**Purpose**: Encourages and safeguards:

- cross-border trade and cooperation
- economic development
- political cooperation between member states
- security
- cultural links and exchanges.

**Membership**: 28 European countries including wealthy nations such as the UK, Germany and France as well as less prosperous countries such as Bulgaria, Greece and Poland.

**UK contribution**: UK Government ministers hold regular meetings with their European counterparts. 78 MEPs represent the UK in the European Parliament. The UK makes a financial contribution to the EU. This was £11 billion in 2015 (11 per cent of the total EU budget.) The UK also receives around £7 billion in rebates and grants from the EU, making the annual net contribution around £4 billion. Each member country's contribution reflects its ability to pay.

**Government policy** (2016): The Government is against the 'ever closer union' favoured by some EU member countries. The UK did not adopt the Euro (European single currency) and has no plans to do so. In February 2016, the Prime Minister negotiated greater independence from the EU and, as part of the Government's policy, arranged a referendum on the UK's continued membership to take place the following June.

**Organisation: Council of Europe (COE)**

**Foundation year**: 1949. Established after the Second World War to promote human rights and justice for all European citizens, and prevent threats to democracy.

**Purpose**: Europe's leading human rights organisation which also supports democracy and the rule of law.

The European Court of Human Rights (ECtHR) enforces the European Convention on Human Rights (ECHR) (see Chapter 1 for more details).

**Membership**: 47 member states from Europe, including all 28 members of the EU. All COE members have signed up to the ECHR. (See Chapter 1 for more details.)

**UK contribution**: The UK was a founding member and has a permanent representative on the COE to represent British interests.

**Government policy** (2016): Increase the effectiveness of the COE and the UK's influence within it. Encourage the COE to do more to improve human rights, democracy and respect for the rule of law.

**Organisation: North Atlantic Treaty Organization (NATO)**

**Foundation year**: 1949. Established after the Second World War as a counterweight to Russia and its allies.

**Purpose**: A military alliance of Western democratic countries. Each country in the alliance agrees to support any other NATO member that is attacked.

**Membership**: 28 independent member countries in Europe and North America. Turkey is also a member of NATO.

**UK contribution**: The UK was one of twelve founding members. UK military commanders contribute to NATO's defence planning. UK armed and civilian personnel contribute to NATO. The UK is the second largest contributor of personnel and weapons to support NATO-led operations.

**Government policy** (2016): NATO membership is the main element of the UK's defence policy and strategy. The UK will work with NATO partners to respond effectively to security threats and crises.

**Organisation: World Trade Organization (WTO)**

**Foundation year**: 1995. The WTO's predecessor organisation was established after the Second World War to encourage trade and prosperity.

**Purpose**: The WTO enables member countries to agree the rules of world trade, settle any trading disputes fairly and promote free trade. WTO's aim is to help producers of goods and services, exporters, and importers to trade efficiently.

**Membership**: 162 member states including More Economically Developed Countries (MEDCs) and **Less Economically Developed Countries (LEDCs)** from all continents.

**UK contribution**: The UK, as a member of the EU, participates in WTO agreements only as part of the EU block. The UK does not have its 'own seat' on the WTO. The UK has made a financial contribution to support least developed countries' efforts to stimulate trade.

**Government policy** (2016): Encourage free trade and oppose attempts by governments to protect their countries' businesses from competition. Support LEDCs to help them access global markets and increase their capacity to trade.

**Organisation: United Nations (UN)**

**Foundation year**: 1945. The UN's predecessor organisation, the League of Nations, was founded in 1920 following the First World War, but failed in its mission to prevent further global conflict. The UN, founded immediately after the Second World War, has helped the world to avoid a third global conflict.

**Purpose**: The UN provides a forum for dealing peacefully with international issues. The UN aims to protect human rights by taking action on issues such as: peace and security; climate change; sustainable development; terrorism; humanitarian and health emergencies; gender equality and food production.

**Membership**: 193 member states. (Only three world states are not members of the UN – Taiwan, Kosovo and the Vatican City.)

**UK contribution**: The UK is one of five permanent members of the UN Security Council – responsible for trying to resolve conflict between states, protect human rights and prevent war. The Security Council can **mediate**, impose **sanctions** or even authorise the use of force to maintain or restore international peace and security. All permanent members must approve Security Council proposals before they can be implemented.

The UK makes a financial contribution of over £90 million a year towards running costs and contributes UK troops to UN peacekeeping missions.

**Government policy** (2016): The UK Government supports:

- all UN declarations and agreements
- UN **millennium development goals**
- all UN environmental targets (by passing the 2008 Climate Change Act, the UK was the first country to set statutory targets for cutting carbon emissions)
- the UN target of contributing 0.7 per cent of national wealth towards overseas development. (In 2016, the UK was the only major world economy to meet this target.)

The UK Government is keen for the UN to provide better value for money by working more efficiently.

**Figure 12.2** The major Commonwealth countries

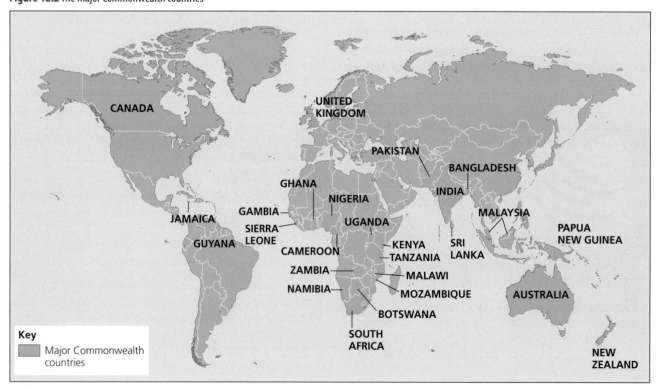

**Mediate** To work with countries to help them settle a dispute.

**Sanctions** Penalties applied to a member state in an attempt to encourage compliance with UN declarations.

**Millennium development goals** International targets, coordinated by the UN, to meet the needs of the world's poorest people.

**Less Economically Developed Country (LEDC)** Relatively poor countries in which many people have difficulty meeting their needs. LEDCs generate wealth through farming, mining, raw materials and manufacturing.

## Websites
- Commonwealth: **http://thecommonwealth.org/**
- Council of Europe (COE): **http://www.coe.int/en/**
- European Union (EU): **http://europa.eu/**
- North Atlantic Treaty Organization (NATO): **http://www.nato.int/**
- United Nations (UN): **http://www.un.org/**
- World Trade Organization (WTO): **https://www.wto.org/**

## Activities

2. Explain why most of the organisations described on pages 184 to 186 were first established.

3. Visit each of the organisation's websites:
    a) Choose a feature or news story from each site that represents a good example of what the organisation does.
    b) Write a short commentary to explain why you have chosen each example.
    c) Make a series of slides or a folder so that you can display your examples to other learners.

4. Use information from pages 184 to 186 to oppose the viewpoint that the UK has very little influence in the world today.

# The European Union

## Key learning
Study the benefits and costs of EU membership. Analyse the impact on the UK of one decision made by the European Union and evaluate different viewpoints on the UK's continuing membership.

The UK has been part of the European Union (EU) since 1973. In 2016, there were 28 countries in the EU with others wanting to join. Membership of the EU affects many of the UK's political and legal relationships with other countries in Europe.

**Figure 12.3** The 28 states of the European Union in 2016

In February 2016, the Prime Minister persuaded other European leaders to support changes to some EU policies and practices in order to give the UK greater sovereignty within the EU. This was in advance of the June 2016 referendum to decide whether the UK would remain a member of a reformed EU or leave the Union.

## Aims of the European Union

The original aim of the EU was to prevent further war in Europe. European nations came together into a cooperative alliance. The EU also aims to promote human rights and democracy in all its member countries and across the world.

The EU aims to bring the laws and systems of each member country closer together (integration). This makes it easier for people to move between countries and for businesses to trade. By 2003, most of the member countries were using the same unit of currency (the Euro) and working towards integration of such things as interest rates and tax levels.

The UK Government decided not to introduce the Euro and to retain its independent economic policy.

Member countries have more power as a group than they would by acting alone. EU members can take joint action to intervene in international conflicts and crises.

> **Summary of the EU's aims**
> 1. *Promote economic and social progress*
>    Help people earn enough money and get treated fairly.
> 2. *Speak for Europe on the international scene*
>    EU leaders hope that a united Europe will have more influence in the world.
> 3. *Introduce European citizenship*
>    Anyone from a member state is a citizen of the EU and is granted four special rights.
>    - Freedom to move between countries of the EU and to live in any nation in the Union.
>    - The right to vote and stand in local government and European parliamentary elections in any EU country of residence.
>    - If you are travelling outside the EU, and your own country does not have an embassy, you can go to the embassy of any other EU country for assistance.
>    - The right to put your side of the story to the European Ombudsman if you think the EU has not acted fairly.
> 4. *Develop Europe as an area of freedom, security and justice*
>    Help Europeans to live in safety, without the threat of war.
> 5. *Maintain and build on established EU law*
>    Make laws that protect people's rights in the member countries.

## How decisions are made in the EU

The citizens of each EU member state are represented by their governments at the **Council of the European Union**. The Council is the EU's main decision-making body alongside the **European Parliament**. EU citizens are represented directly in the European Parliament by the members (MEPs) they elect every five years. This democratic system gives a voice to the governments and citizens of each member state.

It is often difficult to make decisions quickly with 28 separate governments involved. For example, the EU was unable to respond promptly and in a co-ordinated manner to the Syrian refugee crisis of 2015. As a result, member states were forced to make independent

decisions. This led to massive confusion and poor treatment of the refugees.

The EU is at its best when there is time for full consultation and debate across the Union before decisions are made.

## The impact of EU decisions

Although the EU may seem remote, decisions made at European level have a considerable impact on everyday life. Below are just a few examples.

- *Consumer protection and food safety.* EU **regulations** guarantee consumers the same high levels of product information and protection across all 28 states.
- *Employment.* EU laws and regulations guarantee rights to equal employment opportunities and a cap on working hours.
- *Health.* Patients in the UK and throughout the EU have the right to shop around Europe for the best and quickest medical treatment.
- *Information society.* Musicians' performing-rights fees have been simplified to assist satellite, cable and internet broadcasting development, and to give listeners more choice.
- *Innovation.* Two of the UK's biggest car makers were given large loans to help them design and build a more environmentally friendly type of car.

**Council of the European Union** Composed of ministers from each EU member state, the Council works with the European Parliament on main decisions.

**European Parliament** Elected every five years by citizens in each member state to approve the EU budget and to work with the Council on main decisions.

**Regulations** In an EU context, regulations are laws that must be applied across all member states.

# Different viewpoints on EU membership

In 2016 British citizens were deeply divided over whether the UK should retain its EU membership. The Prime Minister had achieved a 'new deal' for the UK during negotiations in the spring but many people wanted Britain to leave the EU. There were massive campaigns – one for the UK to remain in the

EU and one for the UK to leave. Each campaign was supported by members of the UK's different political parties. Most members of the Labour, Green, Liberal Democrat, Scottish Nationalist and Welsh Nationalist parties supported the campaign to remain in the EU while UKIP and the Northern Irish unionists backed the 'leave' campaign. The Conservative Party was deeply divided on the issue. Statements made by the 'remain' and 'leave' campaigns can be found below.

## Activities

1. Design slides or charts to summarise the benefits and costs of EU membership.
2. Research the outcomes of the UK's EU referendum.
   a) Describe the overall result and show how people voted by region, age and gender.
   b) Describe the result's implications.
   c) Explain which way you would have voted in the referendum if you had been able to.

## BRITAIN STRONGER IN EUROPE

 Vote Leave

*Britain is stronger, better off and safer in Europe than we would be out on our own.*

*Of course the EU isn't perfect – but leaving Europe would risk our prosperity, threaten our safety and diminish our influence in the world.*

*The benefits of being in clearly outweigh the costs:*

- A stronger economy *that delivers opportunity now and for future generations – opportunity through growth, trade, investment, jobs and lower prices.*

- Stronger leadership *on the world stage, enabling us to shape the future – influence through participation.*

- Stronger security *in a dangerous world, keeping Britain safe – safety though partnerships.*

*To vote to remain part of Europe is to vote for a stronger, better off, safer Britain that delivers opportunity for individuals and families, now and in the future.*

*To vote to leave is to take a leap into the unknown, risking a weaker economy, the prospects of future generations and a loss of influence on the world stage.*

*Why should we vote to leave?*

*Technological and economic forces are changing the world fast. EU institutions cannot cope. We have lost control of vital policies. This is damaging. We need a new relationship. What should it be?*

*We negotiate a new UK-EU deal based on free trade and friendly cooperation. We end the supremacy of EU law. We regain control. We stop sending £350 million every week to Brussels and instead spend it on our priorities, like the NHS and science research.*

*We regain our seats on international institutions like the World Trade Organization so we are a more influential force for free trade and international cooperation.*

*We stop the current immoral, expensive, and out of control immigration system that means an open door to the EU while blocking people who could contribute to the UK coming from non-EU countries.*

*A vote to 'leave' and a better, friendlier relationship with the EU is much safer than giving Brussels more power and money every year.*

## Websites

Browse the EU website for further information: **http://europa.eu/**

For a summary of EU legislation, visit: **http://eur-lex.europa.eu/browse/summaries.html?locale=en**

Details of the Britain Stronger in Europe campaign for the UK to remain in the EU can found at: **http://www.strongerin.co.uk/**

Details of the Vote Leave campaign can be found at: **http://www.voteleavetakecontrol.org/**

Visit the websites of the UK political parties for news of their position on EU membership. (See pages 84 to 88 for details.)

# Benefits and costs of EU membership

| Benefits | Costs |
|---|---|
| **Peace and stability** | **The UK's status as an independent nation** |
| War between EU countries is much less likely, thanks to cooperation over many years. The EU also attempts to encourage peace and stability beyond its borders. | The UK is a major world economic, military and diplomatic power, and has the world's most widely used language. The UK government may be able to negotiate with other countries more quickly and flexibly outside the EU. |
| **Freedom, security and justice for all** | **Democracy and decision-making** |
| EU citizens have equal access to justice everywhere in the EU. Police and customs officers, immigration services and law courts cooperate to tackle cross-border crime and terrorism. | The UK has lost some important powers to the EU and this limits our sovereignty. Decision-making in the EU is seen to be remote by many UK citizens. |
| **Jobs and growth** | **Regulations and delay** |
| The EU has removed barriers to trade and agreed common European product standards making it easier to do business across Europe. | The EU imposes thousands of regulations each year. Many of these are considered unnecessary. With 28 countries wanting a say, important decisions are often delayed. |
| **Study, work and residence** | **Public opinion** |
| EU citizens can live, work, study and retire in another EU country. More than three million young people have taken advantage of EU programmes to study or train in another European country. | In 2016, public opinion seemed to be evenly split between those who wanted to leave the EU and those who thought the UK should remain a member. It is not good for democracy for the UK to stay in the EU if so many people are against membership, but the June 2016 referendum gave electors the chance to decide. |
| **Travel and shopping** | **Trade and prosperity** |
| EU citizens can normally travel across most of the EU without a passport or border checks. There are no additional taxes to pay on items bought anywhere inside the EU as long as the goods are for personal use. | Some people argue that EU membership limits the UK's potential to trade with the rest of the world, and especially with emerging powers such as India and China. |
| **The environment** | **Financial contribution** |
| EU member states have taken joint action to cut pollution. Europe's rivers and beaches are cleaner, vehicles pollute less, and there are strict rules for waste disposal. | Membership of the EU is expensive even for a wealthy country like the UK. Part of the UK's financial contribution is being used to help develop economies and infrastructure in poorer parts of Europe. The net annual cost of membership is around £4 billion. |

# Responding to international conflicts and crises

## Key learning

Study international agreements to protect victims of conflict and to establish rules of warfare, and evaluate the success of these agreements.

Study the methods (including practical support, mediation, sanctions or force) available to governments that wish to intervene in international conflicts or crises. Analyse and evaluate the role played and contribution made by the UK Government in one international crisis, disagreement or conflict. Evaluate how far the United Nations has fulfilled its aims.

The world is a dangerous place. Wars, conflicts and crises are everyday events. They ruin the lives of many millions of people, especially in Africa and the Middle East. Wealthier countries such as the UK have frequently intervened in wars, conflicts and crises either independently or as part of an EU, NATO or UN international response. UK governments justify intervention by claiming to be protecting national interests or safeguarding human rights. However, such interventions have not always achieved their objectives.

## International humanitarian law

International humanitarian law is a set of rules that aims to protect people's rights in times of war. It protects civilians and those armed personnel who are no longer fighting. It also places limits on the weapons and tactics that can be used in war. International humanitarian law is different from human rights law because it applies only in times of war. Human rights law is far more wide-ranging and applies at all times.

A major part of international humanitarian law is contained in the Geneva Conventions of 1949. Nearly every state in the world has agreed to be bound by these Conventions. Parts of the Conventions also apply to **civil war**.

**Figure 12.4** Even wars are governed by laws to protect civilians and soldiers who have given up fighting. These Argentinian troops surrendered to the British Army on the Falkland Islands in 1982. They were treated humanely according to international law

**Civil war** A war between two or more groups within the same country.

### The seven basic international rules of conflict

1. People not taking part in fighting should have their lives protected by all sides in the conflict.
2. An enemy who surrenders should not be killed or injured.
3. Wounded and sick people should be collected and cared for by whichever side comes across them. The Red Cross or Red Crescent emblem is the sign of such protection and must be respected.
4. All captured fighters and civilians are entitled to respect for their lives, dignity, personal rights and convictions. They shall have the right to contact their families and to receive aid.
5. Everyone shall be entitled to a fair trial if they are accused of doing something wrong. No one shall be physically or mentally tortured, or given physical punishment or cruel or degrading treatment.
6. Weapons or methods of warfare should not be used if they cause unnecessary losses or excessive suffering.
7. Fighters should always respect civilians and their property. Civilians should not be attacked. All attacks should be against other fighters or military targets.

Sadly, there are many examples of international humanitarian law being ignored. In 2016, a group known as Islamic State, fighting civil wars in Iraq and Syria, was deliberately torturing and murdering prisoners so as to scare its opponents. Increasingly, the victims of civil wars are civilians.

However, there are also important cases where international humanitarian law has made a difference by protecting civilians, prisoners, the sick and the wounded as well as restricting the use of barbaric weapons such as land mines.

### Website

More details of international humanitarian law are available at the International Red Cross website: **https://www.icrc.org/en/war-and-law**

### Activity

1. Which of the following actions would be illegal under international humanitarian law?
   - Bombing a factory making weapons.
   - Firing a nuclear missile at an enemy city.
   - Laying land mines outside a village.
   - Leaving wounded enemy soldiers without treatment.

## The United Nations – protecting rights and promoting peace

**Figure 12.5** The United Nations Conference Centre for Africa, in Ethiopia

### The UN's aims

The UN aims to achieve the responsibilities set out in its Charter, which are to:

- maintain international peace and security
- develop friendly relations among nations
- cooperate in solving international problems
- promote respect for human rights.

*Extracts from the introduction to the United Nations Charter signed in San Francisco on 26 June 1945.*

*'WE THE PEOPLES OF THE UNITED NATIONS DETERMINED*

- *to save succeeding generations from the scourge of war, which twice in our lifetime has brought untold sorrow to mankind, and*
- *to reaffirm faith in fundamental human rights, in the dignity and worth of the human person, in the equal rights of men and women and of nations large and small, and*
- *to establish conditions under which justice and respect for the obligations arising from treaties and other sources of international law can be maintained, and*
- *to promote social progress and better standards of life in larger freedom.'*

It was through the UN that countries agreed the Universal Declaration of Human Rights in 1948. (See Chapter 1 for more details.) The Declaration has become a model for national law throughout the world.

### Website

The full text of the UN's Charter is available at: **http://www.un.org/en/charter-united-nations/index.html**

### How does the UN try to achieve its aims?

### Extending human rights and fighting poverty

Eight UN Millennium Development Goals (MDGs) were agreed by all UN member states in 2000. The aim was to achieve these goals by 2015. The MDGs included: halving extreme poverty, halting the spread of HIV/AIDS and providing universal primary education. The UN called for a massive global effort to meet the MDGs in support of the world's poorest people (see page 193).

*The UN's 2015 report showed that much had been achieved to meet the MDGs.*

'*... the world community has reason to celebrate. Thanks to concerted global, regional, national and local efforts, the MDGs have saved the lives of millions and improved conditions for many more ... with targeted interventions, sound strategies, adequate resources and political will, even the poorest countries can make dramatic and unprecedented progress. The report (shows) uneven achievements and shortfalls in many areas. The work is not complete, and it must continue in the new development era.*'

*(The UN Millennium Development Goals Report 2015.)*

## MDG achievements

- In 1990, nearly half of the population in LEDCs lived on less than $1.25 a day; that fell to 14 per cent in 2015.
- 91 per cent of the world's children were receiving a primary education in 2015, up from 83 per cent in 2000.
- Educational opportunities for girls have increased significantly. For example, in Southern Asia, only 74 girls were enrolled in primary school for every 100 boys in 1990. By 2015, 103 girls were enrolled for every 100 boys.
- Even though the number of children in the world has increased, the number of deaths of children under five declined from 12.7 million worldwide in 1990 to less than 6 million in 2015.

- In 2015, 91 per cent of the global population was able to drink clean water, compared to 76 per cent in 1990.
- Aid from MEDCs increased by 66 per cent in real terms between 2000 and 2014, reaching $135.2 billion. (Denmark, Luxembourg, Norway, Sweden and the UK continued to exceed the United Nations' official development assistance target of 0.7 per cent of gross national income.)

### Website

A progress report on the UN Millennium Development Goals is available at:
**http://www.un.org/millenniumgoals/**

## Further progress needed to fight poverty

The UN's 2015 report on *The State of the World's Children* made it clear that '*too many children still confront the future with their needs unaddressed, their rights unrealized and their potential thwarted*'. Most children in LEDCs continue to experience poverty and disadvantage, but many deprived children also live in countries where there is a large gap in living standards between the richest and the poorest. Even in richer countries, child poverty can be found in the poorer parts of large cities and remote rural areas. Children from ethnic minorities and those with disabilities are most likely to be deprived.

### UN report shows more progress still needed on children's rights

- The poorest 20 per cent of the world's children are about twice as likely as the richest 20 per cent to be stunted by poor nutrition and to die before their fifth birthday.
- In LEDCs, nearly nine out of ten children from the wealthiest households attend primary school – compared to only about six out of ten from the poorest households. The gap is most dramatic in countries in West and Central Africa. In Burkina Faso, for example, 85 per cent of children in the wealthiest households attended school, compared to 31 per cent of children in the poorest households.

- Regardless of wealth, girls continue to be held back from schooling. For every 100 boys enrolled in primary school in West and Central Africa, only 90 girls are enrolled. This is worse in secondary school, where only 77 girls are enrolled for every 100 boys.
- Teenage girls are much more likely than boys to be married or with a sexual partner. Girls are also less likely than boys to know about sexually transmitted diseases. In South Asia, boys are twice as likely as girls to know how to protect themselves during sexual activity.

(Extracts adapted from UNICEF: *2015: Reimagine/the Future*)

**Figure 12.6** In Pakistan, young girls show off these notebooks provided by UNICEF.

## Website

For more information on the UN report *The State of the World's Children* and examples of innovative projects to improve children's rights go to:
http://www.unicef.org.uk/

## Emergency aid and long-term development

UN agencies coordinate international responses to natural disasters, famine and war. They also plan and encourage support for long-term development and education projects. For example, the United Nations Children's Emergency Fund (UNICEF) took immediate action to support victims of the Nepal earthquake in 2015 but also continued its longer-term educational projects in that country. Also in 2015, another UN agency, the World Health Organization (WHO), moved quickly to deal with an outbreak of cholera in Iraq.

*'UNICEF was there (in Nepal) from day one, delivering clean water, sanitation and shelter to families sleeping rough, keeping children safe and setting up temporary hospitals so lifesaving medical care could continue. We were there in the tough months to follow, providing nutritional support, helping kids back to school and giving them the psychosocial support they needed to cope and recover. We've been in Nepal for more than 40 years and we'll be there for children as long as we're needed.'*

# CASE STUDY
## UN health agency mobilises immunisation campaign to help control cholera outbreak in Iraq

**Figure 12.7** A health worker administers a cholera vaccine to a child at a refugee camp in western Baghdad, Iraq, November 2015

3 November 2015 – The World Health Organization (WHO) has provided 510,000 doses of oral cholera vaccine for an estimated 250,000 refugees in Iraq, in an effort to stop the cholera outbreak which is now feared to be spreading to neighbouring countries.

The two-dose vaccination campaign is a part of a strategy to prevent a large-scale cholera outbreak in the 62 refugee camps.

WHO has also supported improved sanitation and hygiene practices in high-risk areas and donated further medical supplies to the Iraq Ministry of Health for use in treatment facilities across the country.

(Adapted from the UN website)

## Protecting the global environment

The first UN international conference on environment and development – known as the *Earth Summit* – took place at Rio de Janeiro in 1992. Since then, most countries have taken action to improve the environment and to reduce global warming.

There have been some major successes. Chemicals that damage the atmosphere's ozone layer have been almost eliminated since 1990, and the ozone layer is expected to recover by the middle of this century. But there is still a long way to go if the world is to meet UN targets to reduce the rate of global warming.

The UN's 2015 Paris Climate Change Conference came up with the world's first-ever legally binding global climate change deal. Instead of being asked to sign up to UN proposals, governments were invited to bring along their own national climate action plans. Following some further negotiation, these added up to the strongest-ever global promise to tackle climate change. Nations promised to limit any rise in global temperature to no more than 2 degrees higher than it was in the world's pre-industrial era.

COP21·CMP11
**PARIS 2015**
UN CLIMATE CHANGE CONFERENCE

The Paris conference also provided a much clearer signal to businesses to be more environmentally responsible.

In the years since the first UN global conference in 1992, much has changed, including:

- increased scientific understanding of global warming
- greater support for environmentally-friendly action by governments, businesses and citizens
- more investment in carbon reduction strategies.

There is still a long way to go but, without the UN's work, the world would be facing even bigger problems.

## Resolving conflict

The UN's 163 member states try to agree international laws and treaties to reduce the likelihood of international disputes. Agreement is not always easy because member states often hold very different views. Treaties on limiting the spread of nuclear weapons, care for the environment and the use of the sea have proved particularly difficult to negotiate.

There are frequent disputes between nations in spite of international agreements. These disputes are often about land or resources. The UN's **International Court of Justice**, based in The Hague (Netherlands), has the task of settling such disputes. The UN **General Assembly** elects the fifteen judges, each of whom serve on the court for nine years. This system avoids accusations of bias. In 2014, the court was dealing with several territorial disputes including a long-running argument between Costa Rica and Nicaragua over rights to under-sea oil exploration.

Where people are at risk of violence or where nations need support to make peace agreements work, the UN may agree to send a **peacekeeping mission**. The mission's task is to uphold any peace treaty, make sure former fighters follow international humanitarian law

(see page 191) and help arrange elections to choose a new government.

The first UN peacekeeping mission started in 1948, when the UN **Security Council** sent military observers to the Middle East with the job of monitoring the ceasefire between Israel and its Arab neighbours. Since then, there have been over 70 further UN peacekeeping missions around the world. The UN's priority is for peacekeeping forces not to use violence, but they sometimes do use weapons in self-defence or to protect human rights.

**International Court of Justice** (also known as the **World Court**) Settles legal disputes between countries.

**General Assembly** A meeting of all the UN's member states. It decides UN policies and its budget as well as appointing the non-permanent members of the Security Council.

**Peacekeeping mission** UN officials and armed personnel from different member states entering conflict zones to keep the peace and protect civilians.

**Security Council** The UN body that carries out the policies of the General Assembly by maintaining international peace and security. The Security Council can start peacekeeping operations, impose sanctions and organise military action.

**Figure 12.8** Peacekeepers in Sierra Leone as part of the successful UNAMSIL mission 1999–2006

In extreme cases, the UN Security Council can apply **sanctions** to a national government. This might mean that member states refuse to supply weapons or to trade with the offending government. For example, sanctions were applied to North Korea in 2004 following its development of nuclear weapons and its threats to neighbouring countries.

**Figure 12.9** UN peacekeeping missions in 2016

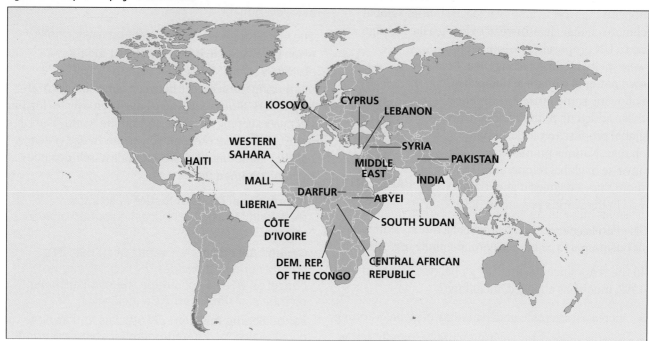

## How effective is the UN in resolving international conflicts?

The International Court of Justice and UN peacekeeping missions have the respect and support of most governments across the world. Nevertheless, UN intervention is rarely straightforward and can only be successful if:

- All sides in a conflict are ready to make peace.
- Members of the Security Council can agree a way forward.

Other difficulties arise where an **insurgency** is taking place or where a terrorist organisation is operating. In such cases, it is unlikely that the groups involved will follow international humanitarian law. The UN has much less scope to use persuasion or sanctions if there is no recognised government to negotiate with. For these reasons, effective intervention did not take place in Syria until 2016, even though violent civil war had raged for over four years and international aid agencies were demanding robust UN action.

The situation was so bad in 2015 that twenty-one international aid agencies considered the UN to have completely failed the people of Syria. The agencies published the scorecard below to expose what they saw as the UN's failings.

**UN SCORECARD: Protection of Syrian civilians. Overall Grade: FAIL**

| What the UN said in February 2014 | What has happened since then | What needs to be done |
|---|---|---|
| • Attacks on civilians must stop.<br>• Weapons should not be used in populated areas without care.<br>• All sides in the war must take steps to protect civilians.<br>• Fighters should not use schools and hospitals as bases.<br>• Civilians should not be taken hostage or tortured. | • 76,000 people were killed in 2014.<br>• 26% more people have been forced out of their homes.<br>• 160 children have been killed in attacks on schools.<br>• Over 1 million more children need aid.<br>• More civilians have been killed by explosive weapons. | • All sides in the war should obey the UN Security Council and members of the UN should take action to make sure this happens.<br>• The governments of UN member nations should stop sending weapons to the fighters.<br>• UN agencies should do more to protect and help civilians. |

(Adapted from *Failing Syria, Assessing the impact of the United Nations Security Council resolutions in protecting and assisting civilians in Syria, 2015.*)

The cost of the UN's peacekeeping missions is well over £5 billion per year, but mission commanders have sometimes found it difficult to obtain further support when they've needed it. When a nation's army is at war, every effort is made to support the army and to take decisions promptly. In a UN peacekeeping mission, a commander's request for additional supplies and reinforcements has to be discussed and agreed by UN officials or even by the Security Council. This can be a long process and delays can put the success of a mission at risk.

Nevertheless, the UN has undertaken many successful missions. Missions are likely to achieve their goals when UN peacekeepers are protecting civilians or supporting all sides in maintaining a peace agreement, as on the India/Pakistan border. In 2015, 300 British personnel were sent to South Sudan as part of the successful UN mission to safeguard civilians there.

## UK interventions in international conflicts and crises

The UK has the fifth strongest economy in the world, a permanent seat on the UN Security Council and is one of nine countries with nuclear weapons. Although Britain now has a much smaller navy, army and air force than in the past, UK governments have been heavily involved in international conflicts and crises. This has sometimes split public opinion and caused heated public debate.

> **Sanctions** Penalties imposed on countries that break international law.
>
> **Insurgency** A rebellion against authority or government.

# CASE STUDY
## UK intervention in Kosovo 1998–2008

Tension in Croatia, Serbia and neighbouring areas was a concern to the UN, NATO and the EU during the 1990s. UN attempts to maintain peace and protect civilians broke down.

Civil war in an area known as Kosovo caused particular alarm because the Serbian government resisted international pressure to stop the fighting. Many hundreds of thousands of people, mainly Muslims, became refugees and civilian casualties were rising. UN peacekeeping operations and sanctions against Serbia had failed to end the conflict, so NATO decided that only armed intervention would prevent further civilian loss of life. (Neither China nor Russia would support military intervention by the UN.)

*'I say this to the British people. There is a heavy responsibility on a government, when putting our forces into battle. I warn: the potential consequences of military action are serious, both for NATO forces and the people in the region. Their suffering cannot be ended overnight. But in my judgement the consequences of not acting are more serious still for human life and for peace in the long term.'*

Tony Blair, UK Prime Minister from 1997 to 2007, in a statement to Parliament, 23 March 1999

In 1998, UK troops intervened as part of a NATO force. At the height of the conflict, the British Army had 3,000 military personnel fighting alongside allies including the USA, Germany, France, Italy and Norway. The Royal Air Force (RAF) bombed Serbian army positions.

**Figure 12.10** British troops in Kosovo as part of the NATO force.

This strategy led to Serbian surrender and the formation of the independent state of Kosovo. British Army personnel remained in the area until 2008 as part of a successful EU peacekeeping force.

While there was criticism of NATO's intervention in the war, there were no military casualties on the NATO side. More than 1,000 Serbian soldiers and police were killed. Over 1 million civilians had to leave their homes and around 10,000 died – 500 of these as a result of NATO action.

# CASE STUDY

## War in Iraq from 2003

The 2003 invasion of Iraq was led by the USA, with substantial armed support from the UK. The UN had been concerned about human rights in Iraq, had imposed sanctions and had sent inspectors to check for the illegal production of weapons, but the UN did not support the invasion.

*'I have indicated it (the invasion of Iraq) was not in conformity with the UN Charter. From our point of view … it was illegal.'*

Kofi Annan, Secretary-General of the United Nations from 1997 to 2006, 16 September 2004

Iraq's leader, Saddam Hussein, had presided over many abuses of human rights in his country. More significantly for the governments of the UK and USA, it was said that he was preparing 'weapons of mass destruction' for use against other states in the Middle East and that Iraq was encouraging terrorist attacks on western countries.

Opponents of the invasion argued that the USA and UK were only interested in getting rid of Saddam. It was claimed that new leaders under American and British influence would be more reliable suppliers of oil to western countries.

A few days after the invasion, most of the fighting was over and Iraq's capital, Baghdad, had been taken. The celebrations were short-lived. Although Saddam Hussein had been deposed, his supporters, and other groups opposed to the American and British occupation, began an insurgency. By 2015,

this had escalated and the RAF had joined a bombing campaign to retake territory for the Iraqi Government that had been lost to the insurgents.

**Figure 12.11** There was widespread protest in the UK about the Government's plan to invade Iraq

The decision to invade Iraq has been heavily criticised, even though it led to the introduction of a form of democracy and to Iraqi citizens enjoying improved human rights. Weapons of mass destruction were never found. Plans to stabilise Iraq after the invasion were inadequate and many thousands of lives were lost, including 179 British military personnel. Conflict continues.

In 2016, Sir John Chilcot presented the report of his independent **public enquiry** into the UK's intervention in the Iraq War. This made uncomfortable reading for politicians who had made the decision to invade thirteen years earlier.

> **Public enquiry** An official review of events or actions ordered by a government. The enquiry hears evidence and conducts its hearings in public.

### Activities

2. List arguments for and against the UK intervening in overseas crises and conflicts. Explain whether or not you think that the UK should intervene only if the whole Security Council has supported intervention.

3. Research the findings of the Chilcot Enquiry into the Iraq War. List its criticisms of the UK Government and describe the lessons that should be learned from the UK's intervention in Iraq.

## The role of non-governmental organisations (NGOs)

Non-governmental organisations include international charities such as Save the Children, Oxfam, the Red Cross/Red Crescent and Medicine Sans Frontiers.

These groups are not controlled by national governments or by international organisations such as the EU or UN. They are independent – controlled by their trustees. They pay for their work with money raised from the general public.

Governments often channel international aid through these independent NGOs. For example, Save the Children worked with the UK Government's Department for International Development (DfID) to help tackle an outbreak of a deadly disease called Ebola when it struck the people of Sierra Leone in 2014 and 2015.

# CASE STUDY
## Refugee rescues 2015

In 2015, hundreds of thousands of refugees began travelling to Europe to escape conflicts in Syria, Iraq, Afghanistan, Libya and Sudan. Refugees tried to cross the Mediterranean Sea in wooden or rubber boats. These flimsy craft were frequently swamped and many hundreds of refugees drowned.

The Royal Navy joined navies from other EU states to rescue people at sea, and to deter smugglers from exploiting the refugees and endangering life.

'*Saving lives means rescuing these poor people, but it also means smashing the (smuggling) gangs and stabilising the region. Now Britain, as ever, will help … and as the country in Europe with the biggest defence budget, we can make a real contribution.*'

David Cameron, UK Prime Minister, speaking before a meeting with other EU leaders, 7 May 2015

### Flying Tigers help save over 1100 lives at sea

'The Flying Tigers' of 814 Naval Air Squadron were poised and ready to launch their Merlin Helicopter at first light from HMS Bulwark's flight deck on Sunday 7 June, a day which would result in the largest Royal Navy migrant rescue to date on Operation Weald.

As HMS Bulwark's 'eyes in the sky', the Squadron's mission was to support the international humanitarian operation by looking out for vessels in distress.

After only 10 minutes airborne, the crew of Merlin – Callsign 'Tiger 1' – spotted an inflatable boat with over 100 migrants crammed onboard and in distress.

A total of five small inflatable vessels each with over 100 people onboard and two wooden boats each with over 300 onboard were found during the four-hour morning sortie.

Royal Marine landing craft recovered the migrants to the safety of HMS Bulwark. Over 1,100 migrants were saved over the course of the day.

(Adapted from the Royal Navy's website, 9 June 2015)

# CASE STUDY
## Save the Children in Sierra Leone

**Save the Children's mission**
- protect children in terrible situations
- prevent unnecessary child deaths from treatable diseases
- deliver sustainable change through education.

Save the Children responded to the Ebola outbreak in Sierra Leone by raising awareness of how the disease passes from one person to another and preventing its spread.

Save the Children also helped to strengthen Sierra Leone's healthcare services where these had been weakened by the outbreak. Their health, child protection, education and child rights work reached almost 4.6 million people, including more than 2 million children.

Save the Children had particular responsibility for the Kerry Town Ebola Treatment Centre (ETC). People diagnosed with Ebola received specialist care here and were isolated to make sure they didn't pass the disease on. The ETC was funded by DfID, and its construction was supervised by British Army Royal Engineers. It was a joint Sierra Leonean Ministry of Health and British Government initiative.

As part of its response to Ebola, Save the Children also trained 300 community healthcare workers who helped families to identify people with symptoms and refer them for treatment.

Sierra Leone was declared free of Ebola in November 2015, but Save the Children made a further three-year commitment to help children and families rebuild their lives.

This longer-term work included:
- reuniting orphaned children with extended family members or finding appropriate care, and getting them back into school
- providing families with food, clean water, soap and household items in cases where a wage-earning adult had died
- training teachers and volunteers to provide long-term emotional support to children whose parents had died.

**Figure 12.12** A Save The Children community health team worker talks to locals on a door-to-door information campaign about Ebola at the Hill Station community west of Freetown, Sierra Leone, 8 October 2014

## Reasons why NGOs can be effective in a crisis or conflict

NGOs such as Save the Children can often be more effective than governments when responding to an emergency.

NGOs:

- do not take sides (they take help directly to the people who need it most and are prepared to support those in need wherever they live)
- are usually trusted by donors, recipients and governments
- do not expect favours, such as military alliances or trade deals, in return for their support
- have clear aims linked to humanitarian values and will stick to their commitments
- act quickly – there is no need for parliamentary approval or favourable public opinion
- have expertise and experience to support people's particular needs
- can appeal directly to the public for extra funds to pay for their aid programmes.

Nevertheless, governments and international organisations can have far more influence than NGOs:

- Governments have massive resources, including finance, food and armed personnel.
- Governments can take combined action through international organisations such as the UN and EU – with considerable impact.
- International organisations can impose sanctions, send peace-keeping forces and deploy armed force in extreme circumstances.

Well-planned joint action by government agencies, military personnel and NGOs can be particularly effective, as the response to Ebola shows.

### Website

For more details of Save the Children's work go to: **http://www.savethechildren.org.uk/**

### Activities

4. Research one of the UN's most recent responses to a natural disaster or humanitarian emergency.
    a) Describe the problem.
    b) Describe the UN's action.
    c) Evaluate the action by checking media coverage. Could anything have been done differently?

5. UNICEF works for children's rights, survival, development and protection. Use the UNICEF website (**unicef.org.uk**) to find three examples of such work. Share these with other learners in your class and choose the most worthwhile projects.

6. Evaluate the viewpoint that the UN is not meeting the aims of its 1945 charter.

7. Use the Save the Children website to check the charity's continuing work in Sierra Leone. Describe what has been achieved and what still needs to be done to support children.

## Practice questions

In the OCR specification, this section will be assessed using objective test questions and questions needing a written response. Below is an example of an extended response question.

Study **Sources 1** and **2** (including the chart at the bottom of the page), and answer the question in the right hand column.

# Source 1
## Extracts adapted from *Top 10 failures of the United Nations*, Listverse, 2013

*The United Nations Security Council consists of fifteen nations, five of which are permanent: France, Russia, China, the United States, and the UK. If any one of these permanent members votes against a Council resolution, it cannot go ahead, even if it has widespread international support.*

*In 2012, China and Russia halted any international intervention in the Syrian civil war. Since then tens of thousands of civilians have died and millions have been forced to leave their homes.*

# Source 2
## Extracts adapted from *Levels and Trends in Child Mortality*, United Nations Children Fund (UNICEF), 2014

*As one of its Millennium Development Goals (MDG), the United Nations aimed to cut the child death rate by 67 per cent from 1990 to 2013. The number of child deaths in the world fell from 12.7 million in 1990 to 6.3 million in 2013. 17,000 fewer children died each day in 2013 than in 1990. (See chart below for details.)*

1. Using information from **Sources 1** and **2**, and **evidence from your studies**, evaluate the following viewpoint:

   The United Nations (UN) has done little to support human rights.

   You should consider:
   - reasons for agreeing with the viewpoint
   - reasons for disagreeing with the viewpoint.
     [12 marks]

| Region | Under 5 death rate for every 1000 live births | | United Nations target for the under 5 death rate, 2015 | Death rate fall 1990–2013 |
|---|---|---|---|---|
| | 1990 | 2013 | | |
| Developing Regions (overall) | 100 | 50 | 33 | 50% |
| North Africa | 72 | 24 | 24 | 67% |
| Africa – south of the Sahara Desert | 179 | 92 | 60 | 48% |
| Eastern Asia | 53 | 13 | 18 | 76% |
| Oceania | 74 | 54 | 25 | 28% |
| Developed Regions (overall) | 15 | 6 | 5 | 58% |

# Index

# Acknowledgements

The Publishers would like to thank the following for permission to reproduce material in this book: **p.16** Adapted from 'Countering terrorism', Liberty, www.liberty-human-rights.org.uk/human-rights/countering-terrorism; **p.22** *t* From the website of the British Medical Association (bma.org.uk), *b* Unite Trade Union. © Unite Trade Union. Used with permission; **p.24** Adapted from the FSB website (www.fsb.org.uk); **p.30** Adapted from The Independent, 21st November 2014; **p.31** Adapted from the Metropolitan Police website, 'Father and sons jailed', 28 August 2015; **p.39** ITN/Channel 4 News; **p.59** Adapted from the GovUK website - https://www.gov.uk/become-magistrate/can-you-be-a-magistrate; **p.61** Extract from Your Guide to Jury Service, HM Courts and Tribunals Service, 2015; **p.67** Figs 3.18, 3.19, 3.20 Ministry of Justice report 'Are juries fair?; **p.68** Juror jailed for researching trial on internet, John Aston, 'Two jurors jailed for contempt of court over use of internet during trials', 30 July 2013, Independent; **p.72** Adapted from Ministry of Justice data; **p.73** Adapted from Prison: the facts, Bromley Briefings Autumn 2015, Prison Reform Trust; **p.75** The Effect of Hate Crime on victims (Adapted from the Stop the Hate website: http://www.stopthehate.org.uk/); **p.95** The Telegraph, June 1, 2015; **p.103** Adapted from 'We'll pay for extra police to stop robbers, say Hampstead residents', The daily Telegraph, 26 Sep 2015; **p.104** Adapted from 'Choice' – a booklet produced by the Scottish National Party for the 2014 referendum. © Scottish National Party. Reprinted with permission from Scottish National Party; **p.105** Adapted from information produced for the 2014 Scottish referendum campaign by Better Together – a pressure group supporting Scotland's membership of the UK; **p.106** *t* Adapted from the original script of George Osborne's speech at the Museum of Science and Industry, Manchester, June 2014. https://www.gov.uk/government/speeches/chancellor-we-need-a-northern-powerhouse, *b* 'A Northern Powerhouse: Does It Make Sense?' presented by John Humphrys. https://yougov.co.uk/news/2014/06/23/northern-powerhouse-does-it-make-sense/; **p.109** https://ourgoverningprinciples.files.wordpress.com/2010/02/uk-fusion-of-powers.jpg; **p.115** Adapted from https://www.gov.uk/government/organisations/civil-service/about; **p.116** Adapted from: https://www.gov.uk/government/publications/civil-service-code/the-civil-service-code'; **p.120** Data from the Office for Budget Responsibility - estimates for 2013-14 r HM Treasury; **p.127** Bedford Free School's website. http://www.bedfordfreeschool.co.uk/about/; **p.129** *l* Adapted from Article 10 of the European Convention on Human Rights Act 1998, *r* Adapted from the Guardian's editorial code – August 2015; **p.133** Missing Milly Dowler's voicemail was hacked by News of the World, The Guardian, July, 2011; **p.134** Adapted from the Hacked Off website (hackinginquiry.org). © Hacked off. Reprinted with permission from Hacked off; **p.135** Steve Hilton, Jason Bade, Scott Bade, 'More Human: Designing a World Where People Come First' © 2015 Random House. Used with permission; **p.136** Biggest rises and falls in the 2014 World Press Freedom Index, Reporters without Borders; **p.137** Amber Rudd, "Secretary of State for Energy and Climate Change on shale gas", Department of Energy and Climate Change blog, August 2015; **p.139** My Political Life. © National Citizen Service. Used with permission; **p.140** *t* Every Child Matters: Change for Children, Department for Education and Skills, 2004, *b* Ashley Brown, Liz Clery, Mehul Kotecha, 'Evaluation of National Citizen Service', May 2013, Natcen Social Research; **p.144** General election turnout 1945 – 2015, UK Political Info; **p.146** Monks: We must modernise voting system, 11 May 2011, The Hunts Post; **p.147** Emily Clarke, https://www.change.org/p/government-of-sudan-don-t-execute-meriam-yehya-ibrahim-for-being-christian-savemeriam; **p.153** Democracy Ranking 2016, http://democracyranking.org/wordpress; © Democracy Ranking 2016. Reprinted with permission from Democracy Ranking; **p.156** Corina Casanova, Swiss Federal Chancellor, 2015; **p.160** Amnesty International, USA. © Amnesty International. Used with permission; **p.170** Non-UK Born Census Populations 1951 - 2011 - Full infographic, 17 December 2013, Office for National Statistics; **p.171** *r* Population by Country of Birth and Nationality tables, January 2014 to December 2014, Office for National Statistics, *l* Emigration from the UK, Research Report 68 November 2012, Office for National Statistics; **p.172** www.migrationwatchuk.org © Migration Watch UK. Used with permission; **p.173** Adapted from Office for National Statistics. https://www.gov.uk/government/publications/immigration-statistics-april-to-june-2015/list-of-tables#asylum (Volume 2 as6); **p.176** Nigel Farage tells Ukip conference in Torquay: UK has lost control of its borders, February 28, 2014, Western Daily Press; **p.180** Team gives UK £90m boost, 19 October 2015, The Prince's Trust; **p.182** *t* Eurostat. © 2012 Eurostat. Reprinted with permission, *b* Romanian protests in Revolutionary Square at Britain's immigration threat, 2 February 2013, The Observer; **p.192** From Charter of the United Nations, International Court of Justice, © 1945 United Nations. Reprinted with the permission of the United Nations; **p.193** From Charter of the United Nations, International Court of Justice, © 1945 United Nations. Reprinted with the permission of the United Nations; **p.193** From The UN Millennium Development Goals Report 2015, by MDG Advocacy Group, © 2015 United Nations. Reprinted with the permission of the United Nations; **p.193** The State of the World's Children 2015: Reimagine the future, UNICEF; **p.194** From 'this the little boy on the beach we can remember with a smile – not lying face down and lifeless in the sand but playing in it with Joyful abandon', by Jacob Hunt, © 2016 United Nations. Reprinted with the permission of the United Nations; **p.194** From Iraq: UN health agency mobilizes immunization campaign to help control cholera outbreak, © 2015 United Nations. Reprinted with the permission of the United Nations; **p.196** *t* United Nations Peacekeeping Operations, Map No. 4259 Rev. 21 United Nations, November 2014 © United Nations. Reprinted with the permission of the United Nations, *b* Adapted from Failing Syria, Assessing the impact of the United Nations Security Council resolutions in protecting and assisting civilians in Syria, http://www.rescue.org/press-releases/report-%E2%80%9Cfailing-syria%E2%80%9D-aid-agencies-give-un-security-council-fail-grade-syria-23832; **p.199** Flying Tigers help save over 1100 lives at sea, 09 June 2015, Royal Navy; **p.201** 'Top 10 failures of the United Nations', Listverse, 2013. © Listverse. Used with permission, *r* Adapted from Levels and Trends in Child Mortality, United Nations Children Fund (UNICEF), 2014.

*t* = top, *b* = bottom, *c* = centre, *l* = left, *r* = right